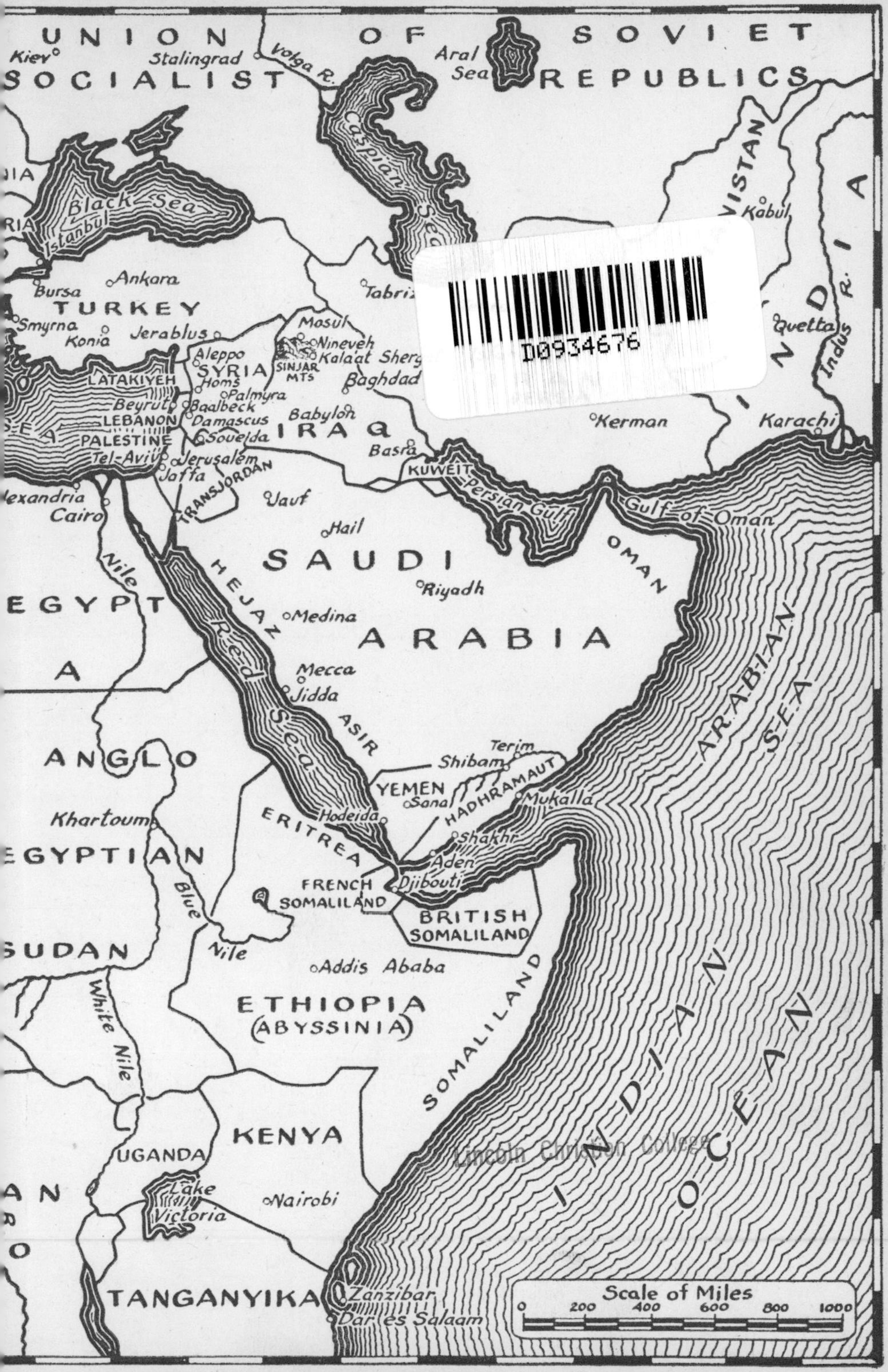
UNION OF SOVIET SOCIALIST REPUBLICS
Kiev
Stalingrad
Volga R.
Aral Sea
Caspian Sea
Black Sea
Istanbul
Ankara
Bursa
TURKEY
Smyrna
Konia
Jerablus
Tabriz
Mosul
Nineveh
Kalaat Sherg
SINJAR MTS
Baghdad
Aleppo
SYRIA
Homs
Palmyra
LATAKIYEH
Beyrut
Baalbeck
LEBANON
Damascus
Soueida
PALESTINE
Tel-Aviv
Jerusalem
Jaffa
TRANSJORDAN
Babylon
IRAQ
Basra
KUWEIT
Persian Gulf
Kerman
Kabul
Quetta
Indus R.
Karachi
INDIA
Gulf of Oman
OMAN
Alexandria
Cairo
Nile
EGYPT
Jauf
Hail
SAUDI ARABIA
Riyadh
Medina
Mecca
Jidda
HEJAZ
Red Sea
ASIR
Terim
Shibam
YEMEN
Sanaa
HADHRAMAUT
Mukalla
Hodeida
Shakhr
Aden
ERITREA
FRENCH SOMALILAND
Djibouti
BRITISH SOMALILAND
ANGLO EGYPTIAN SUDAN
Khartoum
Blue Nile
White Nile
Addis Ababa
ETHIOPIA (ABYSSINIA)
SOMALILAND
ARABIAN SEA
INDIAN OCEAN
KENYA
UGANDA
Lake Victoria
Nairobi
TANGANYIKA
Zanzibar
Dar es Salaam
Scale of Miles
0 200 400 600 800 1000

My heart can assume every form:
The cloister of the monk, a fane of idols,
The pasture of gazelles, the votary's Ka'aba,
The scrolls of the Thorah, the Koran.
Love is the creed I hold; wherever turn
The camels, *Love* is my creed and faith.

— IBN 'ARABI
(*Born in Murcia, Spain, 1165* A.D.;
died in Damascus, Syria, 1240 A.D.)

The World of the Arabs

THE WORLD OF THE ARABS

By

EDWARD J. BYNG

BOSTON

LITTLE, BROWN AND COMPANY · 1944

TO MY MOTHER;
AND TO MY FATHER'S MEMORY

BY WAY OF INTRODUCTION

The object of this book is to give a picture of the life, habits and spirit of the East.

I should be glad if this work, whose author knows the East thoroughly, would help to create abroad correct ideas about one of the most interesting and picturesque parts of the world. After many years of war and suffering, its people feel the strong desire to hold out their hands to the peoples of the West, to assure a common spirit of co-operation in the interest of the entire human race.

Abdul Médjid II

CALIPH OF ISLAM

A FEW WORDS
ABOUT THIS BOOK

$\mathcal{F}$OR THE first time in history, hundreds of thousands of young Americans have established daily contact with the Moslem peoples of North Africa and Arab Asia. The economic and political importance and the geographic location of the countries of Islam are likely to make our contact with them permanent. It is, therefore, of the greatest importance that the American and the Arab should know more about each other.

This book tries to give the American reader an outline of the contemporary life, historical significance, culture, and future importance of the Arabic-speaking East, with those references to Turkey which are necessary to round out the picture.

This is not a "travel book" — that is, its object is not the mechanical description of people, places and monuments. Nor is it a "scientific" book, in the sense of dealing methodically with the more abstract aspects of its subject. The book does strive to be informative; but its principal aim is to appraise the various aspects of the life of the huge Arab community and civilization, to which our Western world owes much.

In an attempt of this nature, we must be constantly

on guard against two chronic sources of error — generalization and emotion.

Generalization is one of the greatest enemies of spiritual growth. When experimenting with some new medicine, we should never be tempted to bring it upon the market on the basis of ten or twenty experiments. Yet often two or three experiences of a similar nature suffice to the average person to formulate a definite opinion about another person, country, or group of people. Generalization is a product of mental inertia. It is the cause of our many totally irrational, unwarranted individual and collective allergies, prejudices and hatreds, from which spring private feuds, bloodshed and war.

The other great enemy of calm and correct observation, and an unbiased evaluation of peoples and problems, is emotion. It often springs from its own twin habit: generalization. Emotion does not impart "color" to a description. It imparts taint.

Our Western picture of Islam and of the Arabs is a pitiful caricature of the reality. It is the result of thirteen hundred years of religious propaganda.

Individuals and communities are clusters of contrasts. We all are guided both by base and by noble instincts. What gives a person and a community its particular hallmark is the *proportion* of these two trends inside the individual, and inside a civilization. On this basis, the civilization of the Arab ranks among the world's highest.

Of course, some caravans still are held up by marauding Bedouins. Conservatively estimated, these cases may compare to the number of bank holdups in the U.S.A. perhaps as one to a thousand. If, in the past, Arabs have indulged in slave trade in West Africa, the Americas have been their best customers. Yet, the Americas have their artists, thinkers and statesmen. So have the Arabs.

If the "howling dervish" looks funny to some Western tourist, our "holy rollers" and "holy jerkers" would look equally funny to some Arab visitor.

To the primitive soul, an unaccustomed environment is a cause for wonderment, criticism, ridicule. To the less primitive, a source of self-education. To the really thinking person, it imparts one of the supreme lessons of life: that the essential nature of the human soul is the same everywhere.

Everywhere, man is a symbiosis of emotion-ridden habits of thought. Feverishly active inside a self-constructed squirrel cage of illusions, he is traversed both by flashes of bestiality and by impulses of divine selflessness.

ოᴚ   ოᴚ   ოᴚ

In connection with the ethnic aspect of my subject, it may not be amiss to refer to an important detail pertaining to the word "Arab."

Racially, the only real Arab is the Bedouin of the

Arabian Desert. As we shall see later, the lands of North Africa and western Asia are inhabited by a very great number of people who are not Arabs, but profess Islam as their religion, use Arabic as their mother tongue, and live inside the great Arab civilization. It is in this broader, cultural sense that this book will use the term "Arab."

A minor point, useful to raise, is that when we refer to the language of the Arabs we should speak of "Arabic." It is customary to speak of "Arabic" numerals, letters, or manuscripts. When referring to something more directly connected with the huge peninsula of Arabia, we should speak of it as "Arabian." It is equally correct, however, to speak of "Arab" or "Arabic" literature.

The expression "Mohammedan" is incorrect and is disparaged by the Moslem. Instead, the term "Moslem" should be employed. When speaking of the religion itself, "Islam," not "Mohammedanism," is the correct term.

In Arabic, "Moslem" means "supporter, follower." It is applied to the followers of the Prophet. The Moslem likes to point out that he considers Mohammed the relatively most inspired among the prophets, but merely one among many prophets. He does not accept the divinity of Mohammed, as the Trinitarian Christian postulates the divinity of Christ. Hence, the Moslem is not a "Mohammedan" as the believer in the divinity of Christ is a "Christian."

A Few Words about This Book

Another point that should be raised here is the matter of the phonetic spelling of Arabic names. I have already said that this book has no strictly scientific objective. Therefore, in rendering Arabic names and other Arabic words, my sole aim is to transcribe them into the Latin script in a way which will, in my personal opinion, enable the Anglo-Saxon reader to come nearest to the original phonetics of the word in Arabic.

Arabic is hard to pronounce. Arabists differ as to the best spelling of Arabic names in English. For example, we encounter the word "Emir" both in this form and as "Ameer." Iraq is spelt "Irak" in many continental European languages. *Rahzoo* — a looting expedition — is often spelt *rhazoo*, and occasionally *ghazoo*, because the initial sound in this word, which is produced by a peculiar contraction of the larynx, resembles the sound *gh*, although it sounds even more like a very guttural *rh*. Other difficulties in the phonetic spelling of Arabic words in English arise from the difference between the Syro-Palestinian and the Egyptian pronunciation of Arabic. For example, "there is none," "it does not exist," is *mahfeesh* in Egyptian Arabic, but sounds like *mehfee* in the Syrian dialect. Salaam is pronounced almost as *selehm* in Syria, and so forth.

In this book, I shall follow certain accepted forms of the phonetic transcription of Arabic into English where that seems to me to come nearest to the original pronunciation, but will completely disregard them where *that* seems to bring me nearer to my objective.

In this connection, as in every aspect of life, we should accept one doctrine alone — not to be doctrinary.

ↄ৯   ↄ৯   ↄ৯

It is customary for authors to preface their books with an expression of appreciation and thanks to those who helped them in their work.

No words could adequately express what I owe to the years I spent in the East. They brought the turning point in my life. The East and West both have their majorities of narrow-minded, ethically and spiritually un-developed people, and their minorities of advanced souls. But, with the exception of a handful of people in the West, really advanced souls in the East actually tower above even the most highly evolved Occidental.

For much valuable information pertaining to the Moslem East, I am indebted to a number of Moslem and non-Moslem, Arab and non-Arab friends. Among these are my old and dear friend, Dr. William Czermak, Pro-fessor of Egyptology at the University of Vienna, with whom I have spent unforgettable days in the Arab East; and my childhood friend, Professor Julius Ger-manus, a famed European Orientalist who became a Moslem and made the holy pilgrimage to Mecca.

Great is my debt to two other old friends, the Ameer Chékib Arslan, one of the greatest scholars of the con-temporary Arabic-speaking world, and that great Turkish statesman and scholar, Abdulhalik Renda, civil governor of Aleppo, Syria's biggest city, at the time when I held the post of a military commander there twenty-six years ago, today Speaker of Turkey's one-chamber legislature.

For spiritual guidance, I am indebted to my late friend, Abdul Hakk Hamid Bey, Turkey's greatest poet in the last generation. For much valuable information, my thanks go to His Excellency, General Ismet Ineunu, President of the Turkish Republic.

Important information pertaining to Moslem culture was given me by His Highness, Azam Jah, Prince of Berar, son and heir of the Nizam of Hyderabad, and his charming and cultured wife, Durru Shéhvar, Princess of Berar.

It would be difficult to try to express in conventional form what I owe to my brother and alter ego, Dr. Maxim Byng, five years my senior in age, many more my senior in matters of the spirit.

In conclusion, I want to do homage to two advanced souls who have honored me by their friendship for over twenty-five years, and to whom I owe a great spiritual debt. One is His Majesty, Abdul Medjid II, Caliph of Islam, artist, linguist, sage, whose hospitality I have enjoyed many times since we first met by the banks of the Bosporus a quarter of a century ago. The other is an Occidental, whom I first met in Asia. That day in January 1917, on which I first met Luigi Dandini, happened to be my twenty-third birthday. Later, it turned out to be the day of my spiritual birth.

CONTENTS

By Way of Introduction. By His Majesty,
Abdul Medjid II, Caliph of Islam   ix

A Few Words about This Book   xi

THE PEOPLE AND THEIR ENVIRONMENT

I   The Peoples of Algeria and Morocco   3
II The Picture in Tunisia, Libya, Egypt   27
III The Bedouin, the Only Real Semite   37
IV Desert Skyscrapers, Devil Worshipers,
    and the Garden of Eden   62

THE RISE OF ARAB POWER

V   The Semite before Islam   91
VI   A Faith Is Born   111
VII The Arab Blitz   128
VIII The Turk Enters the Picture   151

THE TIDE RECEDES

IX   Debacle in Spain   165
X   The West Invades the East   179
XI   The Collapse of Arab North Africa   193
XII World War I in the Levant   206

(xix)

Contents

A LESSON IN HUMILITY: OUR ARAB HERITAGE

XIII The Spirit of Islam   219

XIV Our Debt to Arab Civilization   235

XV What Moslem Thought Can Teach Us   269

THE ARABS IN THE POSTWAR WORLD

XVI The Pan-Arab Federation   285

XVII The Arabs in the Russo-American
Century   300

Index   309

The People and Their Environment

I

THE PEOPLES OF
ALGERIA AND MOROCCO

NATURE is not interested in man-made things. In supreme, timeless serenity, it goes about shaping landscapes and continents. In connection with the soil, we speak of agriculture, horticulture, viticulture, apiculture — never of culture. Yet the soil conditions not only food but also social forms, and, through them, culture.

In other words, man is shaped by heredity, nutrition, tradition.

In sovereign aloofness from man-made history, the physical structure of North Africa has put its indelible mark upon the social forms and the mode of living of its indigenous inhabitants.

But in the spiritual field also has the cavalcade of past and present life in North Africa been overshadowed by major, timeless factors. The fortunes of war and conquest constantly make and break states. Throughout history, frontiers have been, and still are, in a state of flux. Governments, conquerors, political and social forms, come and go.

Civilizations often remain. They survive social and national forms of association by centuries, by millenniums.

For many generations already, North Africa has been broken up into Morocco, Algeria, Tunisia, Libya and Egypt, but its cultural and religious unity has remained unimpaired. The Arab civilization has never lost its hold upon the inhabitants of North Africa, although Arab domination has long disappeared, and only a fraction of North Africa's population has Arab blood in its veins. But, while the major part of the population of North Africa is held together by the spiritual bonds of Moslem-Arab culture and tradition, its ethnic picture is kaleidoscopic.

In Morocco, there is almost no Arab blood in the population. The Moroccans are Berbers, or *Imaziren*, as they call themselves. "Berber," or *Imaziren*, does not denote a race but a mixture of races. The Moroccan of today represents a racial compound, made up of a strong indigenous element going back to prehistoric times, an influx of Ibero-Ligurian blood, and divers other strains. In the veins of the Berbers there flows also a good deal of the blood of the Germanic Vandals, who looted Rome in 455 A.D., crossed over to Africa, and founded a kingdom there, which later succumbed to the Byzantines. There are many fair-skinned Berbers. Many are blond. This feature may be a posthumous present of the Vandals, the only kind of "present" those savage Teutons were likely to give a subject people. In fact, their wanton destruction of art treasures and cultural values, so reminiscent of that of their modern Nazi cousins, gave our vocabulary the word "vandalism."

Major parts of Morocco are mountainous and covered with forests. They are rich in cork oaks and co-
nifers, notably a species of the cedar family. Quite recently, parts of the rugged ranges of the Rif, as the
mountainous northern coastal sector is called, still were
unexplored. The Rif lies mainly in Spanish Morocco,
overlooking the narrow coastline of the Mediterranean.
The Jebel Tiziren, its principal elevation, reaches an
altitude of over eight thousand feet. Deep ravines traverse the region. Many peaks bear colorful *kasbahs*, old
native forts. Protected by powerful buttresses, these
unusually picturesque mountain fastnesses, with their
characteristic sloping walls, prove the uninterrupted survival of the ancient Babylonian style of architecture,
brought here by the Arabs. Below the Rif lie a string
of bays, notably those of Alhucemas, Badis, and Tetuán,
while the important cities of Ceuta and Tangiers are in
the west, just opposite Gibraltar. Tangiers is the center
of a small international zone, with some 230 square miles
and 70,000 inhabitants. Spanish Morocco measures over
60,000 square miles, and has a population of 750,000.

French Morocco, on the other hand, shows a great
variety of scenery. Three powerful, parallel mountain
ranges cross the country from the southwest to the

(5)

northeast: the Mid-Atlas in the north, the High Atlas, with its snow-capped peaks, in the center, and the Anti-Atlas in the south. In the west, between the Atlas range and the Atlantic, stretch the plains and highlands of Morocco, forming the two regions of El Gharb and El Hooz. They were the birthplace of the two ancient rival kingdoms of Fez and Marrakesh, united by Moolay Ismaïl, an ancestor of Moolay Mohammed, present Sultan of Morocco, in the seventeenth century.

Less than half of the 4,500,000 people who inhabit the quarter-million square miles that form French Morocco knows Arabic, which is spoken mainly in the plains and cities. The majority of the population speaks various Berber idioms, which, like the racial types and customs, differ among the three ethnic groups that make up the population. The northern group, known as the Rif people, inhabit the coastal mountain ranges in the Spanish zone. The central group, mostly called Berber, lives in the Mid-Atlas region, its major part leading a nomad life. The so-called Shlooh, who form the third group, live mainly in the High Atlas and the region of the Atlantic coast.

Great numbers among the city folk are direct descendants of the Moorish refugees who left Spain in two major waves. The first followed the conquest of Granada by Ferdinand and Isabella by a few years. The second, equally important, poured into Morocco as late as the seventeenth century, when the fanaticism of the Inquisition drove the so-called Moriscos from Spain. The

Moslem ancestors of the Moriscos had nominally become Christians in Spain, but secretly maintained their Moslem beliefs and customs.

There are also some hundred thousand Jews in Morocco. They live mostly in the cities. In part, their ancestors came here from Palestine more than two thousand years ago, when the Ptolemies ruled Egypt. The rest of Moroccan Jewry is made up of direct descendants of those Jews driven from Spain at the end of the fifteenth century. This group of Moroccan Jews is known to the Moslem Moroccans as "Castilian" — *Gueroosh Castilla*.

The French entered Morocco as late as 1911, setting up a protectorate in 1912. They found a social structure based upon the feudal system. Since the tribesmen of Morocco are fierce warriors, the French administrators of the country have found it wise to placate the population by leaving its tribal and feudal organization unchanged. Major parts of the population outside the cities still live in tribal communities, governed by age-old tribal customs. Over this social system, the French have erected an administrative superstructure. It consists of a French administrative machinery, co-ordinated with the sultanate, and with a measure of authority vested in a number of powerful *kaïds*, or feudal lords. Several of these still wield the power of life and death over their servants and slaves. Entrenched in their *kasbahs*, or mountain strongholds, these men, some of whom hold sway over thousands of armed henchmen, represent a "nuisance value" which the French fully recognize. In fact, following almost twenty years of both open and guerrilla warfare against France's troops of occupation, native armed resistance in the less accessible parts of the Atlas range ceased only as late as 1933.

The three most powerful families who command great numbers of armed tribesmen in the Atlas and the hinterland of Marrakesh are the Goondahfy (usually spelt "Gundafi"), the M'tooggy (spelt "M'tuggi") and the Glaooee (spelt "Glaoui"). The year 1928 brought the death of El Gundafi, powerful head of the clan of the same name, who, in his fortified *kasbah*, and on the snow-covered slopes of the Atlas chain, had defied the French army for many years.

The chief of the M'tuggi clan died in the same year. The death of these two powerful *kaïds* left the most important of the triad, El Glaoui, in possession of the greatest power among all nominal vassals of the Sultan of Morocco.

Therefore, Sidi (that is, "The Lord") Thami El Glaoui, Pasha of Marrakesh and head of the powerful, well-armed clan of the Glaoui, is the pampered child of the French administration in Morocco. The Sultan also regards him with great favor. The reason is that, in the stormy years that followed the arrival of the French in the country in 1911, Thami El Glaoui had proved a faithful vassal of the royal house.

The country had risen in arms against the French, who had to fight the embittered tribal warriors of Morocco simultaneously on five fronts. The Sultan, Moolay

Hafid, escaped capture by the French. Deserted by his army, without money, food or shelter, he sought refuge with El Glaoui, his most powerful vassal. A cold winter night saw the fleeing monarch in his white, hooded robe, standing at the gate of the *Kasbah El Glaoui*, his vassal's medieval mountain fastness in the heart of the snow-capped Atlas. By handing the Sultan over to the French, or even by refusing him shelter, El Glaoui would have greatly strengthened his status and influence with the new European protecting power.

El Glaoui appreciated the value of being popular with the Occidental masters of his country, but appreciated even more Islam's tenets of loyalty and hospitality. The royal refugee found a haven behind the buttresses of the *Kasbah El Glaoui.*

Later, after the French had set up the Sultan's son, Moolay Mohammed, the present ruler, on the throne, they found that it was in their own interest to assure the friendship of Thami El Glaoui, a simple order from whose lips or pen could rouse the Atlas at any time in bloody revolt against Western rule. So Thami El Glaoui resides in his gorgeous city palace in Marrakesh, amid the richly carved walls, cedarwood-and-mother-of-pearl–inlaid doors, marble fountains. His tanned face, with its massive features and aquiline nose, exudes a mixture of dignity, pride and measured friendliness, as he, hereditary Pasha of Marrakesh, receives the dignitaries of the French regime of his country. At the same time, his nephew, Si Hammu El Glaoui, a Berber with a skin as white as that of the French Resident General, lives in the ancestral family *kasbah*, in the heart of the Atlas range. He is known under the proud name "the Eagle of Telouet," from the location of the *kasbah* where Moolay Hafid had found refuge in his hour of supreme distress.

Si Hammu and his warriors are under his uncle's orders, and subsidies, the ribbon of the Legion of Honor, and other favors from the French are intended to keep both Glaouis in good humor.

ↄ₪ঌ   ↄ₪ঌ   ↄ₪ঌ

Aside from their local color, most cities of Morocco resemble our major cities of the West in their combination of splendor and squalor, beautiful residential sections and slums. The ancient city of Fez, and the important religious center of Meknes (pronounced "Meckness"), are picturesque. But Marrakesh, the largest city in the country, with a little under 200,000 people, occupies a unique position. Like Aleppo in Syria, Marrakesh has preserved its unadulterated Oriental character in an astonishing degree. With its flat-roofed houses, colorful mosques, busy streets, palm trees and cactus hedges, the city is enframed in a horizon adorned with the glorious skyline of the Atlas range. Thoroughly Oriental in its atmosphere, tropical in its vegetation,

Marrakesh looks up to peaks eternally covered with snow — an ideal background for some scene from the *Arabian Nights*.

The center of the city's life is the huge square known as *Djemah el Fnah*. On market days, this spot offers a fascinating cross section of Moroccan life. Dotted here and there with the khaki uniforms of French and other Allied officers and the Western clothes of foreign civilians, the famous square teems with natives from every walk of life. Nomads from the Mid-Atlas and warriors of the High Atlas rub shoulders with the city folk. The native's loose, white, hooded robe is in evidence everywhere. The newly arrived Westerner usually wonders how it is that the native, who wears a hood over his turban, is not smothered by the heat. He forgets that the hood creates a layer of stagnant air round the head and neck, insulating it from the heat almost as effectively as a double, or French window insulates a room, or the double walls of a thermos bottle the liquid inside it. In the cold winter days of the High Atlas, the same age-old device protects the Berber's head and neck from the cold. During a railway journey across the highland of Konia, in Asia Minor, in 1917, when I had to spend three days and nights in a sitting position in an unheated compartment with broken windows and a temperature of thirty centigrades below zero, my companions and I saved our feet from freezing off and developing gangrene by taking off our shoes and wrapping a woolen blanket loosely round our feet. The resultant layer of stagnant air protected them perfectly. As in most other regions of the world, in North Africa and Arab Asia also age-old experience has adapted the native dress completely to local climatic conditions.

Among the most colorful features of the *Djemah el Fnah* are the conjurers and the snake charmers. Here, as in Egypt, some snake charmers do not use a flute or other musical instrument to put the reptile into a hypnotic or semi-hypnotic condition. Some dominate the snake, and even induce wild snakes to come to them from their hiding places, by chanting, or uttering rhythmically repeated sounds.

Among many secrets of nature that the Oriental has preserved through the ages, the mysteries of animal psychology, and even of the human Unconscious, rank foremost. I have seen an Egyptian fakir hypnotizing snakes, crocodiles and even chickens, putting them into a state of complete rigidity merely by looking at them. He revived them, without any evil aftereffects, simply by touching their heads with his forefinger.

But Marrakesh can boast of an instance of magic a hundred times more impressive than the subtle psychic artistry of the fakir — the magic of creative artistic genius. It has found sublime expression in that late-sixteenth-century pavilion in the El Bedi Palace, which holds the tombs of the Moroccan sultans of the Sa'adi family.

Granada's Alhambra is justly famous as a shining example of Arab architecture and interior decoration. But some sections of the mausoleum of the Sa'adi family, although much less known, are equal in beauty to any of the glorious details of the Alhambra, or of that Indian funerary monument of world fame, Agra's Taj Mahal.

The screens of carved plasterwork that adorn the entrance and interior of the tombs of the Sa'adis are among the most memorable monuments to the artistic genius of Moslem civilization. In its unrelenting opposition to idolatry, orthodox Islam prohibits the pictorial and sculptural representation of human figures and animals. As a consequence, Islamic art has reached heights of beauty and perfection in adorning walls, arches, windows, capitals of columns, and other architectural elements with ingenious combinations of flowers, foliage, geometric designs, and decorative script.

The tribal structure of Moroccan society, the occasional feuds among rival clans in the Atlas Mountains, represent one aspect of Morocco; the artistic wonders of Fez, Meknes and Marrakesh, another. If we forget this, our picture of Morocco will be just as asymmetric as would be that of our own country in the mind of some Moroccan scholar who may have heard or read about the sanguinary family feuds among our Kentucky mountaineers, but has not seen, or heard of, Gutzon Borglum's sculptures of Pharaonic size and grandeur on Bald Mountain, or of the thoroughly American and thoroughly beautiful forms of New York's Radio City.

(13)

ᴥ   ᴥ   ᴥ

Algeria derives its name from the city of Algiers, and the latter from *El Jerz*, which is its name in Arabic. Algeria, the largest among the countries of North Africa, differs greatly from Morocco in many ways.

More than a hundred years of French rule have left their mark on every aspect of Algerian life. The country was invaded by the French in 1830, but not actually conquered until ten years later, when Abd el Kader, heroic leader of the Moslem defenders, finally had to yield. At the time of the Franco-Prussian War of 1870, the natives attempted an uprising, but were unable to stand up against the superior military equipment of the European troops.

Since those days, France has done much for Algeria economically and socially. The northern part of the country is completely peaceful and, in normal times, prosperous. In the deep south, however, where merely a few oases dot the endless stretches of the Sahara, and among the wild, rugged chains of the Ahoggar Mountains, peace and public security are occasionally menaced by turbulent nomads and other tribal elements.

The French administrative system in Algeria, with its 850,000 square miles and 6,000,000 inhabitants, has been adapted to this situation and to the country's geographic structure. Algeria is not run as a colony. Administratively, its northern region is actually a part of metropolitan France. The Great Atlas, which traverses the country from the southwest to the northeast, and almost parallel to its Mediterranean coastline, roughly coincides with an administrative line of demarcation between the northern and southern parts of the country. The north is divided into three *départements*, those of Oran, Algiers, and Constantine. These administrative units enjoy the same status as the *départements* that make up France proper. In normal times, they send senators and deputies to the national legislature in Paris. The southern region of Algeria is divided into four military territories, under officers of the army, who are both governors and commanders in their sectors. These sectors are known as Aïn Sefra, Ghardaïa, Touggourt, and the "Saharan Oases." Administratively, the whole country is under a governor general. He is usually a soldier, and of a high military rank, so as to be the senior both of the "prefects" of the three *départements* and of the four military governors in the south.

The Algerian coastline on the Mediterranean, about 550 miles long, is steep and rocky. Between it and the High Atlas, and parallel to both, the Little Atlas traverses the country from Morocco in the west almost as far as Tunisia in the east. This northern part of Algeria, between the High Atlas and the Mediterranean, is very fertile, and produces great quantities of wine and olive oil for export. The southern region reaches into the very heart of the Sahara. It consists mainly of huge stretches of barren land. But the region has a few oases rich in water, palms and other vegetation, such as Ghardaïa, Ouargla, and others. Biskra, with its three-mile-long forest of palms, is a famous tourist resort. Like most of the country's cities and oases, it is equipped with hotels that represent the last word in modern comfort. Nothing could offer a more glaring threefold contrast to the visitor than the cities in the north, with their teeming Oriental life, the tiny, forlorn forts, manned by a handful of European and native soldiers, that stand out from the endless sand dunes of the far south, and the gloriously preserved remains of such ancient, once flourishing Roman cities as Timgad and Touggourt. Two thousand years ago these were rich, luxurious centers of commerce and industry, headquarters of Roman legions. Today, their mile-long, lifeless colonnades of columns, their streets paved with stone slabs, their empty theaters, desecrated altars and ruined temples stand there, in the deadly silence of the hot desert. They resemble glorious-hued sea shells from which the spark of life has departed.

Once, the Roman eagles were planted here by the legions of the Caesars. Today, the neighboring forts house units of such crack French colonial troops as the Zouaves, the Turcos, the Foreign Legion, and the Spahis, Algeria's famed native cavalry. Just as a commission in Britain's celebrated Light Blues usually is the hallmark of aristocratic descent, so are the officers of the Spahis often scions of France's most ancient feudal families.

      ᕤ   ᕤ   ᕤ

Racially, about a million of Algeria's inhabitants are European, the other five million being mainly Berber. Many of the latter are of Hamitic stock. There are also many Arabs, who are, of course, Semites. The Kabyles, who inhabit the rocky ranges of the coastal region, also are Berbers. The major part of the Arabs lead a nomad life, although many are sedentary, especially in the coastal region, where they are engaged in agricultural pursuits. Many Berbers still speak their own language, but they write it in Arabic characters. The native population in the cities, a mixture of many races, is referred to as Moors.

Europeans and natives mix freely in the streets of the cities, but they live strictly apart. In justice to the French be it said, however, that in Algeria, and elsewhere in their empire, they do not display that foolish and unwarranted air of superiority which our own light- and thick-skinned mediocrities like to flaunt among darkskinned people. As a matter of fact, the French have shown great ability in creating prosperity in some of their colonies not only for themselves but also for the natives. But they have not been able to bridge the emotional gulf between the colonizer and the colonized.

The cleavage between the lives of the Europeans and of the natives is particularly conspicuous in the city of Algiers itself, with its 200,000-odd inhabitants. Here, two worlds lie side by side inside the city limits. There is the modern European quarter, with its beautiful Boulevard de la République and its two principal squares, the Place du Gouvernement and the Place Bresson. But there is also the famed Kasbah, so called because this spot once bore a *kasbah*, or native fortress. Today, it is the native quarter, a maze of narrow, dark, crooked, dirty streets and blind alleys. The Kasbah, perched atop a 500-foot hill overlooking the port, is also the haunt of both the native and the French underworld of Algiers, and includes the native red-light district.

Many a denizen of the labyrinthine Kasbah is hiding from the *present*. But in Sidi-Bel-Abbès, south of Oran, are those who seek to hide from the *past* — their own private past. It is headquarters of the Foreign Legion, with its four regiments of men who are asked no questions when they enlist but who have helped France to score great military victories. While Sidi-Bel-Abbès is the center of the Foreign Legion, various minor units of that body man the forts in the south, including those in the region inhabited by the Tuareg.

The Tuareg tribesmen form one of the most extraordinary ethnic groups on earth. They are famous as fierce fighters, and also for some unique customs. They inhabit a territory bounded by the Ahoggar Mountains of southern Algeria in the north, Nigeria in the south, Timbuctoo in the west, the so-called Fezzan, in southern Libya, in the northeast, and the Tchad territory in the east. Both men and women are tall, with fine, intelligent features, a very light complexion, and dark, wavy hair. Many Tuareg women are very beautiful.

The social status of Tuareg women is a startling reversal of the practice of Islam, to which the Tuareg nominally profess allegiance. To begin with, it is the men who wear veils, not the women. In fact, they do not call themselves "Tuareg" at all, which is a word coined by the Arabs, but *Kel Tagilmus* — "the people of the veil" — to denote the age-old habit of the Tuareg warrior to conceal his features behind a veil. This veil, the *litham*, actually is a strip of black cloth, which is wound round the head in such a way that it covers the whole face, leaving merely a narrow slit for the eyes. The *litham* helps to protect the camel-riding warriors from the glare of the sun and the whirling sand of the desert, which may account for its remote origin. But the Tuareg share with the Bedouin of central Arabia the belief that human beings are constantly surrounded by evil spirits, seeking to get in through their mouths and nostrils, to gain possession of their souls. It is primarily to ward off this danger that the Tuareg men wear veils. They sleep, and even die, with their veils on, and if they must remove them momentarily to eat, or for any other reason, they usually do it in strict seclusion. Even then they often try to cover their nose and mouth with one hand, to protect themselves from obsession through some *affrit*, or evil spirit.

This unusually colorful ethnic group has a number of regular cities of its own. It has preserved a relatively great measure of independence from outside interference. This is due to the prudent attitude of the French authorities. The reward of French political wisdom is that the Tuareg, although jealous of their independence, maintain an attitude of loyalty and friendly co-operation toward their French political overlords.

Socially, the Tuareg consist of two castes, the nobility, or *imayegh*, and the serfs, or *imghad*. The latter have a good deal of Sudanese and Negro blood. But the most unusual among the many unusual features of Tuareg society is that it represents one of the few surviving examples of the prehistoric institution of matriarchy.

The women dominate the community. Not only do they wear no veils but they have sexual freedom before marriage. They do not abuse this freedom, however, because Tuareg women have an exceptionally high degree of dignity, intelligence, and self-respect. Then again, a commercial motive for sexual freedom is absent, because it is the women, not the men, who own and manage the property of their families. Women attend to all commercial transactions. They alone read and write, and very few women of the ruling caste are illiterate. The wife is the undisputed master in the household. The husband owns little more than his clothes and weapons, and his wife can divorce him without difficulty. The Tuareg trace their family descent in the female line.

But just as if Dame Fortune had wished to empty her whole horn of plenty over the beautiful women of the Tuareg, she gave them also artistic taste and an amazing gift for poetry. They have a faculty, which we find also with the Bedouin men of Arabia, of improvising poetry. They frequently hold competitions in poetry, at which they compose poems of real merit "while you wait," while the men listen in awed, respectful silence.

Until recently, the ethnic origin of the Tuareg was a scientific mystery. They have their own language, the *Targi* (pronounced "targhee"), and their own script, the *tifinagh*. Until quite recently, ethnology classed them as "Hamitic nomads belonging to the Berber group." "Berber" is a very indefinite term, applied to most of those ethnic groups in present-day Morocco, Algeria, Tunisia and Libya which cannot be classed otherwise. Moreover, the origin of the *Targi* language has long been unclear. Only in quite recent years, in fact as late as 1938, have important new facts been found in this connection.

In the light of these discoveries, it now appears that *Targi* is closely related to a language known as *Rong*, still spoken in a geographically restricted area in Asia Minor, not far from the Syrian border. This discovery would point to some prehistoric migration of the Tuareg from Asia Minor to the western Sahara.

In 1938, a French archaeological expedition explored

a number of ancient tombs of Tuareg princesses, held in great veneration by the present generation. The gold coins found in the tombs automatically determined the latter's age, because most of them were Roman coins of the period of Constantine, that is, of the early fourth century A.D. In addition, the tombs held several bracelets of specific, typical Etruscan design. Now we know that by about 300 B.C., some six hundred years before Constantine, the Romans had wiped out the last vestiges of Etruscan life and power. Besides, it is well known to every student of archaeology, or of the history of art, how ancient artistic motifs will survive many centuries, even millenniums, in pottery, architecture, textiles, jewelry, and in other fields. The Greek "Meander motif" has survived some three thousand years in the Western world and in China, where it probably is autochthonous. Various decorative elements in the rugs and pottery of our Navajos, and of Old Mexico, go straight back to the Aztec, Toltec and even Maya periods. We know today that the Etruscans originally migrated westward from Asia Minor, reaching Italy around the ninth century B.C.

Pending further investigation, I should like tentatively to advance the hypothesis either that the Tuareg might be a surviving branch of the Etruscans, which, unlike its brothers, migrated from Asia Minor, not to Europe but to Africa; or that at some time in the pre-Christian era the Tuareg maintained prolonged contact with the Etruscans. It should be relatively easy either to sub-

stantiate or to disprove this hypothesis, once we know
more about the mysterious language of the Etruscans,
long lost to science. Just before the Second World War
began, a European scientist was reported to have de-
ciphered it. Should this be true, Etruscan should be compared with the almost extinct but still living *Rong* language of Asia Minor, and the still flourishing *Targi*
idiom of the Tuareg. An affinity between the three
would have sensational scientific significance.

Another ethnic group in Algeria whose customs are
completely at variance with orthodox Moslem tradition
is the Ouled Naïl tribe. It is standard practice for its
beautiful girls to go to the cities and take up careers as
specialty dancers, with prostitution thrown in.

Incidentally, it may be interesting to mention that,
throughout the Moslem world, women dancers performing for native audiences are always fully dressed.
The flimsy veils and semi-nudity sported by "oriental"
dancers on the Western vaudeville or theatrical stage
are entirely a product of Western imagination. In North
Africa or Arab Asia, they would cause a public scandal.
It is characteristic of the taste of the allegedly superior
"white man" that the clandestine performances of nude
dancers your guide in Algiers, Biskra and Cairo takes
you to see are staged almost exclusively for the Western
tourist. In Algeria, the performers in these clandestine
shows also are mostly Ouled Naïl girls. At these shows,
the musicians, characteristically, usually turn their backs
on the nude dancers. Your guide will whisper to you

with a mysterious smile that they do that because at the sight of the girls in that condition they might lose control of themselves.

This intriguing ethnological "information" from your guide is humbug. The average Moslem is just as human as his Western brother, but, owing to a difference, not in temperament but in traditional methods of education, he usually has much more self-control than the average Westerner. Should the musicians who assist at these nude shows, so diametrically contrary to Moslem usage, wish to lose control of themselves, they would hardly choose the moment when other people are present. Just as their Western contemporaries, they prefer to lose control of themselves in private.

Besides, the last thing the natives who assist at these performances in the nude want to lose is their self-control. They want every bit of it for the lucrative exploitation of the Western tourist's lower instincts and higher gullibility. If they lost their serenity, how could they make the "superior" white man pay through the nose?

With the exception of the Ouled Naïl tribe, it is a rule in orthodox Moslem countries that a bona fide woman artist — actress, singer or dancer — must be chaste, or must lead a respectable life if she is married. Moreover, outside modern Turkey and Soviet Russia, no orthodox Moslem woman dances, sings, or acts in public. In some cities in the conservative regions of Islam, unmarried women artists, regardless of their religion, still have to undergo a medical examination to establish their virginity, before they are allowed to perform. At the time of the First World War, the police doctor in Aleppo, Asia's largest Arabic-speaking city, still had the time-honored duty of examining the native women artists performing on the stage set up in the *Shekhbender*, the city's "Central Park." The star among those artists was a singer by the name of Simhah, a beautiful, graceful and intelligent native Jewess. Like her female colleagues, she submitted to the police test with a great deal of pride, knowing that, by the moral standards of age-old local tradition, a favorable outcome of the medical examination would greatly enhance her personal and professional status.

A few days later, I was listening to the beautiful Arab love songs that Simhah interpreted with real mastery, in the company of Shefket Bey, a local Turkish police officer who had spent many years in Paris. Between two encores by Simhah, Shefket whispered: —

"*Mon cher*, yesterday I got one of the greatest shocks of my life. I looked up the police record of Simhah's medical examination, just to see whether she is chaste. And, by Allah! She is!"

As I have said, the Ouled Naïl entertainer is in a class by herself. She turns her "receipts" into gold and silver coins, which she wears made up in rows round her head. After a few years, she retires to her tribe and hands over the rows of coins as a dowry to an affectionate bridegroom. This dowry is, of course, the exact opposite of the usual practice of the orthodox Moslem, to pay a "purchase price" for a wife to his future father-in-law.

Among the wealthy Moslem of Morocco and Algeria the custom has become purely symbolic, for the bride's father gives her wedding presents equal in value to her purchase price.

II

THE PICTURE IN
TUNISIA, LIBYA, EGYPT

*U*NTIL 1881, present-day Tunisia was independent under its beys. The present dynasty of beys, whose family name is Er-Romdan, was founded in 1705 by Hussein ben Ali, a Christian from Crete who had become a Moslem. Like Algeria, for centuries Tunisia was a pirate state. In 1881 the French conquered it and gave it its present status of semi-independence, in the form of a protectorate.

Tunisia is much smaller than Algeria. It has an area of 48,000 square miles and supports two and a half million people. It is no less colorful than its big western neighbor, Algeria.

The north is mountainous, but very fertile. There are gardens and oases in the south. The central region is rich in good pasture land. The *chott*, or salt-water lakes, are a characteristic feature of the country.

Except for Khaïrouan, the major Tunisian cities are ports. Bizerte and Tunis dominate the north coast. The east coast is studded with the three maritime cities of Sousse, Sfax and Gabes (pronounced "Gahbess"). Khaïrouan is the most important city of the interior, and one of the most important religious centers of Islam.

Roughly 200,000 among the country's inhabitants are

European, 56,000 are native Jews, the rest, some 2,250,-000, being orthodox Moslem. Approximately 90,000 among the Europeans are French, practically the same number Italian. The resultant ethnic, political and economic rivalry between these two groups is Tunisia's principal domestic problem.

The pursuits of the population are conditioned by the structure and climate of the country. Agriculture is the occupation of the people in the north. In the central region, they raise sheep, goats, and some cattle. In the desert in the south, the population is nomad. The Tunisians are a mixture of Berber and Arab blood, but the Berber idioms have died out, only Arabic being spoken.

It is to this part of the world that the entire continent of Africa owes its name. In Arabic, it is *Ifrikeeyeh*. In the days of ancient Carthage, *Ifrica* was the name of that coastal region of Tunisia facing Sicily. Following the Roman conquest of Carthage, this region became the Roman province of *Africa*. Later, the name began to be applied to the entire continent.

Ancient Carthage, for centuries the undisputed master of the Mediterranean, political overlord of present-day Tunisia, Algeria, Morocco, Spain, Portugal, Malta and Sicily, lay ten miles to the northeast of the present-day city of Tunis. Its ruins are a famous tourist attraction. Shortly after the First World War, a Pole, Baron de Prorok, conducted important excavations there. Among the objects found were hundreds of jars, of earthenware. They contained the bones of small children who had been sacrificed to the goddess Tanit, one of the tutelary deities of Carthage. The city's other paramount deity was the sun-god, Baal. Originally the principal god of Babylon and Phoenicia, his ever-recurring cult among the ancient Jews was one of the major concerns of the prophets. But Baal has another connection with the history of Carthage. His name inspired that of the greatest strategic genius of all time, the analysis of whose battles still is "must stuff" in the curriculum of European war colleges. Hannibal was the Roman version of the Punic name "Hanni-i-Baal." But in Punic, which was Carthage's Semitic idiom, Hanni-i-Baal meant "blessed by Baal." To the Romans, Hannibal had another meaning: that of disaster.

An important phase of world history was, and still is shaped by the position of the straits between Sicily and the African promontory that once bore Carthage, and now bears Tunis. It was Carthage's geographic and strategic situation, with the resultant stranglehold on Mediterranean shipping, that made it a world power. Eventually, Rome had to fight Carthage for the "freedom of the seas," and crush it.

But centuries before Rome conquered this part of Africa from Sicily, Carthage conquered Sicily from this part of Africa. In the tenth century of our era, Sicily was once again conquered from the same operation base on the African coast, this time by the Aghlabite princes of Tunisia. In the Second World War, Sicily was once more invaded from the same part of North Africa. Nor is the story of the Straits over yet.

Man lives and writes history. The land shapes it.

        ❧   ❧   ❧

Fully aware of the strategic position of this promontory of North Africa, with its cities of Tunis and Bizerte, the French transformed the latter into a mid-Mediterranean Gibraltar. Bizerte has a population of twenty thousand, which is less than one tenth of that of neighboring Tunis. But as a naval base, Bizerte is so large that its harbor could hold the entire American and British fleets. Its highly modern installations date back only to the nineteen-thirties. It has bomb-proof gasoline tanks, blasted out of the solid rock, dry docks, and modern fortifications.

By contrast, Tunis is an old city, and the political and commercial capital of the country. Its ancient native quarter, with its narrow, crooked streets, teems with life. Its *sooks*, as the alleys forming its bazaar are called, are famous. Even more famous is its beautiful *Zitoona* mosque, known as the "Mosque of the Olive Tree."

The Jewish colony of Tunis is centuries old. It now numbers about thirty thousand. Its founders came partly from Italy, partly from Spain, at the end of the fifteenth century. One part of the Tunisian Jewry, however, actually descends from those who fled there after the fall of Jerusalem in 71 A.D.

The French have built the new city of Tunis side by side with the native quarter, and have laid it out along modern lines. Its mile-long main artery, whose three sections are known as the Avenue Jules-Ferry, Avenue de la Marine, and Avenue de France, has many fine public buildings, and is the business and traffic center of modern Tunis.

But nothing could be more illustrative of the contrasts in which Tunisia abounds than a comparison of modern Tunis, in the north, with its 200,000 people, and Matmata, a city of some 100,000 inhabitants, in the south.

Matmata, not far from the Libyan border, is a city of troglodytes. Its people live entirely underground, in caves called *rhorfa*, dug out of the soft but firm clay which forms the soil. The living rooms always surround a larger room which much resembles a bear pit in shape. The excavations which form the living rooms have barrel-vaulted roofs, shelves for storage jars and raised bed places of clay. Oddly enough, bathrooms are a regular feature in this subterranean world.

Although Tunisia is small, its spiritual significance in the world of Islam is great. Tunis has a famous Moslem university, founded in 732 A.D. The city of Khaïrouan, in the south, is one of the holy pilgrimage centers of Islam. In religious significance, it ranks right after Mecca, Medina, and Jerusalem, whose Dome of the

Rock, built on the spot which once bore Solomon's temple, houses the tomb of the Caliph Omar. Khaïrouan is famous among the Faithful because it holds the tomb of Okba ben Nafi, known as Sidi Okba, "the Lord Okba," who brought Islam to Africa.

The sacred tomb lies inside the Sidi Okba Mosque, one of Islam's holiest shrines. The first part of the mosque was built in 671 A.D., the later building in 703. The city is a sea of white, flat-topped houses, a visit to it a rare experience for the traveler. The beautiful square minaret, with its highly decorative pattern, formed of bricks set edgewise, is a geographic and artistic landmark. Two hundred odd years after this beautiful specimen of Moslem art had originated, it inspired the architect of the great mosque of Moslem-held Seville. Aside from a later, sixteenth-century Christian superstructure, the gloriously beautiful square minaret which he built by the side of the mosque is mainly a replica of Khaïrouan's famed minaret. It still is in perfect condition, is world-famous under the name *La Giralda*, and now is the bell tower of Seville's cathedral.

∾　　　∾　　　∾

Libya differs greatly from its western neighbors both in physical structure and in the relative density of its population. There are a few palm and olive groves around its principal coastal cities and in its oases, but the vast country is mostly barren. The 680,000 square miles which form its area are inhabited by less than 900,000 people. Some fifty thousand among these are Europeans.

The Libyans are mostly Arab and Moslem. Arabic is practically the only language spoken. The Italians divided the country into four administrative units: the provinces of Tripoli, Misurata, Benghazi, and Derna. A little over 100,000 people inhabit the city of Tripoli, 45,000 Misurata. These are the biggest cities. Dates, olives and grapes are the principal products of the country.

In the so-called Fezzan, which lies in the southwest, we encounter small groups of Tuareg. Far down in the southeast lies the large oasis of Kufra or Kufara, traditional stronghold of the famed Senussi, another among those unusual human groups in which Africa and Asia abound.

Fourteen days on camel back will take a caravan from Benghazi, on the shore of the Mediterranean, to Kufra. For three days, the traveler must carry his drinking water with him. When, finally, he sees the palms and the flat-roofed houses of Kufra, he has reached the capital of one of the most picturesque peoples of North Africa.

The Senussi claim about six million adherents throughout North Africa and in certain parts of Arabia. They are not an ethnic group, but a religious sect, forming a confraternity of Moslem puritans. They are pledged to unceasing warfare against the "infidel." In this respect, the Senussi are a Moslem counterpart of our Crusaders, who had pledged unceasing war on the infidel — this time, in the Christian sense of the word.

The founders of the Senussi creed came to Africa from the small country of Asir, which lies between Hejaz and Yemen, on the east coast of the Red Sea. The movement began in the second quarter of the last century, when the Napoleonic aggression in Egypt and Palestine still was generally remembered in the Moslem world, and the European aggression against Moslem Algeria was in full swing. Thus, the fighting creed of the first Senussi resulted from the determination to resist Western aggression.

Ever since the arrival of the Italians in Libya in 1911, the Senussi have nurtured an implacable hatred against Italians, Fascist and non-Fascist alike. They repeatedly rose in bloody revolt against their Italian masters, until Marshal Rodolfo Graziani took their capital, Kufra, some years ago, and "pacified" them, mainly with the help of the gallows.

Before Graziani led his expedition to Kufra, few Occidentals had penetrated to that almost inaccessible Senussi stronghold. The Grand Shaykh (often spelt "sheikh" or "sheik," but *never* pronounced "sheek"), Ahmed, supreme spiritual and temporal leader of the Senussi confraternity, who died in Mecca a few years ago, was one of the most important and influential Moslem leaders of the old school living anywhere between Morocco and India. He led a strictly secluded life.

When we met in Asia Minor in 1923, he told me himself that he had seen only two Occidentals previously, both Americans. The first was a Colonel of the United States Army, who had been sent to the East by President Woodrow Wilson in 1919, to meet and confer with Grand Shaykh Ahmed. The second was the late Charles R. Crane of Chicago, one-time American Ambassador to China and student of Oriental affairs, who toured the Moslem East around 1920.

Nothing could be more illustrative of the Senussi outlook than a remark Grand Shaykh Ahmed made during a conversation. "There is one thing I never allow my servants to do for me," he said, "and that is to clean my rifle. When I was a boy, my grandfather often told me that one of the Senussi warrior's foremost duties, which he should always perform himself, was to keep his gun clean. I have adhered to this rule ever since."

ow   ow   ow

In contrast to Morocco, Algeria, Tunisia and Libya, Egypt has been written and lectured about so often and so exhaustively that the major aspects of its colorful present and glorious past are common property among educated people in the West. Since this is not a travel book, there would be little value in duplicating those more or less generally known facts and data.

Egypt is a sovereign kingdom. It has a strong national movement, whose leaders are firmly resolved to assure the country's continued independence. This national movement is strongly represented in the Wafd party, which unquestionably represents the huge majority of the Egyptian people.

The example of Turkey, which reformed its social, political and economic life from the ground up, has had great influence upon Egypt. But while modern Turkey takes no interest in a pan-Islamic movement, or in any other concerted attitude of Moslem countries, based upon their common religion, modern Egypt plays a prominent part in the spiritual life of Islam. The famous Moslem university of El Azhar in Cairo was founded in 968 A.D. Great is the prestige of its *shaykhs*, or professors — the word *shaykh* has different meanings. Their interpretation of Koranic law and usage carries weight from Morocco to India.

About 10 per cent of the population of Egypt are so-called Copts, a Christian sect. Like the Ethiopians, they still adhere to the school of thought of Arius of Alexandria, who, in the fourth century, denied the divinity of Christ. Thus, the Copts are actually Unitarians.

Fortunately for Egypt, religious animosity is not among its problems. Its strength is not dissipated along such lines.

In the postwar world, Egypt's strength and influence will increasingly make itself felt in world affairs.

III

THE BEDOUIN,
THE ONLY REAL SEMITE

$\mathcal{A}$S WE have seen earlier in this book, the terms "Arab," "Arabian" and "Arabic" are vague in Western usage. We have also seen that "Arabic" should apply to the language and the script of the Arabs, and "Arabian" to the various aspects of life in Arabia proper — that is, outside Syria, Palestine, Iraq, and Arabic-speaking Africa.

The greatest need for clarity, however, exists in the use of the word "Arab." We can speak of "Arab culture," "Arab conquests," "Arab history, science and philosophy," all of which can be traced back to the Arabs.

But who are the Arabs?

When the Occidental speaks of them, he usually means the totality of the ethnic groups whose mother tongue is Arabic. But if used in that sense, "Arab" is a glaring misnomer, just as "Spaniard" would be in the case of a Mexican, Chilean, and Filipino.

Racially, ethnically, the Bedouin of the Arabian Desert alone is an Arab. In a slightly broader sense, the term "Arab" can be applied to the major part of the city population of the Hejaz and of some other coastal regions of the Arabian peninsula. But strictly speaking, only the Bedouin of Arabia is a real Arab. In fact, he

refers to himself not as a Bedouin but as an Arab. When
we speak of an "Arab movement" in the strictly political sense, or of a Pan-Arab Federation, we are referring
to political concepts less than thirty years old, and no
more based upon Arab racial and ethnic homogeneity
than "Spanish-American" or "Ibero-American" movements are based upon the racial affinity of the peoples
concerned.

Racially, the Bedouin, that is, the real Arab, is the
only Northern Semite still in existence. The Jew has
long ceased to be a Semite, although, for purposes of
religious ritual, he still uses Hebrew. But the majority
of the Jews can no longer speak or write Hebrew, and
are just barely able to read the medieval rabbinical script
in which their prayer books are printed.

A "Jewish race" exists solely in the overheated im-
agination of pseudoscientists and German Jew-baiters.
What we call the "Jewish" facial type is not Jewish but
Hittite. And a great part of the Jews of Poland and
Russia descend from the Khazars of the lower Volga,
and other Mongol and Mongoloid peoples converted to
Judaism in the eighth and ninth centuries A.D.

The Jews are not a race but a *people*. They are a people made up of many racial strains, representing a complex mixture of those strains, the Hittite strain predomi-
nating.

Many Scandinavian Jews are blond six-footers. Many
Spanish Jews have more Spanish blood than a Basque
from San Sebastián, or a "Spaniard" from Granada or

Seville, who, racially, is a Berber from North Africa. The Jews of Yemen have aquiline noses and an almost black complexion. As I have said, the Jews of many a Polish village look like, and *are*, Mongols. There are Jews in China who are simply Chinese of Jewish faith.

The Jews are a *people*, and nothing else. The criterion of a people is neither racial affinity nor even religious unity, nor common political frontiers, nor even adherence to one state or government. *The sole criterion of a people is common tradition, including the tradition that it is a people.*

As for the racial characteristics of the Jew, he was a full-fledged desert Bedouin, that is, a full Northern Semite, when he conquered the Holy Land. Aside from the Philistines, who had apparently come from Crete by way of Cyprus, and never seem to have been very numerous, present-day Palestine and Syria were then inhabited by solid ethnic blocs of Hittites.

Again and again we see in history how a handful of determined conquerors overruns a population which sometimes outnumbers it ten to one, but either is less bellicose than the invader, or lives in a decaying political or social order, too weak to resist. The Hittites had a highly advanced civilization in the second millennium B.C. Their territory included the major part of Asia Minor, present-day Armenia, Syria and Palestine. They had two capital cities. One was Heth or Khatti, whose ruins lie near present-day Boghazkeuy, some two hundred miles east of Ankara, capital of the new Turkey.

The other was Carchemish, by the Euphrates, in present-day Syria. Its site is known as Jerablus today. In the battle of Kadesh, late in the fourteenth century B.C., the Hittites defeated the Pharaoh, Ramses II, and retained their mastery over Syria and Palestine.

In the Bible we find several references to the Hittites. In Genesis xxiii, Abraham, speaking to the "sons of Heth," that is, the Hittites, says, "I am a stranger and a sojourner with you." From Ephron the Hittite he buys the cave of Machpelah, "before Mamre, the same is *Hebron in the land of Canaan*," as the Bible describes it. In Genesis xxiii. 11, Ephron the Hittite says: *"In the presence of the sons of my people* give I it thee."

We recall also that Uriah the Hittite was one of King David's generals, and that his wife, Beth-Sheba, became the mother of Solomon.

Racially, the Jewish Semite conquerors must have been completely absorbed by the defeated Hittite population of Palestine as early as the eighth century B.C. Thereafter, the average Jew had the facial construction of the Hittite, not of the Semite.

In western Asia the traveler learns a good deal about the so-called "Jewish type." To his amazement, he finds that the bulk of the Christian and Moslem population of Syria looks incomparably more "Jewish" than many Jews he knows. He is even more puzzled when he discovers that many Armenians look as if they had stepped straight from some ghetto. The reason is that the ancestry of the Armenians, and of many Syrians, is predominantly Hittite. But most Armenians and Syrians have remained in the East, while most Jews live in the West. So, the Jews are almost the only people with Hittite blood the Western Gentile has a chance to see.

Amazingly accurate pictorial records of the so-called "Jewish" but actually Hittite type are available in the perfectly preserved reliefs of Carchemish. They were excavated by Lawrence of Arabia and Sir Leonard Woolley, in 1913–1914. These men had to leave the site in 1914, when Turkey became involved in the First World War. I was able to visit this ancient capital of the Hittites in 1917, and was much impressed with the perfect portraiture of the Hittite kings, courtiers and warriors.

As I have said, the Bedouins of Arabia form the only ethnic group in the world which has preserved the *original* Jewish, more precisely, the North Semitic, racial type. Yet, there is one place in the *West* where the student still can see the Jewish type, as it was when Jew fought Philistine. That place is Córdoba, in Spain. There is not a single Jew in Córdoba today. But the "Cordovese" type, famous in Spain, has been fully preserved in the beautiful city of Córdoba, inhabited by Spanish-speaking Christians.

As a matter of fact, Córdoba forms an anthropological "island" inside Spain. The whole city — men and women alike — has the same type of face. All Spaniards know this. But very few know *why* that face looks like that, and what type it really represents.

When I first visited Córdoba, I might have thought I was back again among the Bedouins of Arabia, so far as the features of the population were concerned. As we shall see later, at the time of the Arab Caliphate in Spain, the bulk of the Moslem population were Berbers from Morocco, that is, not Semites, while for centuries the ruler and the aristocracy in the capital, which was Córdoba, were mostly Arabs of Bedouin descent.

Thus it is that the Córdoba of today is inhabited by Spanish-speaking, Catholic Semites, as distinct from that intellectually and spiritually so highly advanced people of predominantly Hittite blood which we know as the Jews. This is how Nature itself has provided the most eloquent refutation of the asinine racial theory, favorite stand-by of Nazis and other anti-Semites.

∽   ∽   ∽

The Bedouin has not changed for five thousand years — not even in his dress. Besides, he still carries his twelve-foot lance. Merely the bow and arrow have been replaced by the Lee Enfield rifle.

The nomad life of the Bedouin is conditioned by his occupations. His occupations are conditioned by the character of the land on which he lives — another proof that basically history is a cosmic process, is conditioned not by Man but by Nature.

The Bedouin, the Only Real Semite

So, since the Bedouin raises goats, camels and horses, the destinies of these species determine his own. He must move from pasture to pasture, as the seasons change. During this process, only small groups of humans can subsist together in the desert. Hence, Bedouin social life has retained its tribal structure, the tribes being divided into sub-tribes and clans. The Bedouin must always be prepared to move. Hence, he lives in tents. He has no flax, no sheep. So his tents are made of goat's hair, his wide mantle of camel hair. He has practically no furniture. Squatting on the ground cross-legged, he leans against a camel saddle for comfort.

Inside the tribe, criminality is almost nil. The thief, murderer, or attacker of women is not merely punished but excluded from the tribe. In the desert, this can mean death from starvation, because even hostile tribes will not give shelter to a thief, murderer for profit, or rapist. A woman can travel alone through the Arabian Desert. No Bedouin will dare to molest her. Punishment for murder committed for other than base motives is governed by the age-old tribal custom of the blood feud. Usually, however, the affair can be settled by paying the "blood price," which varies among the tribes.

Hospitality is sacrosanct in an environment where death is certain without the mutual assistance afforded by a community. There is no time limit to Bedouin hospitality, but as the life of this people is most frugal, Bedouin etiquette prescribes that normally a visit should not exceed three days. Hospitality actually is nearer the

Bedouin's heart than religion. It is still true that if a murderer took refuge in the tent of his victim's next of kin, he would probably be safe as long as he remained inside the tent.

When visiting a Bedouin, the guest must be very careful to walk *behind* the row of tents, until he reaches that of his host. It would be an unforgettable insult to any member of the tribe if the stranger walked past the open, that is, the front side of his tent without entering it and accepting the family's hospitality.

Poverty is the main reason why the Bedouin is usually monogamous. Besides, his life in the desert makes the seclusion of women impossible. Nor do Bedouin women wear veils.

As a fighter, the desert tribesman is brave but, of course, no match for a soldier equipped by a modern army. As allies or auxiliaries, the Bedouins have military value mainly as scouts and guerrilla fighters. They were used in this capacity by Lawrence of Arabia, who recruited his men chiefly from the Rualla tribe.

As a rule, the Bedouin refrains from killing his enemy unless he meets with resistance. His principal objective is not to kill, or even to score military victories, but to alleviate his eternal poverty by loot. Therefore, the *rahzoo* — raid, or looting expedition — against caravans, hostile tribes, or the villages of the desert rim, is one of his major occupations and sources of sustenance. The word *razzia*, used throughout continental Europe for a police raid, comes from the Arabic *rahzoo*.

When the Bedouin goes to war, he rides a camel, and

uses camels to carry his provisions. But he takes his horse with him and uses it in actual combat. The tribe is under the authority of its *shaykh*, but most tribes and clans elect special leaders, captains, to lead them in war. These leaders are called *ahkyl* — literally, this word means "intelligence," and it therefore shows a candid differentiation between hereditary authority and authority through merit. The election of a leader in war is characteristic of that millennium-old atmosphere of genuine democracy and social equality which pervades Bedouin society. The "Judges" of the Old Testament simply were the *shaykhs* of the Jewish Bedouins, while men like Jephtha were their chosen *ahkyls*, their leaders in battle. Even after the Jewish Judges had been succeeded by kings, with their courts and palaces, Jewish society preserved much of its Bedouin simplicity, including the prophets' freedom of access and speech to their kings. To this day, the desert Bedouin will address his leader, and even his sovereign, such as King Abdul Aziz Ibn Saud, ruler of Saudi Arabia, by his first name, just as if some British workman or farmer addressed his king: "How do you do, George?"

When Bedouin fights Bedouin, he still follows occasionally the ancient habit of challenging some individual warrior in the enemy's camp to a duel, a fight between their parties' champions. Here again we are reminded of a similar habit among the Jewish Bedouins of the Old Testament of which David's fight with Goliath is an example.

As we shall see, the regime of Abdul Aziz Ibn Saud,

present King of Saudi Arabia, has revolutionized Bedouin life in the central Arabian region in more than one respect. In the Syrian Desert, however, it has remained largely unchanged. Inside Saudi Arabia, tribal wars, and all forms of *rahzoo*, have been stamped out. The reward for relapses is not glory and wealth but the headman's ax. But this change dates back to less than twenty years.

Nominally, the Bedouin is a Moslem. Actually, he is very lax in observing the tenets of his faith. He has retained his ancient animistic belief in *jinn*, good, although sometimes impish, spirits, and *affrit*, evil demons. He has also preserved the same belief as the Tuareg of North Africa, that a sleeping person must be wakened very cautiously, lest some evil spirit take possession of him before he recovers consciousness. These traditions have their Western counterpart in such superstitions as the belief in hexing, or witchcraft, among our Pennsylvania Dutch.

But what could be more strikingly illustrative of the Bedouin's outlook and standards of evaluation than his vocabulary? The Arabic language is the Bedouin's gift to the 245,000,000 people who read and follow the Koran. And Arabic has some three hundred different words for "horse," score after score of highly poetic words and of subtlest synonyms to describe horses of almost every age and kind. There are many hundred different words for "camel," many hundred for "sword."

There is, however, one word in the Bedouin's vocabulary which is at once the most symptomatic and the most touching of them all. The Bedouin's life is one endless search for water, coolness and vegetation. And so the Arabic word for "Paradise" is *jennet* — "garden." To the son of the desert, and to the followers of Islam, a faith born in the desert, Paradise is a garden, and a garden Paradise.

The Bedouin tribes are dispersed over the huge Arabian peninsula, and they vary greatly in numbers. As a rule, each tribe restricts the radius of its migrations to a certain area, which can be properly called its territory. Some tribes have colorful names, such as the *Beni Harb* — "sons of war." Others, though bearing less impressive names, are incomparably more powerful.

Among these, the *Anese* and the *Shammar* are the biggest. Each can put many tens of thousands of armed horsemen in the field. The Shammar live in the Jebel Shammar region, in the northern half of central Arabia, the Anese in the Syrian Desert, much farther to the north.

As I have said, the military value of the Bedouin is negligible; but his nuisance value is considerable. It was even more so before the advent of the modern bomber, which makes it possible to police the desert from the air.

But even so, before you punish an evildoer you have to identify him. And that is practically impossible in the vast expanse of the desert. Under the cover of night, a small band of Bedouins can blow up the railway track in a dozen places and retire far into the desert on its *hejin*, the fast, whitish, specially bred riding camels of Hejaz stock, which are never used for carrying freight. The Bedouin can successfully harass a huge military policing force, and only a huge force could even attempt to police land communications in this region. Besides, it would be exceedingly difficult and costly in men and matériel to assure the munitions, food and water supply for such a huge force in the desert. Malaria, amoebic dysentery, dengue fever, typhus, cholera, are the Western soldier's bitterest enemies in this region, taking a huge toll of lives.

It is simply better business to buy the Bedouins off. The tribes of the Syrian Desert, for example, have always felt and behaved like sovereign political entities, although, until 1918, they were nominally under the authority of the Turkish Sultans, and now are nominally under Syrian rule and sovereignty. But actually they feel just as much entitled to be "bought off" as does any sovereign state which habitually cashes in on its nuisance value. The British tacitly recognize this fact. To protect the pipe line that conducts the oil of Iraq to the Mediterranean at Haifa, in Palestine, they have made some *shaykhs* of Bedouin tribes that inhabit the region their business partners. In addition to regular cash subsidies, they gave them shares in the corporations that own the pipe line!

Before the British, the Turkish governments used to pursue a similar policy in Syria and Iraq, both of which were parts of the Ottoman Empire until 1918. During the First World War, long stretches of the Baghdad Railway, which connects Constantinople with Iraq, still were uncompleted. The railway's eastern terminus was Nisibin, a forlorn outpost in the Syrian Desert. From there, merchandise and military supplies bound for Iraq were sent to Mossul by truck, with an overnight stop at Demir Kapu, about half the distance to Mossul. Throughout the war, the Turkish treasury paid the *shaykhs* of the neighboring Bedouin tribes two Turkish gold pounds, then the equivalent of ten dollars, for every truck or other vehicle which they allowed to pass unmolested. Turkish military couriers and truck drivers used to cross this particular part of the desert with mixed feelings, ready to fire, while the Bedouins, in their flowing robes, mounted on their agile little horses, guns slung on their backs and twelve-foot lances in their right hand, were parading their nuisance value along the horizon.

But during the First World War the Bedouin *shaykhs* did business on a much larger scale, too. From time to time, they would receive from Constantinople sacks in which gold coins clinked invitingly. They were to induce the tribe to observe "benevolent neutrality" towards the Sultan's troops. Each time, the *shaykhs* would assure the Sultan of their eternal devotion.

(49)

Then, usually shortly afterwards, mysterious envoys would arrive from the south, pronouncing their Arabic with an Oxford accent, and carrying similar sacks of gold. Thereupon, the *shaykhs* would solemnly assure the British of their eternal devotion. The *shaykhs* had a keen sense of humor, and accepted the money of both the Turks and the British with complete impartiality. It was a case of benevolent neutrality in the most lucrative sense of the word. The *shaykhs* were also very polite people — they never failed upon receipt of money to assure the sender of their eternal devotion.

In a conversation, one of these tribal chiefs explained this attitude to me with perfect candor. *"Wallah,"* he said with a laügh, "we act exactly like most of your governments in the West. We consider ourselves free, subject to no one on earth. The Turks and the *ingilees* [the English] both pay us to refrain from attacking them. We *do* refrain from attacking them. That is a matter of probity. Why do we accept money from both? Because we have no quarrel with either of them. In fact," he added, with a loud laugh this time, "we like them both. They are very good to us. And the only difference between our attitude and that of your Western governments is that in a similar situation they exploit their favorable position a thousand times more effectively than we do."

In the subsequent twenty-five years, I met many Western statesmen, but never did I hear the traditional spirit of so-called "statecraft" in both the East and the

West more clearly and concisely expressed. Had my host been born in Europe, he might have become one of its most famous "statesmen."

∾   ∾   ∾

Outside Syria, Palestine, Transjordan and Iraq, and inside the confines of Saudi Arabia, a peaceful revolution in Bedouin life has occurred since the access to power of Abdul Aziz Ibn Saud, King of Saudi Arabia. Ibn Saud, whose kingdom has the approximate size of California but numbers only a million and a half people, is one of the most unusual and most colorful figures in this prosaic world. Here is a unique combination of a powerful autocrat, an Oriental of Biblical habits, an imaginative reformer, a fearless warrior, and a Bedouin among Bedouins, proud in his Bedouin simplicity, simple in his regal pride.

Abdul Aziz Ibn Abderrahman Ibn Faisal Ibn Saud — Ibn Saud for short — would long ago have become a widely famous figure on the international stage were not his kingdom far removed from the scene of major world politics, in the sun-parched, waterless wastes of Arabia. Recently, however, Ibn Saud, supreme master of a land fabulously rich in natural oil reserves, has become a key figure in the policies of the Second World War and of the postwar world.

(51)

I first heard Ibn Saud's name in 1917, when his star had just risen above the horizon. I was squatting in front of a Bedouin friend's tent, leaning comfortably against a camel saddle. Above us, myriads of stars were blazing away in the crystal-pure night in the Arabian sky — a giant carpet of purple sprinkled with diamond dust.

We were talking politics. "Ibn Saud," said my host, "has definitely cast in his lot with the British."

Saud, and therefore Ibn Saud, meaning son of Saud, is a name as common in the Moslem world as Smith is in Anglo-Saxon countries. So I asked my friend, "Ibn Saud? Which Ibn Saud?"

"Why," he replied, "of course Ibn Saud of Nejd — the *great* Ibn Saud."

The *great* Ibn Saud. That epithet was then just beginning to be attached to the man's name. It has not left him since.

Until a generation ago, central Arabia's ancient Bedouin communities, while nominally under the Turkish Sultans, had never actually submitted to any overlord other than the tribal chief in peace and the *ahkyl* in battle. They knew little or nothing of such concepts as "society" and "nation."

Then came Ibn Saud. With him came astounding changes. For the first time in uncounted centuries, a degree of prosperity, complete order and security came to the population of the central Arabian Desert.

The life of the man whose reforms were responsible for these changes actually is a modern counterpart of the lives of conquest, politics, and individual courage of such Biblical Bedouin chieftains as Saul and David. Like David's, Ibn Saud's life has been linked to the rivalry of two powerful, warlike Semitic groups. In the heart of kingless Arabia there was to be found a striking analogy to some Biblical feuds.

Entrenched in its desert capital, the oasis of Hail, in Jebel Shammar, which forms the northern part of central Arabia, the house of Ibn Rashid, hereditary ameers, or princes, of the Shammar tribes, defied its secular enemy, the family of Ibn Saud. The latter's walled stronghold, Riadh, lies four hundred miles to the south, in the desert territory of Nejd. The influence of the Turkish sultans was nil in both regions. For an army, the house of Ibn Rashid had chiefly the tribes of the Shammar, famed for the number of their warriors and the beauty of their horses and women — which is the proper order of their evaluation among Bedouins. The followers of the house of Ibn Saud, Sultans of Nejd, were, and still are, the Wahhabi. Like the Senussi of North Africa, the Wahhabi form a puritan religious confraternity inside Islam. Like the Senussi, they are fanatical fighters.

In 1891, profiting by a family feud among the Ibn Saud and the resultant weakness of his deadly enemies, the Ameer Mohammed Ibn Rashid swooped down on Nejd and took its capital, Riadh. The few surviving members of the house of Ibn Saud fled. One of their number, with his eleven-year-old son, the Ibn Saud of today, found refuge in a small native state on the shores of the Persian Gulf.

Ten years later, one day in 1901, when the vibrant desert heat conjured up even more mirages than usual, a band of two hundred Bedouins left this refuge and headed west, toward the heart of Arabia. After a strenuous trek, they and their camels squatted to rest near a well a few miles from their erstwhile capital, Riadh.

Fifteen warriors separated from the caravan and proceeded to the city, led by Ibn Saud, now a youth of twenty-one, a six-footer with a body full of muscles. By a ruse, they gained admittance as night fell. Before morning, through a *coup de main* of Homeric audacity and determination, the fifteen men surprised and killed the governor, then captured the citadel.

Next day the jubilant population, which had remained loyal to its former feudal lords, proclaimed young Ibn Saud Sultan of Nejd.

As a leader and fighter, the young Bedouin chief had shown his mettle. Now he was to demonstrate his innate political genius, his vision and perseverance as a statesman. His first concern was to make his realm secure. To this end, he decided to revolutionize the social and political structure of Bedouin society. He was going to transcend the tribal system, sacred in the desert since prehistoric days, and create an Arab nation.

Ibn Saud had not studied philosophy and psychology. But through his innate political acumen and vision, this young statesman of the desert sensed that his great project of molding rival tribes into a nation could be achieved only if the new allegiance was prompted by urges even more ancient and powerful than the tribal instinct.

Ibn Saud found the solution to his problem. He was going to attempt the hitherto impossible: to make Bedouin nomads sedentary, to train them to till the land, to exchange privation for comfort, to transform gardens — *jennet* — from equivalents for the Arab's Paradise into realities on the Arab's earth. Love of plenty was to be one of the deeply ingrained urges of man that would help to transcend the tribal system.

Religious fervor was to be the other. A devout but by no means fanatic Moslem himself, Ibn Saud decided to use his men's ardor for their common religion as an antidote against their tribal tradition.

To popularize his audacious concept of an Arab nation, Ibn Saud coined the slogan, "Back to the Koran and on to the land!" He replaced tribal usage by Moslem religious law, abolished the blood feud, put an end to the *rahzoo*, one of the most sacred among Bedouin customs. Participation in a looting expedition and robbery in any form now incurred the death penalty. As we have seen already, both have been stamped out in Ibn Saud's realm.

In 1912, he founded the first of nearly a hundred Wahhabi agricultural settlements. Inside these communities, members of different, often hostile tribes have forgotten their petty tribal hatreds and settled down jointly to a stable, sedentary form of life.

But their ruler, mindful of the exigencies of political power, was careful to make each agricultural settlement a military unit in his army, in which former enemies, animated by their common religious ardor, now learned to fight side by side. The Wahhabi, so called after the founder of their sect, Mohammed Ibn Abdul Wahab, who flourished about two hundred years ago, call themselves *ikhwan* — brothers. They do not drink alcohol, do not smoke, do not allow music. The rest of orthodox Islam abstains from drinking wine, but does not object to smoking and music. The Wahhabi ban against music is reminiscent of our own blue laws, which still prohibit theatrical performances in certain cities on Sundays.

The Wahhabi regard the worship of saints, and prayer for their intercession with the Deity, as idolatry. They view ornate tombs with the same disfavor. To the *ikhwan*, every other Moslem, whether Sunnite or Shiite, is an unbeliever — an Eastern counterpart of the intolerance between our own religious zealots in the West.

While the Wahhabi are the nucleus of Saudi Arabia's population, they form only a part of it. Through conquest, Ibn Saud nearly doubled the size of his territory between 1918 and 1924. In 1924, he took Hejaz, with the holy cities Mecca and Medina. Already in 1918, he had attacked Ibn Rashid. Two years later, Ibn Rashid lost his life during a hunt, and in 1921 Ibn Saud occupied Hail, the capital of his enemy.

The Bedouin, the Only Real Semite

Aside from such vital necessities as the ruthless elimination of Nazism, "totalitarianism" and militarism, nothing, as a rule, is wiser than moderation in the hour of triumph. In this connection the Bedouin statesman, Ibn Saud, has taught his Western colleagues some valuable lessons. In the nineteen-thirties, for example, he conquered the land of Asir, which lies on the southwestern rim of the Arabian peninsula, between Hejaz and Yemen. El Idrissi, ruler of Asir, fled to Yemen, where he obtained assistance from Imam Yakhya, the king of that country. This led to a war between the Imam and Ibn Saud, in which the latter's army scored a decisive victory. Instead of humiliating his defeated opponent on the European model, thereby automatically laying the foundations for a war of revenge, Ibn Saud sensed that charity and wisdom are twins. Towards the Imam Yakhya he was even more generous than he had been towards the house of Ibn Rashid.

Ibn Saud signed a peace with Yemen, which left Imam Yakhya on the throne, left Yemen its territory and complete sovereignty, and renounced any form of tribute or reparations in money or kind.

In all ages, in the East as in the West, have acts of treachery been perpetrated. But it is a simple fact that the average old-type Chinese and Moslem often represents a higher standard of self-respect and honesty than the average Occidental of corresponding educational or social level. In the light of this undeniable fact, some actions of Moslem statesmen, which recall heroic examples of Biblical days, should appear less quixotic to the Western skeptic. Imam Yakhya himself, the near-Biblical patriarch who rules Yemen, is a case in point.

In 1911, the Imam revolted against Turkish rule, which then extended over the whole Red Sea coast. The Sultan sent Turkey's outstanding strategist and statesman, the late, great Marshal Ahmed Izzet Pasha, to put down the rebellion in Yemen. Ahmed Izzet's Chief of Staff was a young major by the name of Ismet Bey, today, as General Ismet Ineunu, President of the Turkish Republic. The Turks scaled the high mountains of Yemen, defeated the Imam, crushed the revolt. Then, in glaring contrast to customary Western methods, Ahmed Izzet did not declare martial law, did not use the gallows or the firing squad, did not "make an example of the rebel." Instead, all he did was to make Imam Yakhya swear on the Koran that henceforth he would be loyal to Turkey. Then Ahmed Izzet and Ismet went home.

In 1918, the Ottoman Empire collapsed. Turkey lay in ruins. Kemal Ataturk rebelled against the docile Sultan and the Allies, organized an army, defeated the Greeks, forced the Allies to evacuate the country. He organized the new Turkey, made it a republic. Its territory now was restricted to Thrace, with Adrianople and Constantinople, and to Asia Minor. Yemen lay thousands of miles away, with French-occupied Syria, British-held Palestine, and the kingdom of Hejaz in between. The new Turkey, an entirely novel political organism, embracing Turks only and no Arabs, had completely forgotten Yemen.

In 1923, I spent several months in Ankara, capital of the new Turkey, where I visited Kemal Ataturk, President, and Ismet Ineunu, then Prime Minister of the country. During my stay, there arrived in Ankara a delegation from faraway Yemen. In 1911 — Imam Yakhya's emissaries explained to Kemal Ataturk — their ruler had sworn on the Koran to remain faithful to Turkey. After 1918, the Koran was still there, but Turkey was gone. Now that there was again a Turkey to be faithful to, the Imam intended to continue to do so. When the Turkish Empire collapsed in 1918, instead of making common cause with its enemies and making the few Turkish officials and soldiers left in his territory prisoners, Imam Yakhya had kept the Turkish civil servants in their jobs. He had let them continue to run Yemen as a Turkish province. And now, he asked for instructions.

Kemal Ataturk was dumbfounded. This was Harun er-Rashid, "Aaron the Just," come to life. Then the President of the Turkish Republic reminded his visitors that now there was only a Turkey but no longer an Ottoman Empire. He sent words of appreciation and admiration to the Imam, and formally released him from his pledge.

Now, let us be honest: had an Occidental statesman been in Ataturk's place, would not he have jumped at the opportunity to obtain for his country a rich, fertile province or protectorate, that was being offered to him on a silver platter? Can you picture a Western statesman saying "no" in such a situation?

During that same summer, Ataturk said to me in a conversation: "The motto of the new Turkey is: Turkey for the Turks, and nothing but Turkey for the Turks. For centuries, the flower of our Turkish manhood had to die of hunger, thirst and wounds in the deserts of Arabia, thousands of miles away. They had to die so that, in exchange for the maniacal concept of 'glory,' we should have to pour money, foodstuffs and more soldiers' lives into regions that were not self-supporting, hated foreign rule and were ever restive.

"This time, we will give the world an example in self-restraint. We will show other governments that a country can be healthy and great *because* it is small."

"What is the matter with these Oriental leaders?" someone might ask. "Why are they so different? To refuse a rich province or protectorate! And, on the other hand, to offer one's country as a province or protectorate, when no one asks for it! To punish a rebellion through a vow on the Koran! To defeat a rebellious country, and then just go home and forget it! Are these fellows crazy, or just a bunch of Don Quijotes?"

There is an answer to this question. Poison and the dagger have as often made history in the East as in the West. But, as we shall see in a later chapter, in the *Oriental* soul, especially of the higher type, there is no cleavage between practical interests and metaphysical beliefs, which are the mainspring of ethics. An *advanced* Oriental can use an electron microscope, scan the heavens with a modern refractor, operate a big corporation, run a government, and still believe in a supreme force, a World Soul, a Deity, as a stimulus for ethical conduct in interhuman and international relations. The intellectual of the contemporary West cannot, and is deceiving himself if he thinks he can.

Moreover, often in decisive situations the Oriental's age-old "Collective Unconscious" will cause him to transcend *intelligence* and practise *wisdom*. Says one of the sages of the Orient, the great Lao-Tse: "He who restrains others is strong. He who restrains himself, is mighty."

In contrast to their Occidental colleagues, many Eastern statesmen realize *the power that comes from self-restraint* — a political concept totally alien to the West.

Some people may call these Yakhyas and Ibn Sauds eccentrics and dreamers. I call them great.

I like to see Don Quijote and Sancho Panza side by side. But if I cannot have them both, give me Don Quijote every time.

IV

DESERT SKYSCRAPERS,
DEVIL WORSHIPERS,
AND THE GARDEN OF EDEN

*W*HILE the sultanates of Kuweit and Oman, on the eastern and southeastern coast of the Arabian peninsula, and the Bahrein Islands, just off the Arabian coast in the Persian Gulf, are nominally independent states, all three are actually British protectorates. The territory of Aden, in the southwest tip of the peninsula, however, is even officially a protectorate of the British Crown. Kuweit is about 2000 square miles in size, with a population of 50,000. Oman has a population of half a million, inside a territory measuring some 80,000 square miles. Some 120,000 people live on the Bahrein Islands, whose surface is 250 square miles. Aden resembles Kuweit in both size and density of population.

The people of this whole region are Arabs and Moslem. Their land is not wholly barren. Date groves give Kuweit its shade and wealth. Mountains traverse the hinterland of Oman's north coast. Eternal snow reflects the glare of the tropical sun from their 10,000 feet high summits.

Aden's significance is wholly strategic. It is void of any colorful feature. But between Aden and Oman lies

Hadhramaut, one of the world's least known and most colorful regions. Here you have a small community living in a social system that antedates even feudalism. The *hadhrami* actually live in a theocracy.

The ruling caste consists of several hundred families, known as sayids, who trace their common descent back to the Prophet Mohammed, and wear robes and caps of festive white, a color of distinction in Islam. Under the sayids are the simple townsfolk. Many *hadhrami* are extremely wealthy. Most of that wealth was acquired in Malaya, in Java, Sumatra and other parts of the Netherlands East Indies. In times of peace, hundreds of *hadhrami* used to emigrate there each year. These people are astute businessmen, and practically monopolize certain fields of trade in the Netherlands East Indies. It is a habit among them to return to their native Hadhramaut with the fortunes they accumulate. So deep is the attachment of these souls to the sun-parched, shadowless waste in tropical Arabia where they were born that instead of building themselves palaces, or comfortable villas in their adopted homeland, they prefer to spend the rest of their days in primitive Hadhramaut, almost completely isolated from the outer world, lacking any of the comforts that money can buy. "Man does not live by bread alone." The beauty and the comforts of Java, and all the gold it gives these people, are weaker than their nostalgia.

Centuries before Magellan reached the Philippines, the people of Mindanao had become Moslem. As the migration of the *hadhrami* to India and the Malay Archipelago goes back many hundred years, it is not impossible that Islam was brought to Mindanao indirectly from Hadhramaut by way of Malaya. To the sixteenth-century Spaniard, all Moslem still were simply "Moors" — *moros*. This is how the Moros of Mindanao got their ethnic designation.

∞   ∞   ∞

Hadhramaut itself is actually nothing but a wadi, one of the many dry prehistoric river beds of the huge peninsula — the only thing in which Arabia is rich. Rugged, barren, flat-topped hills, not unlike the mesas of our American Southwest, flank the bed of this non-existent river, whose banks they once were. Thanks to the water in its subsoil, the river bed itself is relatively fertile. It is dotted with groves of date palms, the typical economic stand-by of the desert. But inside these oases, which turn the winding Wadi Hadhramaut into a huge emerald necklace, stand cities that are unique in the world. The two biggest among them, Terim and Shibam, conjure up the mirage of some Manhattan surrounded by palms. But the clusters of ten- and twelve-story skyscrapers that form these cities are no mirage. Aladdin's magic lamp did not transfer a part of Lower Manhattan to the south of Arabia. These skyscrapers represent genuine survivals of ancient Babylonian architecture. The Phoenicians transplanted this Babylonian idea to ancient Carthage, which, with its clusters of near-skyscrapers surrounded by palm groves, must have looked like a glorified Hadhramaut.

Not more than half-a-dozen Occidentals have visited Hadhramaut, with its amazing skylines illustrative of the creative originality of the ancient East. But the tall buildings that form those skylines owe their form and height to military considerations. They were built to serve as ramparts against looting expeditions by the marauding Bedouins of the desert. In Hadhramaut as elsewhere, necessity is the teacher of man.

ᢒᠥ   ᢒᠥ   ᢒᠥ

Yemen, a sovereign state whose kings, as we have seen, bear the title of *imam*, is a fertile, mountainous country of 75,000 square miles, with a population of three and a half million. No Occidental is admitted to the country, with the exception of Hodeida, the principal port. Neither xenophobia nor religious intolerance is responsible for this policy. Again and again has the white settler acted as the "Fifth Column" of the West in Asia. The trader was followed by the military spy, mapping the country. Then came the white man's fleet, and another ancient, sovereign civilization would become the prey of the Western invader. That is why the few sovereign or quasi-sovereign countries left in Asia, such as Yemen and Tibet, now regard the white man not as a visitor but as the scout of a future invader. Burned cats fear the fire. . . .

The great central highland of Yemen is famed for its coffee, and the word *Mocca*, which denotes a very high-grade coffee, is actually the name of a port in southern Yemen. Yemen and Saudi Arabia, which now includes Hejaz and Asir, are the only really and truly sovereign states in Arab Asia today.

With the exception of some hundred thousand Christians and about as many Jews, the population of Iraq, five million in number, is solidly Moslem. Slightly less than one half of the people belong to the Sunna sect. The rest adheres to the Shia sect of Islam, as does also the whole population of neighboring Iran. Kerbela and Nejef, the two sacred cities of the Shiites, both are in Iraq. These pilgrimage centers represent the *ne plus ultra* of holiness to the Shiite. They house the tombs of Ali, son-in-law of Mohammed and heir to the Caliphate, who was deprived of his rights to the Caliphal succession, and of Ali's sons, Hassan and Hussein. The Shia looks upon Ali, its great martyr, as an *imam*. In this particular sense, *imam* means an incarnation of the Deity.

Many of the Jews of Iraq are direct lineal descendants of those whom Cyrus the Mede liberated in the sixth century B.C. Their ancestors chose not to return to

Palestine with Zerubbabel, the first "Zionist" in history, who reconstructed the Holy Land as a Jewish "national home" some two thousand five hundred years before the Balfour Declaration advocated a repetition of the process.

Many other unique features characterize the fertile alluvial plain of some 140,000 square miles which the West used to know as Mesopotamia and now calls Iraq.

Tradition places the Garden of Eden in Iraq. It is a fact that the first settlements that could be called cities, and the first civilizations, arose in this area. Ur — the "Ur of the Chaldees" — Eridu, Lagash, were probably the first walled cities of humanity. During his excavations of the remains of Ur, the native city of that historic Jewish *shaykh*, Abraham, Sir Leonard Woolley found bathrooms in private homes that had been used four thousand five hundred years ago. His fabulous finds of art objects in the Sumerian royal tombs at Ur, which date from about 3000 B.C., show a degree of artistic perfection that automatically postulates at least another thousand years of cultural and artistic evolution.

In Iraq stood Babylon, Assur and Niniveh. The ruins of Babylon are not far from Baghdad. Assur's remnants lie near the present village of Kala'at Shergat, by the Tigris. Niniveh was situated on the eastern bank of the Tigris, opposite Mosul.

Before these ancient cities were excavated, they were so many mounds of rubble, covered with sand, and often with vegetation. These artificial hills in the Arab East are known as *tell*. The uninitiated traveler is unaware that each of these innocuous-looking, gently sloping mounds hides an ancient city — sometimes half a dozen or more cities, forming individual layers on each other's ruins.

In Chaldean, which was the Semitic language of Babylon, "Babylon," more correctly *Bab-iloon*, meant "the Gate of the Gods." "Babel" is the ancient Hebrew form of the name of the city, composed of *Bab* — gate, and *el*, meaning "god."

The Tower of Babel is historic. We have actual descriptions of it in Herodotus and in a report of the Greek historian, Diodorus of Sicily, who lived in the first century B.C. In fact, the Tower had a distinctive name, *Etemenanki*, by which it was known throughout western Asia. In Chaldean, *E-te-men-an-ki* meant "the House of the Foundations of Heaven and Earth."

Etemenanki was merely the biggest among the many *ziggurat* — step-towers, or scaled pyramids — which stood in Iraq thousands of years ago. These flat-topped scaled pyramids carried sanctuaries of the guardian deities of the cities in which they stood. The first among them were erected in the fourth millennium B.C., by the Sumero-Akkadians, who preceded the Babylonians in Iraq, and whose amazing civilization the Babylonians inherited.

The *ziggurat* were then introduced to Egypt by the Third Dynasty of that country, in the early third millennium B.C., as evidenced by the *scaled* pyramid of

Sakkarah, in Lower Egypt, which still stands. In contrast to the original Babylonian scaled pyramid, however, its Egyptian copy bore no edifice, being intended to serve not as the base of a temple but as a gigantic funerary monument to the Pharaoh. In keeping with its new use, the Pharaohs of the succeeding Fourth Dynasty built regular pyramids instead of the scaled variety.

Etemenanki, the Tower of Babel, the biggest among the *ziggurat* of the Babylonian Empire, served as a gigantic base for a temple of the sun-god Baal-Marduk, meaning "the Lord Marduk," the principal deity of Babylon. It was first erected in the third millennium B.C. As this region was, and still is, very poor in stone, private homes and public buildings alike were built of sun-baked bricks. As a result, after a few centuries public monuments began to crumble and had to be restored again and again. Various kings of Babylon and Assyria worked on the periodical restorations of the Tower of Babel. The last, and most comprehensive job was undertaken by Nebuchadnezzar, of Biblical fame. Every brick used in this work bore the imprint of Nebuchadnezzar's name.

In an inscription discovered only a few years ago Nebuchadnezzar boasts: —

I prepared to place *Etemenanki's* summit in position, so that it might compete with Heaven. I forced people of all nations to help to build *Etemenanki*. The towering dwelling for Marduk, my master, I caused to be artistically restored on the very top. *Etemenanki*, the Tower of Babylon . . . I restored it with bitumen and burned bricks and brought it to completion . . . a sanctuary of supreme artistry, made of burned bricks with a blue glaze, did I build upon the shining upper storeys.

It is practically certain that the many thousand Jewish slaves carried to Babylon after Nebuchadnezzar's conquest of Jerusalem took part in the gigantic work of reconstruction on *Etemenanki*. Here, they met many thousand other slaves, captured in many lands, engaged in the same work. This is quite clearly implied in that phrase of Nebuchadnezzar's inscription "I forced people of all nations to help to build *Etemenanki*." From their Babylonian captivity, the Jews brought back with them the story of the Tower of Babel and of the confusion of tongues. It is very likely that the variety of languages spoken by the thousands of prisoners of war from many countries gave rise to the passage in the Bible, "And the Lord said . . . nothing will be restrained from them, which they have imagined to do. Go to, let us go down, and there confound their language."

In 1911 and the succeeding years, the foundations of the Tower of Babel were actually excavated to a height of about six feet! In March 1899, Professor Robert Koldewey, one of pre-Hitlerian Germany's greatest scientists, dug the first spade into the drear expanse of rubble and ruins which once was Babylon, the proudest metropolis of antiquity. Then, in 1911, he actually discovered the site of the Tower of Babel.

Six years later, one day in April, 1917, Professor Koldewey sat in the reception room of the old house in the *Aziziyeh* quarter of Aleppo which then was my home. He recalled the greatest thrill of his life, the discovery of the exact site of *Etemenanki*, the Tower of Babel. He gave me a description of the big bridge that spanned the Euphrates in the immediate vicinity of the Biblical Tower. He spoke of ancient Babylon's glorious city gate, dedicated to the goddess Ishthar, which he had also dug up. He described a series of vaulted chambers supporting a large terrace, which, in his considered opinion, probably bore the flower beds, shrubs and trees known as the fabled "hanging gardens" of Queen Semiramis of Babylon, which the ancients counted among the Seven Wonders of the World.

Professor Koldewey gave the original measurements of the Tower of Babel as 99 yards on each side, with a height of 297 feet. Recent researches have confirmed this estimate.

In addition to the story of the Tower of Babel, the Jews have retained another reminder of their life in Babylon. The principal deities of that country were Marduk, the sun-god, and his wife, the goddess Ishtar or Ishthar, who, as her cult spread westward, gradually became the Astaroth and Astarte of the Phoenicians, the Aphrodite of the Greeks, and the Venus of the Romans.

In the Book of Esther, the name of the heroine is, of course, Esther, and of her cousin Mordecai. But in the name "Mordecai" it is easy to recognize the corruption of Marduk, and in Esther, of Ishthar! As we have seen,

Marduk and Ishthar were the paramount deities, not of the Persians, but of the Babylonians, whom the Persians displaced only a few decades after Nebuchadnezzar's Jewish captives had helped to restore Marduk's sanctuary, the Tower of Babel.

In Iraq, I had a firsthand experience of another high light of the Bible, one of the Seven Plagues of Egypt, which still haunts the East.

I had just crossed the Euphrates. Suddenly, the sun was blotted out. Millions upon millions of tiny insects had formed a cloud. They swelled forth out of the horizon with a terrific din, as they flung themselves with a hard, rattling sound onto the afflicted landscape.

A swarm of locusts.

Relentless and inexorable as Fate itself, more and still more hundreds of thousands of grayish-green bodies whirred up from behind the hills, loomed up far above the horizon and fell upon the defenseless plain, gnawing, guzzling, grabbing, digesting, destroying. A few minutes ago, a field in full bloom. The next moment, a desert. And more and still more new masses, new clouds of insect bodies swirled and buzzed and hummed and clattered and rattled upon the dumb earth, messengers of ruin and destruction.

What a revelation of unbridled nature! A cruel, terrifying, and yet gripping symbolic picture of the cosmic circulation of life, which must inevitably nourish itself on destruction. For death is the fuel of life and is a sovereign aspect of Universal Life.

The ancient and the modern are closely interlaced in the present pattern of Iraq. Today, the country has the form of a constitutional monarchy. Lying between Iran in the east, Kuweit in the southeast, Saudi Arabia in the south, Transjordan in the southwest, Syria in the west and Turkey in the north, and with Soviet Russia not far away, the country is of paramount political, strategic and economic importance. In the south, a solid forest of date palms, stretching a hundred miles along both banks of the Shatt-el-Arab, conjures up a tropical version of Paradise. In the north, the fabulously rich oil fields of Mosul now are systematically exploited. A pipe line connects them with the port of Haifa, in Palestine.

Following a native revolt against foreign domination in the nineteen-twenties, Britain renounced its mandate over the country in 1930, replacing it by a treaty of alliance with a sovereign Iraq. Bedouin tribes inhabit the desert area which forms the western part of the country. Among these, the tribe of the Anese is the biggest and most powerful.

The cities of Mosul and Baghdad, while retaining much of their Oriental color, have been considerably modernized. Some modern industries have sprung up in them. Basrah, the "Balsorah" of *Arabian Nights* fame, has important harbor facilities, Baghdad an up-to-date airport.

Like the people of Syria, those of Iraq are strongly nationalist. As in Egypt, old quarrels with Britain have left behind them an attitude none too friendly to the British. But the politically mature part of the intelligentsia understands that Britain intends to respect Iraq's independence, while Hitler's victory would have reduced the country to slavery.

No one understands this better than Nuri Pasha Es-Said, Iraq's most experienced statesman, who became its Premier in September 1941. One of the first associates of Lawrence of Arabia in organizing the Arab revolt against the Ottoman Empire in 1916, Nuri Pasha has remained a friend of Britain. He is, however, primarily an Arab nationalist. As he told me himself a few years ago, he "stands first and foremost for the interests of Iraq."

But Iraq's interests link it permanently to the Anglo-Saxon–Russian group of states.

ᕙ   ᕙ   ᕙ

Transjordan is one of the artificial diplomatic creations of the period immediately following the First World War. It has an area of 35,000 square miles, with a population of 300,000. Its existence as a political entity on the map is warranted neither ethnically nor economically, neither socially nor politically.

The population consists almost exclusively of Bedouin nomads, the land is mainly desert. Economically a dead loss, it could not live, or be governed, without a British subsidy.

Transjordan was set up to serve as a strategic buffer state between Palestine and what now is Saudi Arabia. When the idea of a Pan-Arab Federation materializes, it will probably pass into oblivion.

Before 1918, under Turkish rule, Palestine was merely a *sanjak*, an administrative subdivision, inside the *vilayet*, or division, of Damascus. Fabulously rich in Biblical times, Palestine's fertile region now is restricted to the coastal plain, fifteen miles deep, which skirts the Mediterranean for a hundred miles. The eastern part of the country drops sharply into the valley of the Jordan and the basin of the Dead Sea, some thirteen hundred feet below sea level. Between this eastern strip of Palestine and the coastal plain in the west lies the highland of Judea. The 10,000-odd square miles of the country support a population numbering a million and a half. Natural resources are scarce. Before the collapse of the Ottoman Empire in 1918, Palestine had some 80,000 Jews, a little over 100,000 Christians, and some 800,000 Moslem. Since then, Jewish immigration has changed the proportion of the three communities. Palestine now has about 960,000 Moslem, 475,000 Jews, and 125,000 Christians.

Besides Jerusalem, the most important cities of Palestine are Jaffa and Haifa. Jewish immigrants have made Tel-Aviv, near Jaffa, a flourishing modern city on the Western model. Haifa is known, of course, for its vicinity to Mount Carmel. Near the southeastern end of the mountain lies the plain of Esdraelon, where once stood the city of Megiddo. From the ancient Hebrew term, *har Megiddo* — the mountain district of Megiddo — the Greek-speaking Jews of the Hellenistic period derived the name of Armageddon. It was in this plain that Pharaoh Nekho defeated King Josiah of Judah about 609 B.C., only to go to his own defeat at the hands of Nebuchadnezzar, then Crown Prince and Generalissimo of Babylon, at Carchemish, by the Euphrates.

I have already mentioned Carchemish, then a flourishing city of the Hittites. Today it is a heap of ruins, known as Djerablus, and marked by the big bridge of the Baghdad Railway that spans the Euphrates at this point.

We have seen that Lawrence of Arabia and Sir Leonard Woolley excavated a major part of Carchemish, which the battle of 607 B.C. had blotted out forever. When I studied the ruins in 1917, I found a number of arrowheads among the rubble of the millenniums. Subsequently, excavators actually found Nekho's signet ring. The Pharaoh, who barely escaped with his life, must have lost the ring in the heat of battle. It now rests peacefully in the British Museum. . . .

Oranges are the main agricultural product of Palestine, and Jaffa is their principal port of export. When the ship approaches Jaffa at the time of bloom, the perfume of myriads of orange blossoms, carried out to sea, is almost too strong to bear.

Jerusalem is as sacred to Islam as it is to the Christian and the Jew. Following the failure of the Jewish revolt against Roman rule under Hadrian, Jerusalem's name was changed to *Aelia Capitolina*, Jews were forever barred from it by imperial decree, and a relief, showing a pig, was set up above the main city gate. Subsequently, Jerusalem became Byzantine. Islam conquered it in the seventh century. With the exception of a short period under the Crusaders, the city has been in Moslem hands ever since. Sultan Selim took it for the Turks in 1517, Lord Allenby putting an end to Turkish rule over it exactly four hundred years later.

The Mosque of Omar, built upon the foundations of Solomon's temple, is one of Islam's holiest shrines. The city is also a pilgrimage center for the Greek Orthodox Church. Inside the Church of the Holy Sepulcher, each Christian sect has a section of the building allotted to it. Before the First World War, the question of precedence before the altar on festive occasions was often a bone of contention among the priests of the various sects. Again and again, the squabble would end in a fight, with the Turkish Moslem policemen separating the participants. To the unbiased observer, these scenes were unforgettable illustrations of religious fanaticism.

ოა   ოა   ოა

Syria is history's classic highway. This patchwork of ethnic, religious and cultural groups has been a passage-way and a battlefield from the days of the stone adze, the chariot and the war elephant, to those of the Flying Fortress and the jeep. Every one of its 58,000 square miles of land has been trampled under the feet of march-ing armies. Every one of its 3,500,000 inhabitants has either Hittite, or Phoenician, Assyrian, Babylonian, Per-sian, Greek, Roman, Turkish, or Arab blood in his veins, and in many cases a combination of them.

Before the outbreak of the Second World War, the political pattern of this former Turkish province was made up of four administrative entities. Having created the French-supervised state of Greater Lebanon in 1920, the French, who had been given a mandate over Syria after the First World War, successively organized the other parts of Syria into the state of Syria proper, the "Government of Latakiyeh," and the "Government of the Jebel Druse."

These subdivisions owed their existence in part to ethnic considerations, as in the case of the Lebanon and the Latakiyeh territory; in part, seemingly to ethnic but actually to political and military considerations, as in the case of the Jebel Druse. The state of Syria proper was simply what remained of Syria after the three former regions had been lopped off.

The population of the Lebanon is predominantly Christian, while the major part of Syria's population is Moslem. Arabic, however, is the mother tongue of both groups. Aside from the quarter-million Bedouins of the Syrian Desert, the population, while Arab in speech and culture, is not Arab by blood. There is, of course, Bedouin blood in a number of city notables who trace their ancestry back to the proud, full-blooded Semites of the desert. But, as we have seen, the overwhelming majority of Syrians are the racial product of many thousand years of intermixture, the Hittite strain being dominant. Aramaic, or "Syriac," which was the language of Jesus and his contemporaries in the Levant, still is spoken in three villages near Damascus.

Syria is much more fertile than Palestine. The Hauran, in the southeast, is a rich agricultural region. The mountain ranges of the Lebanon and Anti-Lebanon, the latter crowned by the snow-capped Mount Hermon, run parallel, from north to south, dividing Syria into three strips. The eastern part is the largest, but consists mostly of desert. Between the Lebanon and the Anti-Lebanon lies the unusually fertile Beka'a Valley. The strip of land between the Lebanon and the Mediterranean is mountainous in the north, around Latakiyeh, and flat in the south. The mountains around Latakiyeh are noted for their tobacco, known as *Aboo-r-Reehah* — "Father of the good odor." The Lebanon is dotted with scrupulously clean villages, and is famous for its health resorts, such as Alleih, Brumana, and Aïn Sofar, the latter with up-to-date hotels and a gambling casino. Like the plain of the Beka'a, the Lebanon is one of the most fertile regions in western Asia. Its red wine is famous. The heavy, purple grapes are allowed to lie freely on the dry, sun-baked ground. Throwing the heat of the sun back at them like an incubator, the soil actually helps them to get their rich flavor. The smiling slopes and valleys of the Lebanon are the traditional scene of the saga of Oberon and Titania, with their fairy kingdom, immortalized by Shakespeare and Mendelssohn.

Once covered with forests of its famous cedars, the Lebanon now has some four hundred trunks left, forming a government-protected national monument near the village of Bcherre. Some of these trunks are believed to be two thousand years old. Many of them are dead, like the people who once lived, loved and toiled under them. In the Middle Ages, when forestry was unknown, the Venetians and the Genoese felled most of the cedars of the Lebanon to build their galleys and galleons.

Three among the most ancient cities of antiquity still stand on this coastal strip of the Mediterranean: Tyre, Sidon, and Berytos, the last two called Saida and Beyrut today. Millenniums ago, these coastal settlements of the tiny land known as Phoenicia sent a steady stream of colonists, merchants, warriors, navigators and administrators westward on their puny galleys. We have seen that these Semites of the second and first millenniums

B.C. conquered, and for centuries held, Sicily, Malta and the Iberian Peninsula, that they founded Carthage, and owned a major part of North Africa. They built Solomon's temple. They worked out the formula of a precious blue glass, which has been lost since. They invented the alphabet. From the natives of England's Cornwall, they bought the tin that went into bronze, the primary "strategic material" of the time, and sold it throughout the East.

Near Beyrut, by the Nakhr-el-Kelb, or "Dog's River," there stands a rock. The Pharaoh Ramses II had a relief chiseled into it to commemorate an Egyptian victory won in these parts. Side by side with this war memorial of the fourteenth century B.C., the Assyrian kings Salmanassar II and Asarhaddon commemorated their victories through inscriptions five and seven hundred years later. In 1861, a French military expedition sent here by Napoleon III had *its* calling card chiseled into this rock. The collection was completed by Lord Allenby in 1918.

Such is the past of this coastal strip, two-thirds the length of our Long Island.

America also is represented in this region. But here, as at home, its face is turned not toward the past but forward, to the future. America's calling card is not a lifeless inscription on a rock but a flourishing educational institution, the American University of Beyrut. A model organization, up-to-date in construction and equipment, it is a modern cultural landmark in the Arab

East. In 1917, when I was the guest of Dr. Bliss, president of the college and son of its founder, Jemal Pasha, the Ottoman Empire's all-powerful proconsul in Syria, gave the college his moral support. The attitude of the French administration of Syria has been equally friendly.

On a modern campus that faces the sea stand the clinics, observatory, laboratories and other buildings of Beyrut's American University. By contrast, farther up to the north, on mountain peaks that face the same sea, stand dreadnought-shaped fortresses built by the Crusaders. Some of them, exceedingly well preserved, still have steel arrows sticking high up in the walls.

Some unique ethnic groups inhabit these Crusaders' forts, which have housed them for centuries. Among these are the Ismaïlites. They belong to a Shiite sect of Islam, many of whose adherents live in India and East Africa. They are believed to be descendants of the "Assassins" of Crusades' fame. Their ancestors were a fighting sect of natives, pledged to relentless war against the invading Crusaders, in the form of individual terror and assassination. They were completely dominated by a chief known as the "Old Man of the Mount," and are mentioned in Marco Polo's account of his travels.

The "Old Man" sent his men out to kill prominent Crusaders and also those native Moslem princes who opposed him. Just as shock troops in the First World War were often given rum before storming an enemy position, to drown their fear in the stupefying effect of alcohol, the Old Man of the Mount had his men smoke hashish, a powerful intoxicant made from hemp, before they went out on an "assignment." Hence, this fore-runner of modern Japan's "Black Dragon Society" in medieval Syria became known as *hashishin*, that is, "those addicted to hashish." *Hashishin*, corrupted by the Crusaders into *assassin*, became an equivalent for "murderer" in the Romance languages and in English.

Another little-known sect in Syria is believed to wor-ship the female reproductive organ as a symbol of life. It is said that on festive occasions the devotees of this age-old, prehistoric fertility cult congregate in great secrecy. One of the beautiful young women of the com-munity then sits on a kind of altar, and is worshiped as a symbol of fertility and of the life force which agi-tates the universe. These secret ceremonies, however, are said to be void of any acts of obscenity or promis-cuity.

Two other ethnic, or rather religious, "islands" in Syria deserve attention: the Yezidi and the Druses.

The former, known also, and wrongly, as "Devil Worshipers," are humble, cotton-growing peasants, and live in the Sinjar Mountains, on the Syrian–Iraqi border. Their creed is a maze of nebulous myths and even more nebulous teachings. They have a secret "holy book," which they jealously guard from the curiosity of out-siders. But it seems to be pretty well established that some of the basic tenets of the Yezidi faith go back to the Zendavesta, the Zoroastrian creed of the Achaemenid and, later, the Sassanid Persians. The Yezidi seem to believe in the coexistence of a cosmic principle, or force, of Good, and an equally autonomous force of Evil. Christianity possibly owes its own doctrine of Lucifer, as an autonomous entity in the universe, to Zoroastrian influences. The Yezidi pray and sacrifice to both the good and the evil principle. They claim that they pray to the force of good because it must be followed and obeyed, and to the force of evil because it must be placated. Which sounds like worldly rather than spiritual wisdom.

The Druses represent one of the most interesting religious and social communities inside the Arabic-speaking world. They do not call themselves "Druses," a word which is a derivative of the name "Ed-Deresi." The reason is that Ed-Deresi, one of their early leaders, turned renegade, and therefore is despised by the Druses of today. They refer to themselves as *El Moahideen*, which is the Arabic equivalent of "Unitarian."

The Druses live partly in the Lebanon, but mainly in the Jebel Druse, a mountainous region in southeastern Syria. Certain aspects of their faith represent a considerably modified replica of the so-called mystery religions of antiquity. The Druses are divided into three groups: the uninitiated, the half-initiated and the initiates. The uninitiated think that they are called unitarians because they believe in one single Deity — Allah. The half-initiated believe that Hakim, an eleventh-century Sultan of Egypt, a member of the so-called Fatimid dynasty, was an incarnation of the Deity, just as the Trinitarian Christian professes that Jesus was an incarnation of God. They further claim that Hamza, Hakim's Vizier, was an incarnation of "Universal Mind." To the members of the *third* degree of Druse initiation their epithet of "Unitarian" means belief in the absolute, all-embracing, all-pervading unity of the Deity and the universe, that is, the *identity* of God and creation. They perceive of the Deity's active, dynamic aspect as a World Soul — the Holy Ghost of Christendom in its original, esoteric sense. But they regard this active aspect of the Deity, this World Soul, which they call *El Ahkyl El Kully* — literally, Universal Mind — as *identical* with Man, not as being separate from him or from Nature.

In other words, the initiates among these tillers of the soil, and fierce warriors if need be, are pure pantheists. As a matter of fact, pantheism has never died out among the advanced thinkers of the East, from North Africa to India and China, since the days when it used to be imparted to the initiates of the ancient Egyptian mysteries and of the mystery religions of ancient Greece which sprang from them. We have an excellent account of the secret pantheist teachings of the ancient Egyptian mystery initiates, in the famed book, *About the Mysteries (De mysteriis)*. Its author, Jamblichus, a Syrian philosopher who flourished in the fourth century A.D., lived at a time when Christianity had not yet obliterated the ancient Osiris mysteries of Egypt and the Eleusinian mysteries of ancient Greece.

In fact, not only did the Egyptian and Eleusinian mysteries survive until the fourth and fifth Christian centuries, but early Christianity was their spiritual child. When we quote the first phrase from the Gospel of St. John as, "In the beginning was the Word," we are repeating a time-honored error. "Word" is only one of several meanings of the Greek word "Logos," which is used in St. John. As the late, great Sir Flinders Petrie, father of modern Egyptology, rightly pointed out, in the first two centuries B.C. and A.D. Logos was the accepted term of the educated Greek and Roman for the concept of a "World Soul" or "Universal Mind." This concept of the Deity as an all-embracing World Soul, or Universal Mind, which is *identical* with the universe, including Man, was the cherished secret of the Egyptian mysteries and of their spiritual child, the Eleusinian mysteries.

So the first sentences of St. John should be read as, "In the beginning, there was Universal Mind. And Universal Mind was with God. And Universal Mind *was* God."

In this doctrine, the cultured among the early Christians, Romans, Greeks, and Jews were all agreed. The Jews called Universal Mind *Shekhinah*. Where the Trinitarian Christians differed, and still differ, from the rest is in the *additional* doctrine that Logos, or Christ, or the Holy Ghost, or *Shekhinah*, or Universal Mind, *had incarnated in Jesus.*

As I have said already, those Druses who have been initiated into the second of their three mystery degrees believe that the Deity incarnated in a son of man, who, they claim, was the Fatimid Sultan-Caliph, Hakim. We have seen that the Shiite Moslem also believes in the incarnation of the Deity. The Ismaïli Shiite claims that seven such incarnations or *imams* have appeared in history. Another group inside the Shia sect postulates twelve incarnations of God. The Hindus also believe in incarnations of the Deity, which they call *avatara*. Krishna is one of these *avataras*.

The jealously guarded, secret, sacred book of the Druses is known to them as *kitab el hikmet* — "the Book of Wisdom." Their priests do not read it or show it to those of their people who belong to the first degree, that is, the uninitiated.

The various forms of yoga, including the technique of developing occult powers through specific exercises, are well known to the highest initiates of the Druses, but as unknown to the rest of the community as to any other outsider. Many Druses believe that the souls of their dead "fly to China," by which their *initiates* are said to mean Tibet, land of eternal snow and timeless mysticism.

The Rise of Arab Power

V

THE SEMITE BEFORE ISLAM

*S*EEN INSIDE the mental blinkers of any one generation, humanity as a whole appears to be sedentary, with only occasional ethnic dislocations. In reality, inside the entire human episode of life on earth, man has been nomadic. Just as the particles of water held over a flame are in incessant motion and ebullience, so is humanity, seen historically, in constant motion and ebullience on the surface of that gigantic spherical furnace which is its home.

Viewed from a higher plane of observation, most lands and countries are changing hands at intervals, sometimes of a few generations, sometimes of a few centuries. In many cases the intervals are much shorter. Propelled by its deep-rooted, cosmic urge for self-realization, for self-expression, for exteriorization of energy, humanity is in a state of incessant spiritual, social and geographic motion. This motion takes the form of new religions, new modes of thought, social revolutions, civil wars, external wars, periodical waves of conquerors, refugees, settlers.

Occasionally, these periodical waves seem to follow the rule of the tides. Conquering armies, sometimes entire populations, advance along "isobaric" lines of ethnic pressure, then recede again. Occasionally, their backwash leaves ethnic groups behind it in isolation.

For almost two thousand years now, a bloody tug of war has been going on between Germans and Slavs on the plains and in the valleys of Central Europe, between the Elbe and the Vistula, the Sudeten and the Carpathian chains. Alternately, each ethnic group pushes the other back, then is pushed back itself. Before Charlemagne, the Slavs had reached the Elbe in the west. He pushed them back to the Vistula. The year 1919 brought their advance as far as Danzig. In 1939, they were temporarily pushed back again. One of the results of the Second World War will be probably a new Slav advance westward.

Three times did the German "urge toward the East," the *Drang nach Osten*, menace Russia — under the Teutonic Knights, under the Kaiser, under Hitler. Three times did the Slav dike smash the German wave.

Western Siberia, however, notably the region between the Urals and the Altai Mountains, is probably humanity's most active ethnic volcano. Century after century, it released its lava stream of migrating or conquering populations eastward, southward, westward.

The Mongols conquered China. They overflowed to India, where they became the Moguls. To the west came the Sarmatians, Avars, Huns, Bulgars, Finns, Magyars, Seljuk and Ottoman Turks. To the west roared the Mongol deluge in the thirteenth century, reaching Silesia in the north and western Hungary in the south.

Receding, it left the Tartars of the Crimea, the Kalmuks and various other Mongoloid groups behind in its wake.

There is another ethnic volcano that pours out periodic streams of human lava towards its periphery — the Arabian Desert. As a pebble thrown into a pond will send out a succession of concentric waves, so have, since time immemorial, impulses of mass psychology prompted an almost uninterrupted process of centrifugal migration from the heart of the Arabian Desert towards its northwestern, northern, and northeastern rim, known as the Fertile Crescent.

Individuals and families drift to the villages on the edge of the desert. The nomad becomes sedentary, the Bedouin is transformed into a fellah, or peasant. Co-incidentally, there is a steady flow of fellaheen from the villages to the cities inside the Fertile Crescent.

Aside from these uninterrupted and overlapping twin migrations, the Arabian Desert has periodically propelled powerful collective movements toward the Fertile Crescent. They took the form of military expeditions on a tribal basis, with the women, children, and flocks in the warriors' wake. Characteristically, they were a combination of mass aggression and mass migration.

In the Arabian Desert, as elsewhere, search for food is merely one motive for eruptive ethnic displacement, and not a major one at that. Privation is the Arab's most faithful friend, his only companion who never falters. Yet the Bedouin loves his desert with the abandon of a luckless lover — just another proof that logic is the last thing that governs life. And we have seen how the *hadhrami* emigrant, grown rich in luxuriant Java and Malaya, returns to a frugal existence in the barren wastes of his native Hadhramaut, where a cluster of palms is the *ne plus ultra* of wealth.

No — materialism conditions and corrupts the soul, but does not monopolize it. The human soul is governed by various contradictory trends, synchronized in counterpoint.

Actually, the Bedouin both loves and fears his desert. Undoubtedly, one of the motives for his mass migrations and aggressions is the lure of the wealth and bounty of the Fertile Crescent. But beyond that motive there seems to operate in him, since time immemorial, an unconscious collective claustrophobia that drives him outward, away from the desert that fetters his powerful creative urge more than would the bars of a prison. For, far down in the deeper layers of the Unconscious, where there no longer is a difference between a Bedouin and a professor of history, latent energy constantly seeks polarization, psychic potentials seek release through action.

Five times in recorded history has the full-blooded Semite, that is, the Bedouin of the Arabian Desert, surged outward in mass action, first attacking and destroying, then turning his urge for self-expression into creative channels.

The first wave swept northeastward. It came in the third millennium B.C., when the Chaldean Bedouins overran the Sumerian city states in present-day Iraq, founding the First Babylonian Dynasty.

The second wave, in the eighteenth century B.C., swept westward, when the Hyksos, Semites from Arabia, invaded Egypt.

The third wave was the gigantic maritime and imperialist expansion of the Phoenician Semites westward, round the Mediterranean. The origin of the Phoenicians, like that of all Semites, goes back to the Arabian Desert. Their ancestors had seeped into the Fertile Crescent, finally reaching the Syrian coast. The cities they founded or populated there became jumping boards for the conquest of the lands that skirt the western Mediterranean.

The fourth human wave from the desert brought the invasion of Palestine by twelve allied tribes of Bedouins under a centralized leadership, who worshiped the same tribal deity, Yahveh, then still primarily a war-god.

The fifth ethnic eruption was the conquest of the entire Fertile Crescent, and of Iran, Turkestan, the Punjab, North Africa and the Iberian Peninsula, by armies of Bedouins, again under centralized leadership, who worshiped a common deity, Allah. But this god transcended all tribal affiliations. Since the advent of Mohammed, Allah, once the tribal guardian god of some small group of Semites, had become an all-embracing theological concept. His devotees conceived of Him not as a tribal deity but as everybody's God, the God of all humanity.

Antiquity knew other Semitic civilizations, which

blossomed inside the present territory of Arabic-speaking Asia. Some of these were important, such as the Nabataean, Minaean, Sabaean, Himyaric, Palmyranean. But they were relatively short-lived, or blossomed in minor regions, and influenced history to a much smaller extent than did the five major Semitic waves.

∽   ∽   ∽

This chapter is primarily concerned with the antecedents of Islam, and their influence upon it. In this connection, one of the lessons of history is so important that we must become fully conscious of it before we proceed further. That lesson is derived from the fact that practically every civilization and every religion has freely borrowed from others. Certain peoples, such as the Egyptians, Greeks, Hindus, Chinese, and Semites, have, of course, contributed many basic elements to the civilizations that are attributed to them. But each has taken over almost as many elements from other systems of thought as it created itself. In evaluating any civilization at all, it is decisively important to keep this in mind in order to obtain the right perspective.

The Chaldean Semites who overran the ancient Sumerian civilization in present-day Iraq were no exception to the rule. They built up a colossal civilization, but its nucleus was that of the defeated local population.

Here begins, in recorded history, that process which was to become a cliché in the succeeding millenniums: a minority of alien invaders overruns a sedentary local majority; becomes an aristocratic ruling caste; foists its language and often, though not always, its religion upon the vanquished. Then, inside of a few generations, it is racially absorbed by the politically and socially subjugated majority, and makes the civilization of the vanquished its own. Finally, having found creative outlets for their collective urge for self-realization, the conquerors add products of their own genius to the civilization they have borrowed, giving it added vitality and power of expansion.

The Chaldean Semites are the first people in history known to have done this. They took over the major part of the religion of the local Sumerians, along with their architecture, fine arts, musical instruments, and script, known as "cuneiform," that is, "wedge-shaped." The only conspicuous change in the reliefs and sculptures in the round was that men no longer appeared clean-shaven but had beards. Since his earliest days, the Semite has looked upon the beard as an indispensable symbol of virility and dignity.

The Chaldean conquest of Iraq being completed, the collective urge for self-realization of the new Semitic ruling class now focused upon cultural values. One of the greatest achievements of Semitic originality was the simplification of Sumerian writing. Like the ancient Egyptians and Hittites, the Chinese, the Mayas of Central America, and various other peoples, the Sumerians originally used ideographs, glyphs, not letters. The country was equally poor in marble and other kinds of stone, and in such plants as the papyrus, which grew in abundance in Egypt and from which the ancient Egyptians made their "paper." So clay was used in Iraq for both building and writing. The signs were impressed upon the still wet clay tablet with a kind of stylus, which looked like a wedge-shaped pencil. As the resistance of the clay made the use of curved lines extremely difficult, the glyphs consisted of straight lines and angles. Thereby, they soon lost much of their resemblance to the object pictured, became conventionally stylized. At a later period of Sumerian writing, some signs still symbolized entire concepts, such as God, man, "big man" (meaning king), temple, house, and others. Many signs, however, had begun to have merely sound values, in the form of *syllables*. But the script still was unnecessarily large and unwieldy.

The new Semitic upper stratum of society in the new Babylonian state reformed, and enormously simplified, the Sumerian script. The signs now were formed solely by various combinations of "wedges," imprints of the wedge-shaped stylus in the wet clay, and most of them stood for syllables. This gave the script a vastly greater scope and adaptability to the spoken language, which had become the Semitic Chaldean.

Hand in hand with this development, the Semite's legislative and judicial talent blossomed forth in one of humanity's greatest moral achievements: King Hammurabi's amazing code of civil and criminal law, promulgated around 2000 B.C., and consisting of 280-odd paragraphs. How can that other great product of Semitic ethics and jurisprudence, the Decalogue, glorious as it is, compare with this gigantic achievement, antedating it by many centuries! Even those two admirable landmarks of western civilization, the codification of the whole body of Roman Law under the Byzantine Emperor, Justinian, in the sixth century A.D., and the Code Napoleon, drawn up thirteen centuries later, cannot compare with King Hammurabi's achievement in cultural significance. It is colossal like the Pyramids, without owing its existence to the misery of armies of slaves.

The numerous inscribed clay tablets of this period furnish eloquent illustrations of the amazing economic and social development of Babylonia four thousand years ago. Many of them represent commercial contracts, relating to loans, deeds, mortgages, and other business transactions, such as purchases and sales on the installment plan! Every respectable citizen, illiterate or not, carried his cylinder-shaped personal seal on a string round his neck. Every contract bears the imprints of the seals of the contracting parties, and very often of a third, containing the words, "The public clay-tablet writer" — in other words, a combination of scribe and notary!

The Semitic Babylonian language, with its script, became the accepted official international language of diplomacy, as French is today. A diplomatic note from the Swedish government to the Norwegian, Portuguese, or Swiss, is drawn up in French. Similarly, Babylonian, and cuneiform writing, was used not only between the Babylonian court and other governments, but, for almost a thousand years, almost between any two governments of western Asia, and even in the confidential reports that Egyptian governors, "resident commissioners," and military commanders in Syria and Palestine sent home to their Pharaoh.

Not much is known about the life of those Bedouin Semites known to history as the Hyksos, an ancient Greek word for "shepherd." These fighting nomads raided and conquered Egypt about the middle of the eighteenth century B.C. The flocks of sheep that accompanied them were probably the reason why the sedentary Egyptians gave these nomads from the Arabian Desert the collective name of "shepherds."

For almost two hundred years, from about 1750 to approximately 1580 B.C., these Semitic invaders ruled Egypt. Their leaders became the Pharaohs. They adopted the habits and civilization of the Egyptians. Such names of Pharaohs of this period as are still preserved are Semitic. The best known is that of the great Khayan, or Khyan.

During a visit to the British Museum in 1938, I saw an object which had been acquired only a few years before, and which is unusually interesting in this connection. It is a piece of carved ivory, about three inches

The Semite before Islam

long, a masterpiece of realism. It shows a Hyksos Pharaoh, represented as a sphinx, with a lion's body and a human head. He wears the *pshemt*, the traditional head-cloth of the Pharaohs. Between his claws, he holds an Egyptian. The expression of fear and misery on the victim's face, and the sneer of scorn and triumph on the Pharaoh's, are masterpieces of portraiture. So are the features of the two as illustrations of racial types. As every trained observer knows, the facial construction of both the average Egyptian and the Bedouin Arab, that is, the full-fledged Semite, has remained unchanged for four thousand years or more. If you shaved off a Bedouin's beard today, and stood him side by side with a typical Egyptian of our generation, you would find them portrayed in this little ivory carving, which apparently commemorates the triumph of the Semitic Hyksos over the Egyptians.

A good deal of new material about these "Shepherd Kings" of Egypt and their people has been discovered in recent years. On scarabs of the Hyksos period have been found such Semitic names as *Yekeb* or *Yakub* — Jacob — and *Yekeb-Hor* or *Yakub-Hor* — Jacob-Hur. Besides, some recently discovered names of Hyksos Pharaohs are *Yakub-Hal* (Jacob is God) and *Yakub-Ba'al* (Jacob is Lord)! "Ya," of course, is the root syllable of Yahveh, often used in composite Jewish names, such as *Ya-kub* (Jacob), *Ya-Nathan* (Jonathan), *Ya-Khanaan* (John, meaning literally "blessed by Ya" — that is, by Yahveh).

(101)

In the light of the latest researches, it appears likely that the shepherd people, the Hyksos of ancient Egyptian history, were none other than the Hebrews, and that the Jewish tribes were a subdivision of the Hebrews. Moreover, it is a fair assumption that later, in the fourteenth century B.C., after the last remnants of the shepherds, or Hyksos, had long left Egypt, the same people became known to the Egyptians under the name *khabiri* — Hebrews — which frequently occurs in hieroglyphic inscriptions of this later period.

In the last twenty years or so, Egyptologists have begun to place the Exodus at about 1600–1580 B.C. The idea begins to gain ground that the Exodus was the last phase of the disintegration of the Hyksos regime in Egypt. The access to centralized power by that great native Egyptian dynasty, the Eighteenth, now is generally put at about 1580 B.C. It is very probable that the seizure of power by the Eighteenth Dynasty followed a prolonged war of attrition between native Egyptian leaders who may have held sway in Upper Egypt, perhaps in and around Thebes, and the gradually weakening Hyksos, whose capital and principal stronghold was Havarith, or Avaris, in the Nile Delta, a city later known as Tanis and Saïs. It is now believed that the Jews were the last remnant of the Hebrews, or Hyksos, to be forced out of Egypt.

It is known that, following some hundred and fifty years of Hyksos rule in major parts of Egypt, the remnants of the rapidly disintegrating forces of the one-time Semite invaders were long besieged in their strong-hold, Havarith. On the basis of my own researches, I am inclined to believe that the Exodus, which is undoubtedly historic, may have been the result of negotiations between the victorious native Egyptian leaders and the last remnants of the Hyksos. The latter may have promised to surrender their fortified capital, Havarith, and leave the country, against the privilege of free and honorable retreat with their families, flocks and possessions. If it should be really historic that the Egyptians followed the Jews to the Red Sea to attack them, it might have been done in contravention of the terms of capitulation. This, of course, is a mere conjecture.

                handle

We have seen that the third wave of Semitic conquest was the Phoenician. The fourth overflow of Semitic vitality resulted in the conquest of Canaan by the twelve allied Bedouin tribes of the Jews. Quite recent researches, made in the late nineteen-thirties, seem to warrant the belief that Jericho fell around 1380 B.C., during the reign of the Pharaoh Akhenaton. If we place the Exodus at about 1580 B.C., the Jews must have lived the Bedouins' nomadic life in the Sinai desert not for forty-five but for some two hundred years, before they took Palestine.

In his last book, the late, great Siegmund Freud contended that Moses was an Egyptian. My own researches, which go back to a number of years, lead me to believe that he was not.

Unquestionably, Moses is an Egyptian word, meaning "son of." Two leading Egyptologists, with whom I have discussed my own hypothesis relating to Moses' descent, agree with my assumption that the hieroglyphs denoting his name in the ancient Egyptian language very likely were these: —

In conformity with Egyptian usage, the name of some Egyptian deity must have preceded the word "Moses." The ideographs

which were probably pronounced *mos-e*, or possibly *mos-es*, were often used in Egypt, but invariably in composite names, always in the sense, "son of." For example, the famous name "Ramses" was actually *Ra-mos-e-su*, or *Ra-mos-es-su*, meaning "son of Ra," Ra being the sun-god. The hieroglyphic rendition of *Ra-mos-es-su*, or Ramses, was

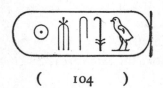

The suffix "su," and the first and second signs from the right, which correspond to it, have no special significance, and do not change the meaning of the word. The name Tutmosis or Tutmoses, which was that of several Pharaohs of the Eighteenth Dynasty, was actually *Thot-mos-e,* or *Thot-mos-es* — "son of Thot" (the god of wisdom and magic, messenger of the gods, and prototype of the Greek Hermes and the Roman Mercury). Its hieroglyphs were

In the case of Ramses, or *Ra-mos-es*, the sign denotes the sun-god Ra. In the hieroglyphs rendering the name of the Pharaoh *Thot-mos-es,*

meaning "Thot," stands for the god Thot, represented as an ibis — undoubtedly originally the prehistoric totemic animal of a part of Egypt.

In each of the above names, we find the signs

meaning "son of."

I personally have no doubt that the original name of

Moses, the historic nature of whose existence we have
no reason to question, was actually some word composed
of the name of a deity and of "son of," because in the
light of classic Egyptian usage, Moses, that is, "son of,"
alone, makes no sense. Later the name of the god must
have been dropped and forgotten. It *might* have been
actually "Ya," the syllabic equivalent for Yahveh. As a
matter of fact, even several decades after the Hyksos
Semites, including the Jews, had left Egypt, a Pharaoh
of the full-blooded native Egyptian Eighteenth Dynasty
bore the name Ya-Mose or Ya-Moses, written like this

and quite obviously meaning Son of Ya or Yahveh! The
Greeks later corrupted the name Ya-Moses into Amasis.
The god Yahveh, whose hieroglyphic sign was
that is, an eye, was probably a tribal guardian deity of
the Jewish subdivision of the Hyksos. The native Egyptians seem to have added this alien god Ya or Yahveh
to the number of their own gods, and to have retained
him among their deities even after the Exodus, as the
Pharaonic name Ya-Moses or Amasis seems to indicate.

It is quite possible, however, that the first part of
Moses' original full name was not Ya or Yahveh but
the name of some native Egyptian deity. This, and the
fact that Moses itself is a pure Egyptian word, would

be no reason to assume, with the late Siegmund Freud, that the great chief of the Jewish Bedouins was an Egyptian. Even many centuries later, under the Ptolemies, many Jews in Egypt had Egyptian names, just as many Jews in ancient Rome bore typically Roman names. Many Jews have Greco-Egyptian and Roman names to this day. For example, so many Jews in Central Europe are called "Marcus" that this name is considered typically Jewish in that part of the world. Yet what name could be more typically Roman than the first name of Marcus Antonius, whom we call Marc Antony, or Marcus Tullius, better known as Cicero?

Another frequent first name among Central European Jews still is Isidore. In fact, in continental Europe Isidore is looked upon as one of the two or three most typical among all Jewish names. Yet Isidore, whose correct form is *Isidoros*, is a Greek name of the Ptolemaic and Roman periods of ancient Egypt, meaning "the gift of Isis"!

So we have no reason to adopt the unconvincing hypothesis that, while trying to escape from Egypt, and while moving among hostile populations in the desert and Fertile Crescent, the Jewish Bedouins entrusted their fate to a *shaykh* of Egyptian descent. Besides, how could an Egyptian have become a Jewish *shaykh*, or chief? This dignity is and always has been strictly hereditary in a Bedouin community. It is the *ahkyl*, the leader in battle, who is elected. But the *ahkyl* of the Jewish Bedouins was Joshuah, not Moses.

We have referred to the great conquests of the Phoenicians. But since this chapter is devoted to the major achievements of the Semitic peoples before the advent of Islam, it must record two other proofs of Phoenician creative originality, which have left indelible marks on the subsequent history of mankind.

One, the invention of the alphabet, has been mentioned already. The other is the invention of the timeless, basic rules of military strategy. Both have greatly influenced the history of the Arabs.

We have seen how the Chaldeo-Babylonian Semites had transformed the Sumerian ideographs into the infinitely more flexible and practicable syllabic signs. Their Phoenician cousins now transformed the syllabic script into a system of letters, the alphabet. In so doing, they literally revolutionized the mechanics of civilization. The Phoenician example inspired the Greeks, Etruscans, Romans, Jews, Sabaeans, Arabs, and a multitude of other ethnic groups. It made literature possible, put an end to the cultural monopoly of a small minority of priests and scribes everywhere, and signalized the first victory of man against illiteracy, handmaid of ignorance and superstition.

The other achievement of the Phoenicians will forever

(108)

be connected with the name of Hannibal, the great general of Phoenician Carthage, and the greatest strategic genius of all time.

Airplanes and tanks have revolutionized military tactics, but not strategy. To win a war definitely, you still have to occupy the country of your enemy. You can do that only if you eliminate his army. When bombed from the air, it can spread out and take cover. Therefore, you can actually eliminate an army only by encircling it. An encirclement is achieved either by going round the enemy's flanks or by breaking through his front line in two places, in a pincers movement.

Hannibal's victories over the Romans at Cannae and on the shores of Lake Trasimenus have gone down in military history as the classic examples of complete victory through the strategy of encirclement. As we have seen, in the war colleges of Europe the study of Hannibal's campaigns still is "must stuff" in the curriculum. Hannibal's strategy laid down the rules for the great battle of Tannenberg in 1914, and for the Russian victories in the Second World War. It inspired some of the Arab generals who conquered North Africa and western Asia, eventually carrying the banner of the Prophet to the Pyrenees and the Sinkiang province of China.

The Arab conquest was the fifth and last among the major ethnic waves originating in the timeless Arabian Desert. Both geographically and culturally, it was the most significant of the five. One of the greatest eruptions of collective energy in the history of man, it set up a powerful and homogeneous civilization that now spreads from Morocco to Nigeria, the Sudan, Bosnia and Albania, the Caucasus, western Asia, India, and Chinese Turkestan, with offshoots in Malaya, Java, Sumatra and the Philippines.

Let us turn to the amazing epic of this Arabo-Semitic conquest.

VI

A FAITH IS BORN

*E*VERY PART of the globe has furnished evidence that in early forms of human society animals are worshiped as the progenitors and guardian deities of tribes. In many instances the place of these totemic animal deities in tribal worship is taken by some other fetish, such as a tree, a stone, or the like.

For uncounted centuries, the pre-Moslem inhabitants of Mecca worshiped a fetish known as the Ka'aba. This black meteoric stone stood, and still stands, in that city. Its age-old veneration made Mecca a flourishing pilgrimage center. Near the Ka'aba stood an ancient shrine. It contained the images of the totemic animal idols and other deities of those tribal communities of the neighborhood that had made Mecca the center of their religious and commercial activities. This brought many visitors to the sanctuary and to the bazaar of Mecca, which was to the Arab tribesmen of the region what Jerusalem had once been to the Jewish tribesmen of Palestine.

Mecca grew rich. And the richest people in Mecca were members of the old, aristocratic tribe of El Qoreish, a name which means "swordfish." This tribe, which traced its genealogy back to the swordfish, its totemic animal, had the hereditary guardianship of the Ka'aba sanctuary, with the right to levy an entrance fee. So both religious and economic interest created strong ties between the Ka'aba and the men of Qoreish. The Ka'aba grew ever richer in fame, the men of Qoreish ever richer in money and influence.

The year 565 A.D. had brought the death of the militant Byzantine Emperor, Justinian, who had spread the Christian faith by offering the vanquished Christianity or the sword. About five years later, in Mecca, a boy was born to Ameenah, widow of Abdallah, a member of the powerful Qoreish tribe, who died before the birth of his son.

Abdallah means "servant of Allah," Allah being the name of some ancient deity of the local polytheistic religion. My own researches lead me to believe that Allah was also a local guardian deity in the powerful Semitic city and state of Palmyra in the Syrian Desert, which flourished almost four hundred years before Mohammed. A ruler of Palmyra, a son of the famous Queen Zenobia, bore the name Vabdalatus. It seems to have escaped the attention of historians and philologists alike that Vabdalatus is quite obviously a bare Romanization of the name "Abdallah."

Both in Mohammed's time and many centuries before him, there was a regular traffic by caravan between Palmyra, Damascus, Palestine, Mecca and Saba — or Sheba — the latter being situated in the southern tip of Arabia, between Yemen and Hadhramaut. This was the famous "myrrh and incense route" between Syria and southern Arabia. It is logical to assume that the cult of the Semitic local tribal god Allah may have been brought to Mecca from Palmyra, or vice versa. At any rate, we have here a clue of the greatest importance for the study of the origins of Islam, and well worth the time and effort of both Western and Moslem students as a subject for further investigation.

The boy born to Ameenah was six when his mother died. His name has never been really established. In the Koran, it figures as both Ahmed and Mohammed, but to Moslem tradition it is known as Mohammed. The boy spent two years in his grandfather's home, when the latter also died. Then, at the age of eight, he joined the family of his uncle, Abu Talib, a prosperous merchant who operated caravans between Hejaz, Syria and Iraq, and often took young Mohammed with him. Against the general background of the boy's brilliant intelligence, this specific experience proved, of course, of great educational value. Mohammed never learned to write. But at that time most people went to the public scribe when they had letters to write or contracts to draw up, while prosperous merchants had their secretary-bookkeepers. Two hundred years later Charlemagne, champion of Christendom, also was illiterate, and in early medieval Europe this was the rule even among princes and nobles.

Physically, young Mohammed was not strong. Besides, he is reported to have had epileptic fits. He was fond of solitude and often meditated in a cave on a hill outside Mecca.

At the age of twenty-five he married Khadiyah, a rich widow of great intellect and high ideals, a member of his own tribe, the Qoreish, and fifteen years his senior. While this marriage freed him from material cares, Mohammed was known to lead a simple, totally unpretentious life. He went more and more often to his beloved cave.

During one of his meditations, he suddenly heard a voice saying: "Thou shalt preach in the name of Allah, the Creator!" As it usually happens with people who have no previous experience of paranormal phenomena, young Mohammed flew into a panic. A few days later, he had a similar experience. Almost crazed with fright, he ran home, hiding under a blanket, only to hear the "voice" saying: "O thou covered one, get up and warn the people!"

After a while, Mohammed got used to the voice, which, he reported, sometimes also sounded like the peal of bells, and sometimes like thunder. Eventually, the voice became his regular companion. He associated it with the Archangel Gabriel. Subsequently, "Gabriel" repeatedly appeared to him and once even "touched" him.

He now was convinced that God had entrusted him with a mission, had made him a Prophet, with a message to his people.

A Faith Is Born

Most of those to whom he spoke about his visions of Gabriel, of the voice that spoke to him, and of his mission as a Prophet of Allah, treated him with scorn. Others looked upon him with the detached sympathy of sane people for lunatics. Only his faithful wife, Khadiyah, his nephew Ali, and another kinsman, Abu Bakr, believed him. Mohammed suffered also from recurrent fever. Very likely it was malaria, common in western Asia, and well-known to the Arab. Often, Mohammed would lie on his bed, covered with blankets, shivering under an attack of the fever, and would repeat the words that "the Archangel Gabriel" was addressing to him. On such occasions his friends thought that if he was not insane he must be delirious.

Mohammed was neither one nor the other. It would be entirely outside the scope of this book to go at length into the physiology and psychology of ecstasy, which often is a highly creative state of the human soul. But in order to understand and properly to evaluate the significance of the prophet-leader type in both Eastern and Western history, we should know more about the nature of ecstasy.

The human intellect is an indispensable *instrument* of cognition, but *not its source*. The sole source of higher cognition is intuition. Intuition is merely a word for that activity of our Unconscious by which it draws upon the transcendental, collective experience of the race, projecting the thoughts so obtained into the focus of our consciousness.

(115)

The essence, the "seed," of every creative thought darts into our consciousness through the medium of intuition, because intuition alone is synthetic, creative, above logic. Then, the analytical, logical, rational aspect of the mind, known as the intellect, performs its indispensable "digestive" functions. It measures the import of the new thought, gives it formal expression, breaks it up into details, labels them and co-ordinates them with that inventory of conscious personal experience, the memory of the individual.

In contrast to intuition, the intellect is not synthetic but analytical, not creative but reproductive, not above, but subject to, logic. As I have said, the intellect is merely an indispensable instrument, and not the source, of cognition, just as the surgeon's carefully sharpened scalpel is an indispensable instrument of surgery, but not the surgeon.

In its higher forms, ecstasy throws open the gates of intuition. During the present, already evanescent episode of super-rationalism and soulless materialism through which the West is passing, the Occidental is cutting himself off completely from access to higher forms of intuition. He has raised the intellect from the status of a much-needed servant to that of an idol. He wallows in facts and figures, which he confounds with culture, just as he confounds the memorization and retention of facts and data with thinking.

Therefore it is only natural that in his ignorance of

the higher mechanics and the higher states of the mind, the Western "intellectual" should look upon every form of ecstasy as a more or less mild form of insanity.

Besides, the average person, even the psychologist, usually confounds that feeling of elation which *accompanies* ecstasy, *but is merely its symptom,* with that *increased* spiritual and psychologic *receptivity to creative and cognitive thought* which is the essence of the higher forms of ecstasy.

As a matter of fact, ecstasy is the bridge between man's human and cosmic, "normal" and paranormal faculties. The degree of intensity of ecstasy can vary from mere elation to ecstatic trance. Its results can vary from a primitive state of spiritual intoxication to the conception and creation of the "Eroica" and the "Pastoral" Symphony, of the Archimedean Theorem, the Pyramids of Gizeh, the Copernican System, the basic tenets of Judaism, Buddhism, Christianity, Islam.

Buddhists know four distinct stages of ecstasy, which they call *jyhanah.* To Moslem mystics, ecstasy is known under the Arabic term, *rhaboobah.* Christian and Jewish mystics use austerities, such as fasting, to bring about ecstasy. In India, austerities form merely one of several alternative techniques for creating ecstasy.

Many details of Mohammed's life have been preserved that stand the test of historic criticism. There is no doubt that he was humble, natural, and thoroughly truthful in his account of his subjective experiences. When reading of his visions of the Archangel Gabriel, and the Archangel's "voice," we naturally think of Moses' visions of his god in the burning bush, and how the Lord's voice constantly gave him instructions. But, oddly enough, so far nobody seems to have called attention to the close analogies between Mohammed's ecstatic experiences and those, much more recent, of such famous Western mystics as Jeanne d'Arc, Luther, Swedenborg, or Bernadette Soubirous, of Lourdes fame.

Yet the hallucinations which accompanied the ecstatic states of these Christian mystics bear perfect resemblance to those Mohammed told his friends and followers about.

The acoustical experiences of Jeanne d'Arc, her famous "voices," urging her on her mission, are a case in point. So is the voice of the Virgin Mary, which, Bernadette said, had spoken to her. Bernadette claimed to have seen the Holy Virgin besides hearing her. Swedenborg actually lived amidst visual and acoustical experiences of a paranormal nature. In the Wartburg, in Germany, tourists still are shown the spot in Luther's room where the inkstand he threw at the apparition of Satan hit the wall.

Mohammed's account to his confidants that he often heard sounds like the tinkling of bells, and others resembling thunder, is amazingly accurate. In some secret methods of *sâdhana*, or spiritual training, as practised in India, it is a familiar symptom of certain forms of ecstasy to hear "the tinkling of bells" and "thunder."

A Faith Is Born

ᴄᴡᴐ   ᴄᴡᴐ   ᴄᴡᴐ

We have seen in a former chapter that the Arab is a born poet. Today, as in the days of Mohammed, the simple, illiterate Bedouin expresses himself with an eloquence, poetic power and rhetoric elegance of speech that tower above those of an Occidental of similar station. Mohammed had this gift in the highest degree. Once he had gained the conviction that Allah had ordained him a prophet, he began to preach his creed of pure monotheism to his fellow citizens. His message was that all idols must be discarded because there was only one god, Allah. Unlike the Yahveh of the early Jews, a stern war-god, visiting the sins of the fathers upon their children down to the fifth generation, Mohammed's god resembled the later Jewish conception of the Deity, as it developed during and after the Babylonian exile. Allah is constantly referred to as *er-rahman, er-rahim* — the merciful, the compassionate.

As we have seen, at first only Khadiyah, the Prophet's wife, Ali, his nephew, and his kinsman Abu Bakr believed in his mission. Gradually, he made a few more converts, who were impressed by his imposing countenance, powerful personality, and simple, austere life. Among these first Moslem (the word means "supporter") was Omar ibn el Khattab, Omar for short, who

(119)

was to become one of the great figures of early Islam.

Mohammed was unselfish, fearless, and insistent — three great weapons in any environment. The solidarity of the Meccans in opposing him began to weaken, then to crumble. This fellow could not be assailed on moral grounds. He claimed no divine status. He merely called himself the latest in a long line of prophets of the human race. When some of his followers tried to idolize him, to keep the hair his barber clipped off his head and beard, as a charm, he nipped the attempt in the bud. The number of his followers grew.

Mohammed ibn Abdallah ceased to be the laughing-stock of the Qoreish. He had become a dangerous agitator. The influential citizens decided to kill him.

But among Arab tribesmen murder is a dangerous thing for both parties concerned. People think twice before starting a blood feud. So the men of Qoreish made haste slowly, discussed the project at length, finally decided to share the responsibility for the deed equally. Meanwhile, of course, the plan had become an open secret.

Mohammed decided to flee. When a deputation from Medina invited him to make that city his home, he accepted. First, he sent a couple of hundred of his followers to Medina, then followed himself. After a long trek, made necessary by the man-hunt of which he was the quarry, he reached Medina on September 24, 622 A.D. Mohammed's flight is known in Islam as the *hejira*, and the Moslem era is figured from that date.

A Faith Is Born

With Mohammed's escape to Medina, Mecca's old political and economic rival, the religious quarrel became a civil war, and the Prophet a general and statesman.

For its very existence, Mecca depended upon its caravan traffic with the outer world. It was at this life artery of his enemies that Mohammed decided to strike. He and his men organized a *rahzoo* against a powerful caravan, homeward bound from Syria to Mecca. The caravan's escort of a thousand men suffered a crushing defeat at the hands of Mohammed's three hundred fighters.

A year later, the Meccans sent an army of several thousand men against Mohammed's followers and defeated them. Mohammed himself was wounded. Only nine hundred years later did the world see another religious reformer who backed his teaching with his sword — Ulric Zwingli, champion of Protestantism, who fell in a battle between the citizen armies of his native Zurich and of its rival, Berne.

To give incipient Islam and its leader the *coup de grâce*, the Qoreish now organized an army outnumbering the Prophet's in a ratio of five to one. Among Mohammed's greatest assets were his common sense and appreciation of well-meant advice. One of his aides, a military genius of the first magnitude, recommended that the Moslem army dig a trench and meet the enemy's charge under its protection. Trench warfare as a part of military tactics was subsequently rediscovered during the Russo-Japanese War of 1904–1905, becoming a basic feature of the war of 1914–1918! In addition, Mohammed himself had another idea, which the German General Staff unconsciously revived during the blitz of 1940 in France. The prophet-general sent a number of his men secretly into the enemy's camp, where they played the part of "Fifth Columnists." They actually weakened Meccan morale by spreading greatly exaggerated rumors about the size, strength and ruthlessness of Mohammed's army.

Trench warfare, disruptive propaganda, and last, but not least, the fanatical courage of Mohammed's Moslem army inflicted a decisive defeat upon the Meccans.

Then, six years after his flight to Medina, the Prophet marched against Mecca, but made a generous peace with the city. An Arab Cincinnatus, he did not need the pleas of a mother to show moderation towards his native city in the hour of his triumph. This man was an unusual combination of religious reformer, general and statesman. He was fully aware that a victory followed by moderation is likely to result in a peace covenant followed by loyalty.

Two years later, in 630, he entered Mecca, smashed the idols of the Qoreish, but treated them and the rest of the Meccans with exemplary magnanimity.

Then, in 632, he led a pilgrimage to Mecca, which he had restored as a pilgrimage center, though no longer in the service of pagan gods. This proved his last visit to Mecca, and during his stay in the holy city he preached a last sermon, embodying his religious and political testament. In its spirit, it is curiously reminiscent of Washington's Farewell Address and political legacy.

Mohammed exhorted his followers to be united. He laid down the axiom that every Moslem is the brother of every other Moslem, that Islam is one brotherhood.

The Prophet then returned to Medina, where he died in the same year.

His doctrine that all Moslem are brethren, and that every Moslem's property is sacrosanct to every other Moslem, decreed a social revolution. Literally for thousands of years, the tribes of Arabia had been making war upon one another. As we have seen, the *rahzoo* was an age-old and perfectly honorable institution. It was a source of gain, but even more was it the Bedouin's traditional outlet for the general human urge for self-assertion. Mohammed's doctrine of Moslem brotherhood was a public condemnation of the ancient tradition of tribal separatism and rivalry. Islam had transcended the status of a religion. It had become a social system, a state.

⁓   ⁓   ⁓

At this point, we reach the very core of the spirit of Islam. Following their subsequent contact with the Byzantine and the Asiatic autocracies, Moslem communities often emulated these tyrannical forms of government. Autocracy was, of course, the customary form of government in the Roman Empire and throughout the Orient, and prevailed in Europe even in modern times, as in Tsarist Russia, in France under the various Louis', and in Germany under Hitler. But regardless of any autocratic form of government, and side by side with it, there survived inside Moslem society, and inside the various Moslem states, the Bedouin's genuine, privation-bred sense of equality, the democracy of the desert.

To understand the social and political aspects of Islam as a state, and the difference between them and later Western forms of government, we must realize a fact of fundamental significance. It is that *democracy*, in its *Western* form, *was born of the struggle not between rulers and the people but between rulers and oligarchies.*

Brutus and his fellow conspirators were members of the oligarchic party, not men of the people. To attain his ends, Julius Caesar leaned on the plebeians, worked hand in glove with the tribunes of the people, checkmated the aristocrats who had monopolized the republic. So the aristocrats killed this shrewd politician of aristocratic descent who opposed his own kin in order to monopolize himself the power and the spoils which had been their *collective* privilege.

King John gave the Magna Charta not to the people, but to the oligarchs whose formerly unchecked privilege to run and exploit the social system had been curtailed by the kings. The Prince Electors of the German-Roman Empire elected the penniless little nobleman,

Rudolph of Habsburg, Emperor, because he was too weak to curb their exploitation of the people. For the same reason, following the death of Ivan the Terrible and of Boris Godounov, did the powerful *boyars*, or oligarchs, of Russia make the penniless and therefore powerless little nobleman, Michael Romanoff, Tsar of all the Russias.

Yes, the history of the early Roman Empire and of the Western monarchies was one long fight between the ruler, who wanted to exploit the people on a monopolistic "trust" basis, and the hereditary aristocracy, which wanted to exploit it on a collective "cartel" basis. The few revolts of the people, such as the *Fronde* in France and the *Bundschuh* revolt of the serfs in Germany, were put down with a bestial cruelty duplicated only centuries later, in Nazi Germany's concentration camps. Not until the middle class, the intelligentsia, asserted its rights, through tenacity in England, through revolution in America and France, did the *people* attain modern democracy, that is, emancipation from oppression by both kings and oligarchs.

In major parts of Asia, however, beneath the superstructure of an autocratic monarchy, democracy has long existed in the sense of social equality independent of birth. In these regions of Asia, autocracy had won decisive victories over the oligarchies even before the beginning of the Christian era. In China, the Han dynasty, which reigned in the last two pre-Christian and the first two Christian centuries, abolished the class of big landowners, that is, the oligarchy. The Mandarins were a class of intellectuals, hand-picked and highly trained civil servants, not hereditary nobles.

Inside the social structure of the early Moslem state and later Moslem empire, democracy was an age-old legacy of the desert. Mohammed incorporated the Bedouin's sense of social equality in the structure of Islam. He made equality among the Moslem a tenet of their religion. The average Western historian of Islam is inclined to overlook *this sanctification, this "canonization," of social equality inside the community* — Mohammed's supreme achievement, formally established during the Prophet's "farewell pilgrimage" in 632 A.D.

1776, less 632: a time difference of eleven hundred odd years.

Like every system and form of human association, whether Oriental or Occidental, the Moslem social system and the structure of the Moslem state eventually deteriorated, lost much of its original ethical texture. But in diametrical contrast to Christendom, an organized oligarchy, systematically exploiting the people, never existed in the gigantic Arab empire that was presently to arise on the ruins of Byzantine and Sassanid-Persian power. Nor did it ever exist in the various Moslem states that later emerged from the ruins of the Arab empire, or in the Ottoman Empire, in which most of them were subsequently absorbed.

Unquestionably, the Arab empire, its divers regions that later assumed sovereignty, and the Ottoman Empire before 1908, all had autocratic forms of government. It is equally true that the whims of some Caliphs and sundry Sultans often raised slaves to the Grand Vizierate and often handed Grand Viziers over to the executioner. Tyranny is a somber and pathetic technique of social equalization, creating an equality of fear, hazard and misery. But in the West, the peoples found themselves between the devil of oppression by the king and the deep sea of oppression by an organized class of privileged nobles, which did not exist in Islam. Moreover, in Moslem autocracies those directly exposed to the dangerous whims of the ruler were a small minority of courtiers and others living inside the radius of the autocrat's attention.

VII

THE ARAB BLITZ

*B*ESIDES being a religion, Islam had become a social system, a state. But true to the intentions of its founder, *Islam never became a Church*.

Mohammed had been anxious to assure that the new religion had no privileged priesthood, no organized clergy that could attempt to dominate the citizen through the medium of his religious inclinations or fears. To this day, anybody in Islam can be an *imam*. Here, this word of many meanings is used in the sense of "he who leads in prayer." Any Moslem can lead in prayer. And that is the essential function of the Moslem priest. The word *hojah*, used in Turkey for "priest," means "teacher."

Here we come to another source of erroneous beliefs about Islam — the nature of the Caliphate.

Khaleefah — Caliph — merely means "successor." Successor to the Prophet. Mohammed had never claimed to be either a vicar or an incarnation of Allah. He proclaimed himself a *messenger* of God, and merely one in a long line of such messengers, or prophets. Neither was he deified after his death. Says the *rayk'ah*, the Moslem's famous creed: *"La ilahah illa'llah, Mohammedoom rasooloo'llah."* (There is no God but Allah — Mohammed is the messenger of Allah.)

So there could be no successor to Mohammed in the spiritual or religious sense of the word. There was no class of priests, no religious hierarchy. There was not even a vacancy left in the Church that someone else could fill, because there was no Church. No Moslem would have dreamed of claiming succession to Mohammed's status as a prophet, or as a messenger of Allah, because by that very act he would have violated the spirit and creed of Islam and become an apostate.

In other words, the term, and the post, of *Caliph*, or "successor," *involved no special religious status or privilege whatever*, with the exception of being mentioned in the prayers of the Faithful on Fridays. *The status of the Caliph was wholly temporal.* He was indeed looked upon as a successor to Mohammed, but solely in the latter's capacity as the head of the state which he first founded in Medina, and which, at Mohammed's death, included also Mecca and other territories.

Nor was this initial Moslem state, and the subsequent empire of the Caliphs, wholly Moslem! Mohammed himself had followed up his triumph over the Christians of Aqabah and the Jewish tribes of Jarbah, Maqnah and Adrooh, by *treaties guaranteeing them liberty of religious worship, local self-government, and complete security*, against disarmament, political allegiance to the new state, and payment of a combined head and land tax. No proof of Mohammed's statesmanship could be more eloquent than this treaty, made more than thirteen hundred years before freedom of religion and freedom from fear were incorporated in the Atlantic Charter.

So the Caliphs were temporal rulers of a community only partly Moslem. Not until the latter part of the eighteenth century, following a treaty between Russia and Turkey, did the idea become general in the Christian world that the Caliphate was a Moslem counterpart of the Papacy. The famed, time-honored Arabic title of the Caliphs, *Ameer el Mumeneen*, leaves no doubt as to their status. It means "Commander of the Faithful."

Bedouin usage applied to the appointment of the first Caliphs. They were elected, preferably, but not necessarily, from among the members of the Chief's family. Usually, but again not necessarily, the dead leader's oldest male relative would be chosen. Later, in the Ottoman dynasty, this mode of succession became hereditary, the oldest male member of the house of Osman succeeding to the throne of the Ottoman Empire. This rule remained in operation right up to 1918, when the Ottoman Empire collapsed.

The first Caliph was Abu Bakr, Mohammed's father-in-law, and one of his first converts. He ruled for two years, being succeeded by Omar, next to Mohammed the most popular figure in the history of Islam.

Omar was a typical Bedouin *shaykh* of the old school, frugal in his private life, stern in character, with the moral standards of a Biblical patriarch. He owned only one shirt and one mantle, both copiously patched. When visiting Jerusalem, which his warriors had conquered, the Caliph, surrounded by his gorgeous retinue on their richly caparisoned camels and horses, got off his camel and entered the Holy City on foot. Twelve centuries later, in 1917, this gesture of humility was repeated by Lord Allenby, British conqueror of Jerusalem, as a bid for his country's popularity in Palestine.

The first Caliphs resided in Medina. Abu Bakr ruled from 632 to 634, Omar from the latter year to 644, Othman from 644 to 646. He was succeeded by Ali, Mohammed's son-in-law, husband of his daughter Fatimah.

Othman was murdered by a faction of religious zealots of a type quite common in the history of both the West and the East. It was this faction which made Ali Caliph. These events precipitated a civil war between the followers of Moaviyyah, Moslem governor of Syria, and those of Ali. Moaviyyah defeated his opponents and became Caliph, making Damascus his residence. He founded the dynasty of the Omayyads. But regardless of its political antecedents, Ali's claim to the Caliphate had been lawful. Moaviyyah, an astute diplomat, bought off Hassan, Ali's eldest son, who formally renounced his claims to the Caliphate. But the Moslem of Iraq and Iran continued to look upon Ali as the only rightful successor to Mohammed, and considered all the Caliphs who came after him impostors. This split exists to this day. More than half of the Iraqis, and all Persians, belong to the dissidents. Their sect is known as the Shia, a word meaning "party." Today, the Shiites are regarded as a purely religious sect in Islam, separated from the majority, the Sunna, by the same kind of animosity which reigns between Catholics and Protestants of the intolerant type. But actually, as we have seen, the Caliphate was a purely temporal office, and the schism between the followers of Moaviyyah and those of Ali and his sons, Hassan and Hussein, was definitely a political issue revolving round a dynastic quarrel. It is useful to realize this clearly if we want to evaluate the deeper psychologic causes of the violent animosity of the Shia, and especially of the people of Iran, against the rest of Islam.

Moaviyyah used Othman's violent death as a welcome pretext for carrying out his scheme to seize the Caliphal power. Similarly, the political and dynastic quarrel about Ali's rights to the Caliphate was a welcome crystallization point for the pent-up opposition to Arab rule among the people of Iraq and Iran. These two regions had formed integral parts of the culturally highly advanced Persian Sassanid Empire, which had been overrun and conquered by the Arabs less than fifteen years before Ali's accession to the Caliphate. Few Western, or even Moslem, historians realize fully to what extent the Shiite schism in Islam, under the thin veneer of religious opposition, was actually a Persian national and cultural rebellion against alien rule. Besides, while Arabic became the lingua franca of the peoples of North Africa, Arabia, Palestine, Syria, and of a part of Iraq, the Persians accepted the Arabic script but used it for their own Persian tongue, which they retained. And the recrudescence of a Persian national monarchy eight centuries after the inception of the Shia sect was merely the formal political manifestation of a Persian cultural nationalism which had never died out. We shall see in a later chapter how the unquenchable spirit of Persian civilization consistently disregarded some of the strictest tenets of Islam, to give expression to its own concepts of art and culture in its own way.

To a certain extent, the Irish problem offers an illustrative analogy to the Shiite-Persian. Religious antagonism between the Catholic Irish and the Protestant English is bitter, but it is only one aspect of the national and emotional antagonism between the two peoples. Like religion-infused Persian nationalism, religion-infused Irish nationalism has culminated in the re-establishment of political independence.

But we should see Moslem life and culture in the wrong perspective unless we first followed Islam in its unique "blitzkrieg" conquest of the vast region bounded by the Pyrenees and the Atlantic in the west and central India and China in the east.

સ>   સ>   સ>

To the Occidental, spectacular generalship is associated with such names as Alexander, Caesar, Napoleon. It is owing to traditional religious antagonism between primitive souls in the West and East, with the resultant ignorance of each other's history, that the names "Khalid ibn-el-Walid" and "Amr ibn-el-As" are unknown to the West. Yet these two men rank with Alexander and Caesar among the greatest conquerors of all time. In extent, their conquests far exceeded those of Napoleon, being themselves exceeded only by those of the Romans and of the Mongols.

After the death of the Prophet, a major part of the new, small Islamic state seceded. On behalf of the Caliph Abu Bakr, Khalid ibn-el-Walid put down the revolt. Then he set out to conquer territory outside the confines of the Moslem state.

The Moslem wave first swept forward against Syria, which formed a part of the Byzantine Empire. A powerful Byzantine army was defeated, Damascus besieged and taken. Khalid crushed another Byzantine army in Palestine. Byzantine power in the Levant collapsed like a house of cards.

The Arabs next attacked the Persian Empire of the Sassanids. In one major operation in 637, they wiped out the Persian army sent to stop them. Iraq fell into their hands. In a panic, the Sassanid Emperor, Yezdegerd, fled from Ctesiphon, gorgeous capital of his empire. He was murdered by one of his own men during the flight. The conquest of the huge Sassanid Empire lasted ten years, but it was complete.

A number of Persians refused to submit to the conquerors. They fled to the islands of the Persian Gulf, thence to India. Their direct lineal descendants are the

Parsees of Bombay, who still are Zoroastrians, and number about three hundred thousand.

The Moslem conquest did not stop at the eastern borders of present-day Iran. It engulfed Afghanistan, and the regions of Sind and of the Punjab in India. It swallowed up Bokhara, Khiva, Samarkand — the Turkestan of today. As a faith, Islam spread even to the Chinese province of Sinkiang, to Sumatra, Java, and Mindanao, in the Philippines.

The laurels of Pompey had given Caesar no rest. Neither did the laurels of Khalid give rest to his great rival, Amr ibn-el-As, early Islam's other military genius. In 639, with four thousand Bedouin riders, he advanced against Egypt, then a flourishing province and the granary of the Byzantine Empire.

The story of the Arab conquest of Syria was repeated in Egypt. The Arabs crushed the Byzantine field army sent against them. Amr laid siege to Alexandria, then one of the world's richest and most imposing cities. It was also the base of the Byzantine fleet, thirteen centuries before it became the base of the British Mediterranean Squadron.

Alexandria fell. Amr's Bedouins pressed forward. They took the rest of Egypt, and present-day Libya as far as Tripoli. Only a few years later, subsequent Arab commanders took Carthage and Tunis, Algeria and Morocco.

The Omayyad Caliph in Damascus had appointed Musa, one of his generals, governor of North Africa. It was he who extended the Caliph's empire from Tunis and the neighboring Carthage, then a flourishing Byzantine Christian city, to the Atlantic.

At this time, Spain was under the sway of the Western Goths, or Visigoths, Germanic barbarians who had succeeded their Teutonic cousins, the Suevi and Vandals, in the mastery over the Iberian Peninsula. The native Ibero-Roman population disliked the Visigoths. Besides, dynastic squabbles divided Spain's Germanic overlords.

Musa thought that the chances were favorable for a successful *rahzoo*, a large-scale looting expedition to Spain. He sent a small reconnaissance force over, then, in 711, dispatched his Berber freedman, Tariq, with 7000 men to the peninsula. Tariq crossed over at the foot of Gibraltar's famed rock. This gave the place its Arabic name, *Jebel Tariq* ("Tariq's Mountain"), which the West corrupted into Gibraltar.

Not far from Xerez de la Frontera, in the southern tip of Spain, Tariq's forces, now numbering about 12,000, were met by the Visigothic army, exactly twice as large. The wild onslaught of the Moslem cavalry and its greater mobility decided the battle. The Visigoths were literally wiped out. Spain was lying at the feet of the conqueror, a ripe fruit waiting to be picked up.

Tariq's orders had been to carry out his *rahzoo* and bring back the loot. Now, he was unable to resist the temptation to advance. He may have been quite sincere in interpreting his orders to mean that he should bring back *all* the loot he was able to get. In this event, the logical thing to do was to follow up his overwhelming victory, and to loot as many cities as he was able to conquer. On the other hand, he might have been dominated by an idea similar to that which guided Cortéz in his Mexican adventure eight centuries later: to conquer a big country in order to be made its governor and actual ruler, with direct responsibility to his sovereign, and not to an intermediary superior.

Actually, we have no reason to doubt that when Tariq saw that his *rahzoo* had developed into a promenade through Spain, he simply pushed on in order to do as much looting as possible.

Arab historians report that the Caliph in Damascus was angered and dismayed at the news of the expedition into Spain. "I don't want Moslem people to go beyond the sea!" he is reported to have cried. The Caliph was a statesman. Apparently, he felt that in the long run to maintain Arab rule in so far advanced a position as Spain, with the sea in one's back, would be a liability, not an asset.

The first phase of Arab history in Spain seemed to give these fears the lie. But in the end, they proved well-founded. Spain was the only country in the world where Islam, once introduced, failed to stay.

For the civilization of the Christian West, the Arab rule in Spain turned out to be a boon. As we shall see in a later chapter, our Occidental civilization is largely a legacy from the Moslems of Spain.

∞ ∞ ∞

Inside of a few weeks, Tariq had occupied a great number of cities. Some were taken by storm, others opened their gates before the conqueror. Musa, governor of North Africa, Tariq's direct superior, was either dismayed about his subordinate's action or jealous of his successes. At any rate, he set out for Spain himself. He laid siege to a number of important cities, conquering one after another. Having taken them, it never entered his mind to give them up again. Musa disregarded his ruler's major policies just as completely as had Tariq. In the vicinity of Toledo, which had fallen to Tariq, Musa assumed supreme control of the Spanish campaign, continuing to overrun most of what Tariq had not had the time to conquer. Then he staged a triumphant march, through the whole of North Africa, to Damascus, to give an account of the situation. To win the good graces of El Walid, who now sat on the throne of the Caliphs, Musa brought back with him many thousand slaves, a retinue of Visigothic nobles and princes of royal blood, and loot of such value as had hardly ever been seen before. El Walid seems to have forgiven Musa and Tariq, but both suffered iniquities at the hands of a succeeding Caliph. Tariq's further fate is unknown. Musa died in exile and poverty in the Hejaz.

But the fate of Spain's conquerors did not change the fate of Spain. It had become a province of the huge Caliphal empire, now extending from the South of France to the West of China.

For a while, the empire of the Caliphs extended even into France. In 720, following earlier Arab incursions north of the Pyrenees, Es-Samh ibn Mahlik el Khowlah-nee conquered Narbonne, in the South of France. The Moslems held this city for almost forty years. They transformed it into a powerful stronghold, arsenal, and strategic base for *rahzoos* deep into France. They temporarily held Avignon, raided Bordeaux and Lyon, and made their deepest thrust into France in 732, when their *rahzoo* extended as far as Tours and Poitiers. This is the famous battle of Poitiers in which Charles Martel is supposed to have saved Europe north of Spain from Arab domination. Actually, historic evidence seems to indicate that the initial momentum of Arab conquest north of the Straits of Gibraltar had spent itself, and that looting expeditions were the principal objective of the minor Arab armies which crossed the Pyrenees from time to time, or sallied forth from their base at Narbonne.

The battle of Poitiers was a draw. Charles Martel's men repulsed the charge of the Arabs, with great losses to both parties. The Arab commander, Abd-er-Rahman ibn Abdullah, fell in the battle, and during the night, unnoticed by the Franks, the Arabs withdrew southward. But their raids into southern France continued for almost twenty years.

Most of Tariq's men had been Berbers from Morocco and Algeria, while Musa's army consisted mainly of Arabs and Syrians. Following their conquest of the Iberian Peninsula, many of the Arab soldiers became settlers in the newly won territory. The Arabs transformed the country from a temporary home of Teutonic barbarians into one of the greatest cultural centers of all time, the cradle of our present Western civilization. The first bloom of Arab culture in Spain is connected with the name of Abd-er-Rahman — not the Arab commander at Poitiers of the same name. Abd-er-Rahman and his immediate successors would rank in our minds with the spiritually most advanced rulers, the most inspired cultural and temporal leaders of all time, had a thousand years of religious propaganda in the West not surrounded us with a wall of ignorance with regard to the achievements of Islam.

Like Napoleon, the first Abd-er-Rahman found his crown on the wayside and picked it up with the point of his sword. As we have seen, the dynasty of Caliphs founded by Moaviyyah and known as the Omayyads, resided in Damascus. For a hundred-odd years, that city was the center of a huge Arab empire. But once the pace of the initial conquests of the Arabs had slackened, political intrigue and dynastic strife among rival groups became as common in Islam as they were in Christendom.

In 747, civil war broke out openly. The powerful family of the Abbasids, who were lineal descendants of Ibn Abbas, an uncle of the Prophet, overthrew the

Omayyads. In 750, they seized the Caliphal power. They transferred the capital of the huge Moslem empire to Baghdad, which they built in the neighborhood of ruined Ctesiphon, onetime capital of the defunct Sassanid Persian Empire. Shortly, Baghdad was to have a rival in Córdoba, which became the capital of a rebellious province. But the political rivalry between Baghdad and Córdoba became incidental to a much finer kind of rivalry. By the tenth century of our era, both Baghdad and Córdoba had outdistanced Constantinople in cultural significance. One became the cultural center of western Asia, the other a spiritual beacon that shed its light far into the night that was medieval Christian Europe. Abd-er-Rahman of Córdoba, a Moslem Prometheus, had brought the light of Eastern culture to the West.

Shortly after the Omayyads had been overthrown, an Abassid general perpetrated one of the treacheries so common in both Western and Eastern history. Eighty members of the deposed house of the Omayyads were invited to dinner, and, once inside the hall, were massacred to the last man. One of the Omayyads, Abd-er-Rahman, was staying with some Bedouins by the bank of the Euphrates, when his executioners arrived. He had just time enough to jump into the river and swim to the other bank. For five years, he wandered through North Africa, hiding from his enemies. Finally, he found refuge with his mother's relatives, Berber chiefs in Morocco. Here he got into touch with the leaders of

Syrian troops stationed on the European side, just across the Straits of Gibraltar. They accepted him as their leader.

Abd-er-Rahman crossed over to Spain and soon won the allegiance of its cities and garrisons. He established his capital at Córdoba, and assumed the title of Ameer. In Spain, Sicily, and North Africa, this title later became the equivalent for "king," although in the Moslem world it actually has the significance of prince or duke, its literal meaning being "commander."

In connection with the Arab conquests, we often read that the Moslem army burned the famed Library of Alexandria. Actually, the major part of the Alexandrian Library perished during Julius Caesar's battles in Egypt, in 48 B.C. The remainder, which had grown once again into an important depository of Greco-Roman philosophy, science and literature, was destroyed in the second half of the fourth century A.D., following the death of the Emperor Julian, known as the "Apostate," in 363. This act of vandalism was a part of that deluge of destruction of "pagan" culture which then swept the Roman Empire from end to end. A few years later, the Emperor Theodosius had the last remaining manuscripts of the once-famed library destroyed.

On the other hand, history knows two *authentic* instances of libraries being burned down by soldiers — in both cases by *Western* soldiers. In October 1943, the Germans set fire to the famous library of the Italian Royal Society in Naples. A generation earlier, when the

Chinese rebelled against their exploitation and domination by the white man, and rose in the Boxer Rebellion, the Western powers sent a "punitive expedition" to China. It was made up of contingents of all major European powers, under the command of the German general, Count Waldersee.

The troops representing the "civilized" West among the "pagans" of the Orient burned the unique imperial palace of Peking, a triumph of Chinese architecture and art. They looted the public buildings. Then they deliberately and wantonly laid fire to the famous Library of Peking, one of the glories of civilization, which it had taken many centuries to create.

The soldiers of the "superior West" were hardly able to walk back to their barracks. What slowed them up was the loot they had stolen in the palace and the library. It was heavy. It was "the white man's burden."

This happened in 1900 A.D. — not in 632.

That is the story of the Library of Alexandria.

ળ   ળ   ળ

Another sacred tradition of Western history writing is the affirmation that the slogan of the Arab conquests was "The Koran or the sword." The truth, however, is that the advancing Arabs did not give Christians and Jews the alternative of apostasy or death. But before looking at the evidence in the case, let us look at the jury, that is, at ourselves.

We cannot readjust that caricature of the East which we take for its true picture unless we recognize that we are the victims of millenniums of sustained propaganda. Take, for example, the traditional way in which we are taught the history of Alexander the Great. Here you have a Macedonian war lord invading the Persian Empire of the Achaemenids. On the other side, you have an empire which happened to have a religion incomparably loftier than the primitive polytheism of the Greeks — Zoroastrianism, with its abhorrence of idols. You have an empire with a highly advanced, flourishing civilization, with a postal courier system so perfectly co-ordinated that it took a letter only five days from the Dardanelles to Susa, in the south of Iran. Today, except by airplane, it takes much longer.

Yet is it not a fact that, as we were taught the story of Alexander's campaigns, and as we recall it now, as adults, the whole thing looks like some wonderful adventure, in which that shining Western hero Alexander, oddly enough, was repeatedly checked in his laudable efforts by those sinister Oriental Persians? What have you and I in common with Alexander and his Macedonian mercenaries? Yet Occidental propaganda has made our version of the story axiomatic, by repeating it through the centuries.

But, through repetition an untruth becomes not a truth but a prejudice. Twenty-two centuries of propaganda have made us blind to the real history of the Persians. Thirteen centuries of propaganda have blinded us to the true history of Islam.

So much about the jury. Now let us look at the evidence. The story that the Moslem armies advanced with the motto "The Koran or the sword" is as colorful and as untrue as the one about the Library of Alexandria. The Arab conquerors actually treated Christians and Jews with leniency. For this, they had a very definite reason.

Mohammed himself knew the Bible, and held it in great respect. We have seen that he looked upon Moses and Jesus as highly inspired prophets, and upon himself merely as one of many prophets. To this day, the pious Moslem never mentions the name of Musa (Moses), Da'ood (David), Suleiman (Solomon), or Issa (Jesus), without preceding it by the epithet *hazret* — something like "His Highness," or "the Illustrious."

Originally, Mohammed decreed Saturday as the Moslem Sabbath, made the praying Moslem turn towards Jerusalem, outlawed pork. After the Jews of Medina had refused to recognize him as a new Prophet, he changed the holy day to Friday and made his followers turn towards Mecca instead of Jerusalem, while maintaining the taboo on pork. But he continued to assign a special status to the "peoples of the Book," by which term he meant the Jews, Christians, and Sabaeans. He specifically provided that they were not to be forced to give up their faith, by decreeing, in one of the *soorahs*

(145)

of the Koran: "Fight those who have been given the Book, until, humiliated, *they offer tribute*."

Eventually, this provision of the Koran assumed fundamental importance. It had a far-reaching effect upon the subsequent social and political status of the Jews, Christians, and some other sects inside the empire of the Caliphs, and later, also, inside the Ottoman Empire. The pious Moslem, filled with deepest reverence for the rules and precedents set up by his Prophet, came to feel that Christians and Jews, although inferior to the Moslem, ranked next to him in nearness to God's favor. Besides, the Prophet had made it a fundamental tenet of Islam that no Moslem shall pay tribute to another. It was, therefore, better business to let the Christian and Jew retain his faith, liberty and property, and make him pay a land and head tax, than to force him to become a Moslem and lose an important source of revenue. After all, the money for the maintenance of the state had to come from somewhere.

This is why the Christians, the Jews, the Sabaeans of southern Arabia, who subsequently disappeared from history, and some minor non-Moslem sects, were not given the alternative of the Koran or the sword. They gained a special status inside the Moslem state, and were known as *dhimmi*.

When Amr ibn-el-As conquered Egypt, the Coptic Christians retained their religion and liberty, and have continued to live under the authority of their Patriarch ever since. When Tariq took Toledo from the Catholic Visigoths, he actually installed their Bishop, Oppas, in the cathedral. Seven centuries later, when the Turkish Sultan, Mohammed II, styled *Fatih*, the Conqueror, took Constantinople from the Byzantines, he formally recognized the Roman Catholics, Greek Catholics, and Greek Orthodox Christians in the Turkish Empire, including the Balkans, as a "nation." Their official designation in Turkish was *millet-i-Rûm*, "the Roman Nation." He respected their freedom of religion and their personal liberty, and put them under the authority of their own Patriarch, who became their temporal as well as spiritual head. Except in cases of litigation where one party was Moslem, the Patriarch even acted as judge between them. This privileged status of the Christians was respected by all subsequent Sultans. The Armenians had similar rights, being known as *ermeni millety* — "the Armenian nation." Until the days of Abdul Hamid II and the First World War, they remained unmolested. The massacres of Armenians under the "Red Sultan," and in 1914–1915, were due to political, not to religious reasons.

The Jews also enjoyed freedom of religion and of their persons and property in Islam. Under the Caliphs, the Jews of Iraq and Iran were governed and judged by the Grand Rabbi of Baghdad, who bore the title *Resh Glutha*, "Prince of the Captivity," a reference to the Biblical captivity of the Jews in Babylon.

Nor was there in the Caliphal empire any such thing

as anti-Semitism or "anti-Christianism" as a basis for political, social or economic discrimination. Some rulers, such as the Omayyad Caliph Omar II, ordered Jews and Christians to wear a distinctive dress, and forbade them to ride horses. Abd-el-Mumen el Moahid, ruler of Morocco and Spain in the twelfth century, a member of the so-called Almohade dynasty of Morocco, also decreed vexatious social measures against Christians and Jews. But most of these measures were disregarded, and all of them rescinded after the death of their originators.

The fact is that at various periods of the Omayyad and Abbasid rule, and of Arab history in Spain, Christians and Jews vied with the Moslem in the liberal professions, as teachers, physicians, savants, lawyers, civil servants, and in other fields. Many Christians and Jews held highest administrative positions in the Moslem state. The case of Rabbi Samuel, famed Grand Vizier of Granada, has several parallels under the Abbasids. In Baghdad, some Caliphs had Christian Grand Viziers. In Moslem Spain, the name *mózarabes* denoted the numerically important Christian element which had voluntarily acquired the Arabic tongue and culture but was allowed to retain its faith. And, so far from being suppressed, various Christian sects which flourished under the Caliphs actually sent out missionaries to other countries. Under the Abassid rulers, for example, Nestorian missionaries from Syria and Iraq made converts as far away as China.

ৄৄ৹   ৄৄ৹   ৄৄ৹

But let us revert to Spain. It was the third ruler of that country by the name of Abd-er-Rahman (912–961), who formally proclaimed himself Caliph. Thereafter, for about two hundred years, Islam had two rival Caliphs. They do not offer a close analogy to the protracted episode of rival Popes in medieval Christendom. The Roman Popes wielded temporal power over the small Papal State, the Counter-Popes at Avignon had no temporal power at all. By contrast, the Omayyad Caliph in Córdoba was master of most of present-day Spain and Portugal, while the Abbasid Caliph in Baghdad held sway over a vast empire.

The extent of the Caliphal state of Córdoba fluctuated between the near-totality of the Iberian Peninsula and a small region round Córdoba itself. During the same period, however, the Cordovese Caliphs built up a civilization in many ways unique in human annals. That dynamic collective urge for self-expression, self-realization, which is the principal motive power of history, had carried the Moslem warriors like a whirlwind through western Asia and North Africa. Now, this urge found new, creative outlets in the fields of exact science, the humanities, philosophy, social and hygienic reform, scientific agriculture and horticulture, and every other branch of civilized life. The ninth and tenth centuries of our era were the golden age of Moslem civilization. This Moslem civilization permeated and fertilized the barbarian Europe of the Middle Ages. Centuries later, it penetrated into Europe once again, this time by way of the Balkans. There, Destiny chose for its vehicle a warlike Mongoloid people from the plains of Central Asia. It had gradually drifted west, and had adopted the creed, *La ilaha illa'llah Mohammedoom rasooloo'llah.* (There is no God but Allah — Mohammed is the messenger of Allah.)

The advancing Turk carried the Arab civilization in his camp kit, as the Roman legionary had carried the Greek. No picture of Islam can be complete without a look at its most powerful proselyte, the Turk.

VIII

THE TURK ENTERS THE PICTURE

$\mathcal{U}$NDER the Omayyads, the empire of the Caliphs had reached its greatest expansion. Soon, it began to disintegrate.

In Tunis, early in the tenth century, there arose the powerful dynasty of the Fatimides, which claimed descent from Fatimah, the Prophet's daughter, wife of Ali, the Caliph whom Moaviyyah had displaced. The Fatimides were Shiites. Their power extended over major parts of North Africa, including Egypt, which became their permanent residence.

Morocco saw the rise of a strong local Berber dynasty, the Almoravides. Originally, these men were a militant Moslem religious confraternity, an early precursor of the Senussi of Libya and the Wahhabi of central Arabia. In the eleventh century, following the fall of the Caliphate of Córdoba, the Almoravides seized that city, besides taking Seville and major parts of Spain.

The Almoravides were followed by the Berber dynasty known as the Almohades. "Almohade" is an Occidental corruption of the Arabic term *El Moahid*, meaning "Unitarian." We have seen that the Druses refer to themselves as *El Moahideen*, which is the plural of *El Moahid*. But the Berber line of kings known as the Almohades had no connection with the Druses. The

(151)

designation of a Moslem as a "Unitarian" usually means that he is a pantheist. Pantheism is the basis of the Moslem mystic school of thought known as Sufism, and there are reasons to believe that the founders of the Almohade dynasty professed ideas of this kind.

The Asiatic part of the Caliphal empire showed no greater cohesion than the African. By the end of the ninth century various Moslem princes inside the empire had assumed virtual independence, calling themselves either Ameers or Sultans. They merely allowed the time-honored habit to continue whereby a public prayer for the Caliph's welfare was said in the mosques every Friday. That was all they had to do with the Caliph.

The second decade of the thirteenth century brought the terrible onslaught of the Mongols against the West. Jinghiz Khan conquered the flourishing Caliphal provinces in Turkestan, taking Bukhara, Samarkand, and other famous centers of Moslem culture amidst wholesale slaughter and destruction. It was his grandson, Hulagu, who dealt the deathblow to the Caliphate itself. In 1258 he took Baghdad. The Caliph, his family and entourage were butchered. So was a major part of the population of Baghdad. Palaces, mosques, libraries, whole quarters of the city, were razed. The surviving members of the Abassid family fled to Egypt. There, Caliphs merely in name, they were actually glorified captives of the local Moslem rulers.

Two hundred years earlier, the Omayyad Caliphate in Spain had fallen. Now, the Abbasid Caliphate ceased to have temporal power, became nothing but a name. The stage was set for the Turk.

ono   ono   ono

In an earlier chapter, we described that region of Central Asia situated between the Ural and Altai Mountains as the most powerful ethnic volcano on earth, through whose eruptions dozens of peoples rocketed into history. The Sarmatians, Avars, Huns, Slavs, Magyars, Kumans, Jazygues, Petchengi, Mongols, came westward. Under Jinghiz and his successors, the Mongols marched also southward and eastward, and once again southward and westward under Tamerlane, around 1400. Under their seventh Khan, the Mongols became Moslem. One of their offshoots conquered a major part of India, founding the dynasty of Moguls, a corruption of the word "Mongol."

The migrations of the Seljuk Turks and Ottoman Turks both represented explosions of the ethnic volcano of Central Asia. The Seljuks were the first to appear. They wrested from the Byzantine emperors those parts of Asia Minor that the Arabs had failed to conquer in the seventh century. By the end of the eleventh, the Seljuk Sultans held practically all of Asia Minor, and various adjacent territories. Their capital was Iconium, the Konia of today. The Seljuk Turks adopted Islam,

(153)

and left behind them cultural monuments of great beauty and importance, such as the wonderful Tsarataï Mosque in Konia, still in a perfect state of preservation, and the important ruin of the once glorious Mosque of Selim at Ephesus, not far from Smyrna. But the Seljuk Turk proved to be merely the forerunner of his cousin, the Ottoman Turk, who made his appearance in Western history in the fourteenth century.

The name Ottoman — *Osmanli* in Turkish — comes from that of Othman, or Osman, ruler of a tribe of Turks whom his grandfather, Suleiman Shah, had consolidated into just a little more than an aimless horde of nomads. Suleiman's son and Osman's father was Ertoghrul Shah, whom the Turks of today look upon as the actual founder of the Ottoman dynasty. It is with him that they associate the origin of the Star and Crescent as the famed emblem on the Turkish flag, and of Turkish rule everywhere.

I often recall those glorious starry nights in Turkey when, sitting round a campfire with my troop of native Boy Scouts, I would give the "tenderfoot" scouts the traditional explanation of the origin of the Turkish flag.

"And then *Hazret-i-Ertoghrul*, His Highness, Ertoghrul, decided to lead his warriors into the country of his cousins, the Seljuks, whose great *jahmee* (mosque) those of you who know Konia have surely seen. He was going to offer his services to the Seljuk Sultan. And one night, after he had entered the land of *Anadolu*, whose capital was Konia, he looked up into the sky. There, he perceived a most propitious omen. The Moon was in its first quarter, and the Evening Star, blinking like a brilliant, many-faceted *elmass*, was just inside the scythe of the Moon. *Hazret-i-Ertoghrul* exclaimed: '*Allahu Akbar!* Great indeed is God! He has sent us this sign of encouragement. Let us continue on our course!' And since those days, the Star and Crescent have indeed been a propitious omen for you Turks. *Euylah dayilmy* — is it not so?"

"*Euylah yah, Beym!* It is indeed, my Bey!" the boys would shout in chorus.

ᐁ   ᐁ   ᐁ

By the end of the fourteenth century, the Osmanli, or Ottoman Turks were masters of both Asia Minor and the Balkans. Their capital was Bursa, also known as Brusa, still one of the most beautiful cities in Asia Minor. The Serbs, as heroic then as they are now, faced the onslaught of the powerful Turkish army in 1389, in the celebrated battle of Kossovo Polye, in which their King, Lazarus, perished with his whole army. The murder of the Turkish Sultan, Murad, by a Serb, did not halt the Turkish progress.

In the initial period of their history in Europe, the Turks were often accompanied in battle by their women, who were not veiled and rode their horses with the same consummate skill as their men, and whose presence was a great morale builder for the Turkish army. Only later did the Turks borrow the institution of the harem and the eunuch from Christian Byzantium.

The victorious advance of the Star and Crescent suffered a temporary setback when Tamerlane, the Mongol, inflicted a catastrophic defeat upon Sultan Bayazid near Ankara, the present capital of Turkey, in 1402. But a few years later, following Tamerlane's death, through a miracle of psychological resilience the Turks continued their forward march as if nothing had happened.

The Byzantine Empire now consisted of little more than the city of Constantinople, a jewel of natural and artistic grandeur at the confluence of the Bosporus, Golden Horn, and the Sea of Marmora. Here, at this spot of fairylike beauty, three sheets of water meet in a sun-drenched maze of islands, palace-studded shores, many-domed mosques, cypress groves, and intertwined civilizations, in an atmosphere created by millenniums of cultural effort.

The Turks had conquered the Balkans, with its checkered pattern of peoples. They had taken the whole of Asia Minor. Constantinople had eluded them. Its walls were impregnable. A huge iron chain had been drawn across the Golden Horn, between what now is the Turkish quarter of Stambul and then was the city of Byzantium proper, and Galata, a suburb founded by Genoese merchants, and the commercial center of Constantinople to this day. A similar chain had prevented the fleet of Moaviyyah, founder of the Omayyad Caliphate, from getting near the walls of the city eight centuries earlier. This one stopped the Turkish fleet now.

Mohammed II, a young man thirsting for glory who had ascended the Ottoman throne, offered the last Emperor of Byzantium, Constantine XII, of the house of Palaeologos, respect for Byzantine sovereignty in the Peloponnesus in exchange for the surrender of Constantinople. Constantine reversed the offer. He would cede the Peloponnesus to Mohammed if he could keep Constantinople. The Sultan refused.

Before the formal siege began, the Turkish sentries did not prevent the population of the city from going about their business outside the city walls. When challenged by the Turkish outposts, the Byzantines would usually reply that they were on their way *eis ten polen* (pronounced "ayiss tayn polayn") — "to the city." Istanbul, the Turkish name for Constantinople, originated from the corruption of these Greek words by the Turks.

But philology was the last thing that interested the Sultan at the moment. He broke off the negotiations. One of the bloodiest sieges in history followed.

Politically and ethically, the Byzantine Empire had been probably the most corrupt state the world had ever seen. Every form of vice was popular. Graft was the very basis of public life. An ancient heritage of loftiest culture had been trodden into a quagmire of decadence, moral depravity, and political despotism, known as "Byzantinism" to this day. Yet Byzantium, a community whose spirit was believed to have departed long before its body was slain, now gave a fifteenth-century version of "Praise the Lord and pass the ammunition."

In the churches, the priests chanted. On the walls, the people fought the numerically superior, fanatically brave Turkish army to a standstill. Wave after wave of the Anatolian shock troops was hurled back from the scaling ladders. The struggle continued. Still no decision. Mohammed's loss in men and matériel was too big to bear. The siege could no longer be maintained.

Then the Sultan decided upon one last, desperate attempt. If it failed, he would raise the siege.

The last assault began. The Byzantines stood their ground. In the hour of its agony, the once great, now merely big city grew to heroic stature. So did its leader, Constantine. He had lived as an emperor. Now he was going to die like a man.

Still the Turks could make no headway. Then, by what a soul in despair might call the treachery of Fate, some Turkish soldiers, making their way along the city wall, discovered a small door in a hidden nook. Amazed at this unusual sight in a city wall, they leaned against it. It flew open. They found themselves in the inner precinct of the city, without encountering anyone. Apparently, the Byzantines had long forgotten the very existence of this tiny, hidden door in their impregnable wall. It was the heel of Achilles, the vulnerable spot of the Byzantine colossus, an accident inside a five-foot radius that changed the face of Europe. Today, five hundred years later, that opening in the wall, known as the *Kerkaporta*, still stares at the tourist.

The janissaries ran back, brought reinforcements. Caught in the back, the Greek garrison went down before the twofold attack. The Emperor was last seen on his charger, hewing down his attackers. His body was never found.

Mohammed II, now known as *Fatih*, "the Conqueror," entered the city. He made a mosque of the splendid Hagia Sophia, the Church of the Holy Wisdom, at whose completion, nine centuries earlier, the Emperor Justinian had cried: "Solomon, I have prevailed over thee!" But the Sultan left a number of other churches to the Christian population. As we have seen in an earlier chapter, instead of applying the slogan "The Koran or the sword," he confirmed the personal and religious freedom of the Christian population.

Mohammed did not stop at Constantinople. He decided to take Vienna, capital of the German-Roman Empire of the Habsburgs, and then the rest of Europe. He gathered a formidable army and laid siege to the key fortress of Belgrade, present capital of Serbia, then a Hungarian frontier fortress. The victory of the Christian army under its leader, John Hunyadi, saved Europe. The Pope decreed that the event should forever be celebrated in all churches of Christendom by the peal of bells at noon. The custom still is observed, although hardly anyone seems to be aware of its origin.

It was Sultan Selim who, half a century later, turned his attention to the southern boundaries of his empire. He conquered Egypt, along with Syria and Palestine. This brought about a decisive change in the history of the Caliphate.

We have seen that, following the capture of Baghdad by Hulagu the Mongol, the surviving Abbasids and their descendants lived as refugees at the court of the Sultans of Egypt and that nothing remained to them but the title of Caliph. Following his capture of Egypt, Sultan Selim took El Mutawakkil, the last in the line of these nominal Caliphs, with him to Constantinople. The Caliphate now passed from Arab hands into those of the Ottoman Turk. Thereafter, the Sultans of Turkey bore the title of Caliph right down to 1923, when the national assembly of the new Turkey elected Crown Prince Abdul Medjid Caliph, but without the temporal power of the Sultans. In the following year the Turkish legislature abolished the Caliphate, and Caliph Abdul Medjid II went into exile. But many Moslem jurists and laymen regard the abolition of the Caliphate as invalid, and continue to look upon Abdul Medjid II as the rightful Caliph, on the grounds that the legislative body of one single Moslem state has no authority to abolish an office which has existed since the death of the Prophet and applies to Islam as a whole.

From Selim's days to 1918, the Caliphate was once again in the hands of Moslem rulers of a big empire. The extent and power of that empire reached its zenith under the next Turkish Sultan, Soliman (Solomon), to whose name a hostile but admiring Christendom attached the epithet, "the Magnificent."

Soliman conquered Persia and Iraq, and the major part of Hungary. In Africa, he extended Turkish power as far as Algiers. A Barbary state, Algiers was then ruled by the pirate Haïreddin, known as Barbarossa because of his red beard. Soliman accepted Haïreddin's offer of allegiance, made him an admiral of the Turkish fleet, and assumed suzerainty over Haïreddin's kingdom, leaving his vassal almost complete freedom in its administration. Seven times did Soliman personally lead an army into Central Europe. He died during one of these campaigns, at the age of seventy-two.

It was Soliman who gave the huge Ottoman Empire its first workable administrative structure. Towards Christians and Jews he was even more considerate than Mohammed the Conqueror after the fall of Byzantium. He gave them practically extraterritorial status, something no Christian power ever dreamed of doing to non-Christians.

Soliman's love for his favorite wife, Roxelana, daughter of a Christian from the Crimea, has become famous in history. Roxelana's death was responsible for the construction of the Suleimanieh Mosque in Istanbul, one of the glories of Turco-Byzantine architecture, and still one of Istanbul's most impressive sights. The grief-stricken Sultan had the mosque built in memory of his beloved wife, whose body still lies side by side with his own in the *türbeh*, the funerary chapel, of the mosque. Here we have a Turkish counterpart of that other great monument of a polygamous ruler's marital love, India's fabulous Taj Mahal, built at Agra by the Mogul Emperor, Shah Jahan, in memory of his wife, Mumtaz Mahal.

In 1683, little more than a century after Suleiman's death, the Turks made their greatest lunge forward into Christian Europe: they besieged Vienna. The capture of that key city might have completely changed the subsequent history of Central and Western Europe.

The siege failed. Vienna's hard-pressed garrison, led by Prince Rüdiger von Starhemberg, was saved by the arrival of King Yan Sobieski of Poland, whose army forced the Turks to raise the siege.

The second apogee of Islam had passed. Now, the pendulum swung back.

The Tide Recedes

IX

DEBACLE IN SPAIN

*C*HE disintegration, and even the rise, of Turkish power was preceded by the disintegration of Arab Moslem rule in the Iberian Peninsula and in Sicily.

In Spain, the Arabs had made the political mistake of failing to eliminate the various small feudal states in the mountainous north of the peninsula that survived the Moslem invasion. It was in these small centers of Christian resistance that the doom of Moslem power in Spain was engendered. For centuries, the little counts and petty kings who ruled these small patches of Christian land were fighting and looting one another. Profiting by the famed slogan of the one-time Roman masters of the peninsula, "Divide and rule," the Caliphs of Córdoba maintained their own power. But in 1031, the Caliphate of Córdoba fell in one of the many civil wars that raged periodically inside the Cordovese Caliphate's own territory. The realm of Córdoba broke up into more than a dozen local principalities and petty kingdoms. Seville, Granada, Córdoba itself, now formed small states. Arab Spain became a Moslem counterpart of Christian Spain, a conglomerate of petty autocracies constantly at war with one another.

Then came the first wave of Berber rule in the Iberian

Peninsula. Present-day Tunisia, Algeria and Morocco had come under the sway of the so-called Almoravides, a Berber Moslem fighting confraternity. Their rulers crossed over into Spain at the end of the eleventh century, took over and consolidated Moslem power there, and temporarily eliminated the various local Arabo-Semitic dynasties from the political scene. Seville, which was known to the medieval Arabs as Homs, was inhabited and governed by Syrians, whose ancestors had originally come from Homs in Syria. In Córdoba the dominant ethnic layer was almost purely Semitic, with a basic strain of Bedouin blood. Now, the Berber conquerors from North Africa brought with them an entourage of their own kin, which was temporarily superimposed upon the Semitic element.

The Berbers at this time were adherents of the Shia sect of Islam. Their sultan, Yussuf (Joseph), had an army of a hundred thousand men, many of whom were of Tuareg extraction. They wore the same kind of black veil, or *litham*, which Tuaregs wear to this day, and the Christians they fought in Spain came to know them as the "Veil-Wearers." They disliked the Arabo-Semitic Sunni Moslems of Spain, because they differed from them both racially and in their religious orientation.

Yet, it had been King Motamid of Seville who called Yussuf to Spain. This time, it was the Christian who profited from Moslem disunity. Seville and other Moslem principalities were in immediate danger of conquest by the King of Castile. Motamid, warned of Yussuf's own plans of conquest, motivated his appeal to the Berber ruler for aid with words that have become famous in the Arab world: "I would rather be a camel driver in Africa than a swineherd in Castile."

Soon there followed a second wave of Berber conquest in Spain. The Almoravides were succeeded by another dynasty from North Africa, the Almohades. Abd-el-Mumen, the first Almohade ruler of Spain, was a friend of learning. His son, Yussuf, was one of the greatest patrons of culture and the arts who ever sat on a throne. We shall see in a later chapter that the very basis of our Western culture and knowledge in almost every branch of science and industry comes from the Arabs. It was during the reign of Yussuf that Seville, which was his capital, got its wonderful mosque. Later the mosque was razed by the Christians. Fortunately, its beautiful square minaret was spared. It now forms the major part of the famed bell tower, *La Giralda,* to which we have already referred.

Yussuf was the protector of the famous Averroës, whom he made governor of Seville. Averroës, a genius whose actual name was Ibn Rushd, is mainly responsible for the preservation in the Christian West of the teachings of Aristotle, whose greatest commentator he was. Besides, he was an accomplished jurist, a famous physician, and an even more famous philosopher, who profoundly influenced Christian thought. We shall meet him again later.

Under Yussuf's grandson Mohammed, the resentment between the politically dominant Berbers and the culturally much more evolved Arabo-Semitic element inside Moslem Spain led to an Arab national tragedy, the decisive defeat of the Moslem army at Las Navas de Tolosa.

The Popes had called a Crusade against the *Christian* communities of the Albigensians, in the South of France. For a whole year, Christian knights of the West had massacred the Albigensian Christians, looted and burned their cities. Many of these knights then flocked to Spain, where the rich Moslem cities promised even more plunder.

The Moslem and Christian armies met at Las Navas de Tolosa. Both parties fought bravely. But in the Moslem camp prudence succumbed to hurt pride: the Berber commander-in-chief had punished the Arab commander of a city which had been taken by the Christians, and the Arab part of the army refused to fight. The Berbers were wiped out. So were the Arab contingents. The way was open to the Christian conquest of Moslem Spain.

Ferdinand of Castile had already united the crowns of Castile and León by conquest. Now, his armies surged forward. Córdoba fell in 1236, Seville in 1248. Between 1238 and 1260, Murcia, Valencia, and more than a hundred other cities, fell to the Christians.

Granada alone, with its hinterland, including Málaga, Almeria, Lója, Ronda, and minor cities, withstood the

Spanish onslaught for another two hundred years. Surrounded by an ocean of surging and rejuvenated Christian vitality, it held out, a flourishing center of Moslem culture to the very end. It was as late as the middle of the thirteenth century, under Granada's so-called Nasrid dynasty, a family of pure Arabs, that the nucleus of the glorious Alhambra rose on the hill that governs the city, and it was only a hundred years later that this wonder of the world reached its completion.

The agony of Granada began several years before 1492. It was hastened by a fratricidal civil war and incessant political intrigues between the last rulers of that Moslem kingdom. This family feud dragged on over a number of years, and paved the way for the ultimate victory of Ferdinand and Isabella.

Mohammed Abu Abdallah, known to the Spaniards as Boabdil, was the last of the rulers of Granada, and one of the most pitiful figures in history. Ferdinand and Isabella took the various cities of the kingdom of Granada one by one, almost in each instance through starvation. Methodically, the flourishing fields and orchards surrounding the Moslem cities were burned by their army, the fruit and olive trees felled, the peasants massacred, their herds driven away. When the Spaniards took Málaga, two thirds of its population were sold into slavery, with the full consent of Ferdinand and Isabella. Hundreds of beautiful Moslem virgins were bought by the Queens of Portugal, Spain and Naples!

The end came to Granada itself on January 2, 1492.

Culturally, the end, not of Moslem Spain but of Spain itself, began seven years later, when the culturally incomparably inferior Spaniards, fired by religious fanatics, began to exterminate Moslem culture in their country.

Ferdinand had signed a solemn treaty of honorable capitulation with the people of Granada, guaranteeing them and their successors freedom of religion, the preservation of their customs, continued administration of justice by their Moslem judges under Moslem law, and security of their persons and property.

In 1499, seven years after this solemn treaty had been signed, it was openly flouted by the Spaniards, upon the instigation of the Franciscan monk, Ximenez de Cisneros, who had been appointed Archbishop of Toledo. The Moslem population was forcibly baptized. Tens of thousands of Arabic manuscripts, of unique cultural value, were collected and publicly burned, just as Joseph Goebbels burned books in the squares of Germany's cities four centuries later.

A fine wood carving of the period, which forms a part of the altar of Granada's cathedral, shows one of a thousand similar scenes that had become the order of the day: monks are seen pulling the turbans from the heads of intimidated, defenseless Moslem men, and pouring baptismal water upon their heads. Behind them are seen Moslem women in a queue, holding one end of their wide robes over their faces. In an age-old Oriental feminine gesture of modesty, they are trying to hide their features from these strange men, while awaiting their turn to be forcibly baptized, "or else."

Then came the Inquisition, that institution unique in the history of humanity whose motto, "Orthodox Christianity or the stake," became the nightmare of every independent soul. If the "heretic" recanted, he won the right to the act of "clemency" of being garroted at the stake, before the wood pile was lighted. If he was stubborn, garroting was considered too good for him, and the slow-burning fire consumed him for the higher glory of God.

Ferdinand, personally, was not a Moslem- and Jew-hater. He was merely a cynic, yielding to pressure from those fanatics, Tomás de Torquemada and Ximenez de Cisneros, and similar backward souls. He did this the more readily as the Inquisition was a source of considerable revenue to the Crown. In fact, it is not too much to say that Ferdinand financed his last campaigns mainly with the help of the Inquisition's sinister activities.

It has passed almost entirely unnoticed in the annals of history that one of the rules under which the Inquisition operated was the provision that *anyone accused of heresy automatically forfeited his property, whether he was found guilty or not.* This was the "catch" behind the activities of the *Santísima Hernandad,* the "Most Sacred (!) Brotherhood," as the Inquisition was officially called. It was one huge "machine" of graft and corruption. If a person was put under accusation by the prosecutor of the Inquisition, his fortune was seized *even if he was acquitted!* It was then divided between the Spanish Crown and the funds of the Inquisition, while a percentage of it was paid as a reward to the informer. This was, of course, a standing invitation to the population to make money simply by accusing a wealthy converted Moslem or Jew of heresy.

Throughout Europe, under medieval law, nobody accused of a criminal action could be convicted without a confession, unless at least two credible witnesses gave testimony against him. Heresy, of course, was considered the acme of criminality. Since the alleged secret practice of Moslem or Jewish rites automatically excluded the presence of potential hostile witnesses, the Most Sacred Brotherhood had to extort the "confessions" through torture. Until the middle of the eighteenth (!) century, torture was an official, integral part of judicial procedure in Catholic and Protestant Europe, but not in the world of Islam. In fact, Arab writers of the *twelfth* century in Syria wrote satiric pieces, in which they ridiculed the administration of justice through ordeal and torture, which prevailed in the Christian Crusader states of the Levant. In the United States, it was actually our Bill of Rights which abolished the practice of torture, of forcing an accused person to be "a witness against himself."

While a handful of religious fanatics at the head of the Inquisition sincerely believed that they were serving the Lord, most of the members of that institution, and also the kings of Spain, welcomed the wholesale accusation of "heretics" because it was a gold mine for the treasury and the pockets of hundreds of people in and around the Inquisition, and in court circles.

As we have said, the long and exceedingly costly siege of Granada was almost entirely financed from the seized fortunes of converted Jews accused of heresy. Long before the fall of Granada, Spain had hundreds of thousands of *conversos,* as the converted Jews were known. Most of them were descendants of the forcibly converted survivors of the massacres of Jews in Valencia and many other cities held by Spanish Christians in the fourteenth century. There exists a scientific theory about Columbus' origin which maintains that he was the child of *converso* parents who had migrated from the Balearic Islands to Genoa. It is, however, a historic fact that possibly the majority, but undoubtedly a very large minority of the aristocratic Christian families of medieval Spain had intermarried with *conversos,* many of whom were rich and highly cultured. Later, in the eighteenth century, the kings of Spain repeatedly decreed a general investigation of their subjects' ancestry, to discover who had Jewish blood in his veins. The practice was a Spanish precursor of Hitler's search for Jewish grandmothers. When the King of Portugal planned a similar decree, his Prime Minister, the Marquis of Pombal, a great liberal of that great eighteenth century, foiled the plan by remarking: "Sire, if we begin to look for people with Jewish blood, Your Majesty, the Grand Inquisitor and I will be among them."

The Inquisition was founded in 1478. It operated only against *converted* Jews and converted Moslem, on the theory that they practised secret Jewish and Moslem rites. This would make them merely lip-Christians, and actually heretics. After the fall of Granada, the plan of expelling the unconverted Jews from Spain was openly discussed. The Jews offered the Catholic Kings a huge sum for "protection," in the best manner of the victims of our present-day gangsters and racketeers. Ferdinand and Isabella discussed the question in newly won Granada in March 1492. It seems that they were inclined to accept the money and abstain from expelling the Jews. But eventually they yielded to the fanatic insistence of Torquemada, the Grand Inquisitor. They decreed that every Jew must either become a Christian or leave the country. Whether Adolf Hitler studied the details of the expulsion of the Jews from Spain, or whether intolerance inspires similar thoughts in similar situations, cannot be determined in this connection. But there is an astounding similarity of technical detail between the exodus from Spain and the twentieth-century exodus from Germany.

Theoretically, the Spanish Jews were given a few months wherein to realize their property, but they were not permitted to take any gold or silver out of the country. Just as in Germany in 1933–1939, the sudden wave of forced sales of valuable property naturally caused that property to change hands at ludicrous prices.

The number of Jews who refused to give up their

faith for safety was probably around two hundred thousand. Some sources speak of half a million. They sought refuge in North Africa and Turkey. In Constantinople, Smyrna, and especially Salonika, their descendants still live in communities. These so-called Spanish Jews of today still speak the pure Castilian of the fifteenth century among themselves, with an admixture of relatively few Hebrew words. Many of them later moved from Turkey to Christian Europe. They brought traditional forms of Arab, or so-called "Moorish" architecture with them. That is why practically all synagogues in the Western world are built in the "Moorish," actually the Arab style.

The next oppressive measure against the defenseless population of formerly Moslem Spain was the decree ordering the forcible conversion of all followers of Islam, the alternative in this case also being their expulsion from Spain and the confiscation of their property.

The previous centuries had seen intermittent warfare between the various petty Christian and Moslem states inside the peninsula, but also many decades of continuous peace between Christian and Moslem princes. During this period, millions of Moslem lived inside Christian principalities, millions of Christians were subjects of Moslem lords. The former group was known as *mudéjares*, the latter as *mózarabes*. As a rule, perfect peace reigned between the Christian and Moslem communities inside the individual kingdoms, ameerates, or sultanates. Now,

following the elimination of Moslem power in the peninsula, and the resultant forcible conversion of Moslem
people, converts from Islam came to be known as Moriscos, "little Moors." The totally arbitrary Spanish designation, *moro*, or Moor, for a Moslem, came from the
Latin *maurus*. This, in its turn, comes from *Mauretania*,
the name of a North African kingdom which flourished
briefly under the Romans. The traditional association of
a Moor with black skin is equally arbitrary and erroneous, because neither the Arabs nor the Berbers, who
once inhabited ancient Mauretania, are black. As we
have seen in earlier chapters, many Berbers, or "Moors,"
are white-skinned, many even blond and blue-eyed.

For centuries, the Moriscos, like the *conversos*, were
the daily quarry of the Inquisition. The Moriscos spoke
a Romance dialect, but had retained the Arabic script.
They never really gave up Islam. The public baptism
of a Morisco child would often be followed by a secret
Moslem rite of "purification," the Catholic marriage of
a Morisco couple by a secret Moslem marriage. To this
day, the spiritual hold of Islam upon its followers is such
that one can safely say that almost never is a Moslem
converted to another faith through real conviction.
Later, we shall see why.

During more than a century, right up to the first
decade of the seventeenth, the authorities tried to stamp
out "crypto-Islam," the secret Morisco form of Islam,
through terror and other vexatious methods. Literally
hundreds of thousands of precious Arabic manuscripts
were seized and burned. Unique scientific instruments,

constructed by Arab scientists and engineers, cherished heirlooms in Morisco families, were smashed. King Philip II actually decreed the formal suppression of pub-, lic baths, particularly dear to the Moriscos, who still followed that famous adage, so often quoted among Moslem people, and attributed to the Prophet himself: "Cleanliness is an integral part of religion."

Hundreds of thousands of Moslem private homes in Spain had had bathrooms, the major Moslem cities actually hundreds of public baths, smaller cities having scores of them. Now, bathing was looked upon as typical of the "infidel." Only as late as the seventeenth century did the aristocrats of Spain begin to wash their hands before meals. The major Moslem cities of the peninsula had had complete sewer systems. They were allowed to crumble and collapse, were no longer used. The Duke of Saint-Simon reports that even in France, as late as the reign of Louis XIV, the courtiers and the fair *marquises* would squat just anywhere in the corridors of the royal palace at Versailles to answer a call of nature. And we know from the same firsthand source that Louis XIV, like millions of his subjects, literally took a bath about once a year. The liberal use of perfume by men and women at the European courts of this period was a direct "antidote" against the results of their disdain for the dirty Moslem habit of bathing.

All attempts to convert the "converted" Moslem population having failed, the Spanish Crown, upon the counsel of its ecclesiastic advisers, decreed the expulsion of all Moriscos from Spain in 1609. Once again, the

Western world witnessed the wholesale ruin of a flourishing and highly cultured community. The Moriscos had been the economic backbone of Spain. They were its artisans, farmers, merchants, and were known for their industry and integrity. Now, they were driven out of the country. The soldiery assigned to protecting them indulged in orgies of looting and rape among its "protégés." Again, Moslem Africa was a haven for the unfortunates.

The expulsion of the Jews and Moriscos proved to be a boomerang. It is a simple historic fact, not contested by unbiased Spanish historians, that the Arabs and Jews had represented the culture, industry, agriculture, and learning of Spain. The Spaniards had been primarily warriors. While the Spanish governors and viceroys enslaved the unfortunate Peruvians, Mexicans, Filipinos, and other foreign peoples, and while the Inquisition established branches in Mexico City, Lima, Cusco, and elsewhere abroad, the Spanish mother country began its dismal slide down the slope of history. Culture in Spain took a nose dive. Never before has fanaticism proved as effective a method for the cultural and economic suicide of a nation as it has in Spain.

With the Moslem, the Moriscos, and the Jews gone, Spain became the country of bullfights, cockfights, misery and ignorance, with a sullen population periodically terrorized and decimated by military cliques and other reactionary adventurers.

X

THE WEST INVADES THE EAST

$\mathcal{A}$T THE other end of the Mediterranean, Syria and Palestine had been the scene of a similar struggle, the Crusades. But this historical episode was compressed into two centuries. The wars in Spain can be viewed as a protracted Christian defensive against Islam, the Crusades, as a prolonged Christian offensive.

The first Crusade was caused by a request for help against the Seljuk Turks, addressed to the Pope Urban II by the Byzantine Emperor, Alexios Comnenos, in 1094 A.D. Various, widely different reasons were jointly responsible for the favorable reaction that the Pope's appeal evoked in Europe. The Pope hoped to reunite the Roman and Greek Churches; religious fanatics hoped for the salvation of their souls through fighting the "infidel." Many penniless knights hoped for loot. Some of the more powerful nobles and "second sons" hoped for countries for themselves and their successors to govern — that is, to exploit. Thousands of criminals were released from prison, the trials of thousands quashed, in exchange for participation in the Crusade. Thousands who were in debt took the Cross because that saved them from financial ruin.

Most of the knights were Franks and Normans. In the

German Rhineland, the Crusade began with a wholesale pogrom of Jews, "because they had crucified the Lord." The Jewry of most of the German cities along the Rhine — Worms, Treves, Cologne, and the rest — were given the alternative of conversion to Christianity or death. The major part preferred martyrdom. Tens of thousands of Jewish men, women and children were slaughtered and burned alive, their homes looted. In many cases, to escape both baptism and death through torture, the Jews killed their own wives and children, then committed suicide.

Then the knights' camp followers, who had been recruited from the rabble of the streets of Europe's cities, began to loot German, Austrian, and Hungarian cities and villages that lay on the route of their march. Reports of their deeds preceded the Crusaders. To save his subjects' lives and property, King Colomannus of Hungary, Catholic monarch of a Catholic country, known to history as "the Bibliophile," laid his books aside, gathered his warriors and inflicted a resounding defeat upon the Crusaders' army, killing many, and exacting formal vows that the security of his subjects would be respected.

It is worthy of note that, as early as the eleventh century, this member of the royal family of the then still Mongoloid Hungarians forbade witch-hunting in his country. Braving the wrath of the Western world, he decreed: "Let there be no talk of witches. They do not exist."

In Islam, no such decree was necessary. It is a simple fact that the "problem" of witches, one of our most shameful memories in the West, never even arose in the Moslem world.

The crusading army, some hundred and fifty thousand strong, eventually assembled in Constantinople, the Byzantine capital. The Emperor Alexios, recalling the experience of the Christian Hungarians, and harboring no illusions as to the motives of the crusading princes of the West, made them swear feudal allegiance to him before they passed on into Seljuk-held Asia Minor.

Considerable portions of Asia Minor were wrested from the Seljuk Turks. Godefroy de Bouillon himself resided for over ten years in the citadel of Ankara, present capital of Turkey, which still is well preserved. Following the conquest of Aleppo and other cities in Syria, the Crusaders besieged Jerusalem, garrisoned by some thousand men. The actual combatant force of the Crusaders, as distinct from the many tens of thousands of camp followers, craftsmen, serfs, and prostitutes, was over twenty thousand. On July 15, 1099, they took Jerusalem. The storming of the city was followed by one of the bloodiest massacres of a civilian population in history. The major part of the inhabitants of the Holy City, men, women, children, were butchered. Heads, hands, were cut off. Men were emasculated. Pregnant women had their bellies slit open. Contemporary Western chronicles proudly report that the warriors of Europe were wading ankle-deep in gore.

About a hundred years later, there arose in Islam the famed Saladin. The name is a corruption of the Arabic *Selah-ed-Din,* meaning "the Sword of the Faith." This was an honorary title, not the man's name, which was Yussuf (Joseph). He put an end to the Fatimid Caliphate in Egypt, abolished the domination of the Shia sect in that country, and made himself Sultan of Egypt and Syria. The famous Jewish physician and philosopher, Maïmonides, who had left Spain, was Saladin's personal physician.

In the East and West alike has the noble figure of Saladin been sung about, his life been chronicled. In 1187, in the battle of Hattin, he captured practically the entire Frankish army and most of its leaders, including Guy de Lusignan, King of Jerusalem. On October 2, 1187, the Holy City surrendered to the Moslem army. Now came Saladin's chance to avenge the horrible massacre that the Crusaders had perpetrated among the Moslem population a hundred years before.

Saladin made sure that the Christian population was unharmed. He maintained discipline in his victorious army. According to the Christian and Moslem custom of the time, he held several thousand military prisoners for ransom. Upon the plea of the Christian Patriarch of Jerusalem, he freed those who were unable to pay. Seldom in history has anyone wrought a revenge at once nobler and more humiliating than this response to cruelty by self-restraint.

The West Invades the East

The fall of Jerusalem resounded through Europe. It brought Richard the Lionhearted, Philip, King of France, and Frederick, surnamed "Barbarossa," the Hohenstaufen Emperor, to Asia. Frederick was drowned while crossing a river in Asia Minor. The rest of the Crusaders failed to take Jerusalem, but took Acre. After a siege that lasted two years, Acre's Moslem garrison surrendered in July 1181. Richard captured some twenty-five hundred men. He held them for ransom. A month passed, the ransom had not yet been paid. Richard had the twenty-five hundred prisoners butchered.

Saladin's tomb, covered by a beautiful cupola, still is a landmark in Damascus. It was Shaykh Saïd, a Moslem scholar, who showed me round Damascus. We stood in front of the building that houses the tomb, discussing the Arab version of the history of the Crusades.

"Why did our ancestors fight so bitterly? Why do so many Christians and Moslem still hate one another? Why do so many people hate one another in all parts of the world?" asked the bewildered young Westerner.

Saïd looked in the direction of the cupola of the sanctuary. Actually, he was looking into space, not at men and things, but beyond them. He spoke, slowly: —

"Hatred comes from ignorance, lack of tolerance from lack of vision. We all are potential Richards and Saladins. Spiritual progress can come only from the realization that the peculiarities of environment are incidental, the basic traits of human nature identical everywhere. This truth is so obvious that it is almost banal. Yet, it is amazing how few are those among you and among us who realize it."

ᕕᕗ   ᕕᕗ   ᕕᕗ

The Crusades of the French King, Louis, in Tunis and Egypt failed. The "Crusade" led by Enrico Dandolo, Doge of Venice, got as far as Christian Constantinople, where the Crusaders indulged in one of the greatest orgies of pillage and destruction in history. They overthrew the Greek Orthodox Emperor and founded a short-lived Catholic Latin Kingdom, setting up King Baldwin on a shaky throne.

The end of the Crusader states in the Levant came in the second half of the thirteenth century. It was brought about by the so-called Mameluk dynasty of Egypt, several among whose members, oddly enough, combined enthusiastic patronage of the arts and sciences with the most bestial cruelty. In 1263, Baybars, the powerful founder of this dynasty, marched against the Crusader states. He took city after city — Nazareth, Jaffa, Acre, Antioch, Tyre, Sidon, Beyrut. Baybars was no Saladin. Both the garrison and the civilian population of Acre were slaughtered. So were the defenders of Antioch, about fifteen thousand men.

Fortunately, human nature, and therefore history, has constructive aspects too.

In Sicily we find a most impressive and admirable example of co-operation between West and East. In Sicily Islam actually laid the basis and gave the direct inspiration for our Renaissance in the Christian West.

Medieval Sicily offered the world a unique spectacle. Following the elimination of Moslem political power by Christian conquerors, Moslem culture, incomparably higher than the contemporary Christian, was greatly encouraged by the Christian rulers of the island. In fact, under their protection it soared to heights greater than those it had scaled under Moslem political rule in Sicily.

The Aghlabites, Moslem rulers of Tunisia, conquered Sicily in 827 A.D. They proceeded to besiege Naples and Rome, failed to take them. But they captured Malta, and the important city of Bari on the Italian mainland, on the heel of the Italian boot. They held Bari for thirty years, using it as a base for their sallies and looting expeditions into southern Italy. Palermo was the capital of Moslem Sicily, and the seat of its ameers. In Sicily, as in Spain, the Arabs introduced a living standard based upon much higher conceptions of hygiene, comfort and general culture than those that had previously prevailed.

It was the Normans who took Sicily back. Count Roger, son of Tancred of Hauteville, took Messina in 1060. Inside thirty years, Roger took Malta, Syracuse, Palermo, and the rest of Sicily. He granted his Moslem subjects complete freedom of religion, language, and customs. A major part of his army was recruited from the Moslem element. He surrounded himself with both Moslem and Christian intellectuals. His son, King Roger II, went even farther. He wore Moslem clothes, encouraged the Moslem philosophers, geographers, physicians, physicists, scientific chemists, mathematicians, in their work. No cultural treasures were destroyed in Sicily under the Normans, no Arabic manuscripts burnt as works of Satan. Moslem savants held high offices at court. Byzantine Christian and Arab Moslem architects worked side by side in building churches, mosques, palaces, other public buildings. Mosaic work had been developed to highest artistry in Byzantium. Byzantine artists created the gold mosaics of the glorious Palatine Chapel inside Palermo's still undamaged royal palace, and those of the cathedral at Monreale, near Palermo. Moslem art inspired the cloisters of that same cathedral, still one of the wonders of Europe. The combination of Norman and Moslem style gives Palermo unique charm, the co-operation between Christian and Moslem genius gives humanity an inspiring lesson.

The climax of cultural development in Sicily, and also of the island's significance as a political factor in world affairs, came with the reign of the great Frederick of

Hohenstaufen, King of Sicily, ruler of Germany, Emperor of the Holy Roman Empire, King of Jerusalem. Frederick was undoubtedly the most enlightened monarch of his age, and one of the greatest rulers of all ages. In religious matters, he was a freethinker. At his court in Palermo, he happily blended Christian and Moslem culture. Being Emperor of Germany, and feudal overlord of great sections of Italy, he had many German and Italian officers, civil servants, scholars, merchants, and functionaries in his entourage. In addition, Frederick had literally hundreds of Arab Moslem savants, artists, architects, engineers, physicians, philosophers on his payroll. These children of two worlds met daily. Each found out that the other fellow was human. The material and spiritual products of the soaring Moslem civilization and culture were carried from Sicily to every corner of Italy, and to Germany. They kindled the flame of the spirit in the barbaric North.

The Renaissance is a part of our Arab heritage.

We left the story of the Ottoman Empire at the point where the Turkish attempt to take Vienna failed.

The first Turkish Sultans had been strong men, the Turks always remained a virile people. But, basically, the Turks had one great asset and one great liability.

The asset was ethnic unity. The liability was the corrupt administrative system of the Byzantine Empire, which the Ottoman Empire had inherited.

Before the inception of the Pan-Arab movement, less than a generation ago, if you asked a person in the Levant: "What are you?" he would name his *religion*. "A Moslem," "A Maronite Christian," "A Greek Catholic," "A Jew," would be the reply. But if you put that question to a Turk, his reply was, and still would be, "A Turk." The average Turk used to look upon himself as a pious Moslem, but he was, and still is, a Turk first and a Moslem afterwards. During their march of conquest, the Turks derived from this ethnic cohesion a psychologic and political momentum which the Arabic-speaking world had lost as early as the ninth century.

On the other hand, the sad heritage of Byzantine corruption caused the political weakness, the chronic and fatal illness of the Ottoman Empire. The reckless squandering of money by the Byzantine emperors and the resultant chronic bankruptcy of their treasury caused them to make graft quite openly the basis of public life. Their civil servants received totally inadequate pay, often had to go for months without it. On the other hand, they were actually encouraged to accept bribes, because that relieved the emperors from paying their salaries. This graft-ridden administrative machinery of the Byzantine Empire had actually muddled through ten centuries, a sad illustration of how much mismanagement an empire can stand before it collapses.

The West Invades the East

Following their conquest of the Byzantine Empire, the Turks stepped right into its administrative mechanism. At first, it seemed neither necessary, nor logical, nor even possible to turn this centuries-old machine inside out and create a new one. Besides, the minority of Turkish warriors and leaders who now tried to govern the vast realm had no experience that could have helped them to reorganize its administration along new lines. The administrative reform which Soliman the Magnificent introduced to his huge empire gave the political units of the state new names but left the Byzantine system of government almost unchanged.

So, the virile Turk found himself enmeshed in the web of the Byzantine administrative system. Thereafter, Ottoman history was an incessant struggle between the momentum of Turkish virility and the inertia of Byzantine corruption. The battle between the two psychologic factors lasted six hundred years. In the end, the phantom of dead Byzantium won. In 1918, it dragged the Ottoman Empire into the abyss.

Then followed the miracle of Turkey's rebirth. Turkey, long known as "the sick man of Europe," proved to an astonished world that its virility had not actually died. But this miracle came only after the complete collapse of the gigantic Ottoman Empire.

Only three years after the Turkish attempt to take Vienna, the tables were turned, and a Christian army conquered Buda, the Budapest of today, then still the strongest frontier fortress of the Ottoman Empire in the West. The Turks now were forced to evacuate Hungary, whose major part they had held for a century and a half. But they held on to the Balkans for another hundred to a hundred and fifty years. Serbia gained partial freedom through a successful rebellion early in the nineteenth century. Full independence came to it as late as 1867. Greece got its liberty in 1829, after many years of heroic fighting against the Turks and unheroic intrigues among the various Greek factions. In 1856, Rumania followed, and made Karl of Hohenzollern-Sigmaringen its ruler.

Russia had a hand in the liberation of Serbia and Rumania. Along with England and France, it also actively intervened in the military and diplomatic events that preceded the liberation of Greece. The independence of Bulgaria was a direct present from Russia. Hence the traditional pro-Russian attitude of the Bulgarians. There had been a Bulgarian revolt in 1876. Abdul Hamid II had just ascended the Turkish throne. He had some fifteen thousand Bulgars, men, women and children, massacred in reprisal. Thereupon Tsarist Russia declared war on Turkey. Officially, to punish it for this terrible massacre. Unofficially, to conquer the Dardanelles. The Turks fought bravely, as usual, but lack of supplies and disorder inside their leadership sealed the fate of the campaign. Russia was brought to a halt at San Stefano, at one hour's distance from Constantinople, not by the Turkish army but by the diplomatic intervention of the

British, who wished to prevent the Russian conquest of the Straits.

Bulgaria now got its freedom, the Turkish Sultan retaining only nominal suzerainty over it. In 1908, Ferdinand of Coburg, then only "Prince of Bulgaria," shook off his nominal allegiance to the Sultan and proclaimed himself "Tsar of the Bulgarians." By now, the Turkish administration was so feeble that it could do nothing in retaliation. Profiting by Turkey's helplessness, Austria-Hungary, which had occupied Bosnia and Herzegovina in 1878, now proclaimed the official annexation of these provinces to the Habsburg Empire.

The Ukraine and the Crimea had long been lost to Turkey. The first went to the Poles in 1699, the second to the Russians some seventy-five years later.

In every one of these wars, the Turks fought with their customary valor. But the curse of Byzantine corruption, which their military and civil administration had inherited, hamstrung every attempt at the effective organization of the army and its commissariat. There was nothing left for them to do but to recede step by step, yielding their former conquests piecemeal.

From 1683 to 1918, the Ottoman Empire was fighting one long, almost uninterrupted rear-guard action through the expanse of history.

By 1908, all it had left in Europe was Constantinople, Adrianople, Thrace, Macedonia and Albania. Soon, it was to lose all this too, with the exception of a small strip of land that included Constantinople. But just before this new catastrophe happened, the Turks made a major attempt at modernizing their country and putting an end to Abdul Hamid's crafty and cruel despotism. Already weakened and crumbling, the empire now was tottering under the impact of a revolution. Its organizers, the so-called Young Turks, hoped that the concussion would shake the country out of its lethargy and invigorate it through Western, democratic concepts.

It was a heroic effort. It came too late.

XI

THE COLLAPSE OF
ARAB NORTH AFRICA

℘HE FIRST three mem-
bers of the Young Turkish Revolutionary Committee,
officially known as *Ittihat wa Tarakki*, Committee for
Union and Progress, were Rahmy Bey, son of a distinguished family of Salonika, Midhat Shukry, and
Mehmed Talaat, the latter a clerk at the telegraph office
in Salonika. The secret regulations and bylaws of the
committee were drawn up by Rahmy and Midhat
Shukry. The country was overrun with Abdul Hamid's
informers, and greatest secrecy was necessary. To protect themselves against the Sultan's spies, the members of
the originally secret committee wore masks at their
meetings. Therefore, none among them knew the identity of any other member except his own sponsor, who
had brought him into the committee, and vouched for
him.

The committee grew rapidly in members and influence. When it felt strong enough, it shed the cloak of
secrecy. Enver Bey, Jemal Bey and other popular officers of the army and navy were early members of the
committee. The Sultan no longer felt sure of the armed
forces. He lived in constant fear of assassination. He

was actually stampeded into giving in to the revolutionary democrats. In July 1908, the "Red Sultan" proclaimed a constitution, known as *Hürriyet* — "Liberty." Thereupon, reactionary elements in the country tried to stir up a counterrevolution. The motive force behind this attempt was a group of elderly officers, rich people of reactionary views, and religious fanatics, who accused the Young Turks of hostility to Islam.

The counterrevolutionary *Putsch* failed. It was quelled by an army led by Young Turkish officers. Then a delegation of three men forced the Sultan to abdicate. Abdul Hamid was interned first in a villa in Salonika, then in the fabulously beautiful Beylerbey Palace on the Bosporus, where he later died a natural death.

He was succeeded by his brother, Mehmed Reshad, whom he had kept interned for twenty years. The Young Turks now set about reorganizing the country along Western lines. Mehmed Talaat became Minister of the Interior, later Grand Vizier. Rahmy assumed the Governorship of Smyrna. Enver later became a lieutenant-general, and Minister of War, Jemal being made Minister of the Navy. Having seized the helm of the heaving ship of state, the Committee for Union and Progress became feverishly engaged in a series of far-reaching reforms.

It was too late. Dark clouds had long gathered on the political horizon of the Balkans. Abdul Hamid had been a past master at playing the Serbs against the Bulgarians,

the Bulgarians against the Greeks, the Greeks against
the Albanians, and everybody against everybody else.
Through sheer diplomatic intrigue, he had been able
to neutralize the anti-Turkish policies of the Balkan
countries and checkmate their policies. The Young
Turks lacked his experience. The country was in a state
of reconstruction and resultant impotence. In 1911, the
Italians invaded and took Libya, which then was a
Turkish province. In the same year, the Imam Yakhya
of Yemen rebelled against the Turkish administration.
Serbia, Montenegro, Bulgaria and Greece had long been
planning a concerted attack against what was left of
Turkey in Europe, including Constantinople. Now,
they felt, the propitious moment had come.

They struck. It was the First Balkan War. The year
was 1912.

The Ottoman Empire was caught napping. Until
then, its territorial integrity had been due in great measure to the jealousy between the British and Russian governments. The Tsarist regime had already conquered
huge Moslem-inhabited areas. As we have seen, the
Crimea had been attached to Russia as far back as the
eighteenth century. As recently as the second half of
the nineteenth, the Tsars had annexed major portions

of Turkestan, including the Moslem regions of Bukhara, Ferghana and Samarkand. The conquest of Merv, during the reign of Alexander III, father of the last Tsar, Nicholas II, threatened Britain's hold on India, by bringing Russian power to the gates of Afghanistan, Britain's "buffer state" protecting India from the northwest. Iran also had become a diplomatic arena between Russia and Britain, each power setting up a "zone of influence" inside that country.

Then, there was the problem of Russia's access to the Mediterranean, known as the Straits Question. British diplomacy of the old school wanted to keep Russia away from the Mediterranean. It looked upon a Russian Mediterranean fleet as a direct menace to Suez, upon Russian maritime trade as dangerous economic competition.

As a consequence of this attitude, Great Britain pursued a pro-Turkish policy, aimed at keeping Russia's army, navy and trade out of the Levant. By contrast, Russia sought to weaken Turkey and wrest the Straits from it. The Balkan nations were bent on establishing their complete independence from Ottoman suzerainty, and later, upon conquering the entire territory still left to the Turks in Europe. Therefore, in accordance with its own interests and policies, Tsarist Russia looked upon the Balkan states as its natural allies, and supported their anti-Turkish projects.

One generation earlier, every major Russian move in the Balkans had been foiled by British diplomacy, and we have seen how, during the Russo-Turkish War of

1877, the intervention of Lord Beaconsfield, then British Premier, actually brought the victorious Russians to a halt at one hour's distance from Constantinople.

But since those days, the European atmosphere had changed. The Kaiser had acceded to the German imperial throne, and initiated a big naval building program which threatened Britain's dominant position on the seas. Later, the Berlin-Baghdad scheme began to take shape. Britain felt that Germany, not Russia, now was its most dangerous rival. The direct result of this new British attitude was the Entente between England, Russia, and France, the latter country acting as the intermediary between the two former rivals. The Entente was formed in the first decade of the present century. It resulted in a change in Britain's customary anti-Russian attitude in the Balkans.

It was this change in traditional British policy that gave the Balkan countries the right of way to Turkey. Encouraged by Russia and unchecked by Britain, they attacked.

As usual, the Turkish army fought with great valor. As usual, disorganization led to its doom. Within a few weeks, the Ottoman Empire lost all it still had left in the Balkans, with the exception of a narrow strip of land west of Constantinople, bounded by the villages of Enos on the Aegean and Midia on the Black Sea.

Then, in 1913, came the Second Balkan War, actually a bloody squabble between Bulgaria, Serbia and Greece over the division of the spoils. Serbia and Greece felt that Bulgaria wanted too much of the territory taken from Turkey. They attacked Bulgaria. Rumania then joined in the fight, invading Bulgaria from the north. This sealed the fate of the Bulgar army. In the ensuing peace treaty, Macedonia, which Bulgaria had tried to annex, was divided between Serbia and Greece. Rumania took the Dobruja, that strip of land which skirts the Black Sea to the north of the Bulgarian port of Varna.

The Turks profited by the free-for-all by taking back the key city of Adrianople, which still belongs to the small region that Turkey owns in Europe.

Italy also saw its chance to indulge further in the favorite European political game of grab and seek. During the First Balkan War, while Turkey was being attacked from all sides, Italy simply seized the Dodecanese Islands, inhabited mainly by Greeks but then a part of the Ottoman Empire.

ονᵊ   ονᵊ   ονᵊ

In 1913, humanity escaped a world war by a hair's breadth. Austria-Hungary had mobilized and Tsarist Russia was on the verge of "counter-mobilization," as one aspect of the traditional preliminaries to Europe's periodical massacres is known. Then, the catastrophe was averted, rather through luck than through the sagacity of Europe's statesmen. But the blood bath had been merely postponed.

The Balkan Wars furnished one of the causes for the First World War, which finally dismembered the Ottoman Empire and amputated its huge Arabic-speaking provinces from the Turkish trunk. But one of its major causes was the famed Berlin-Baghdad plan, Germany's own project for the exploitation and even the colonization of the Ottoman Empire. Actually, this plan was a belated phase of the wholesale scramble for colonies and "spheres of influence" that had been going on throughout the nineteenth century. The most dramatic aspect of that scramble was the rivalry between Britain and France. Germany arrived rather late on the international scene, but succeeded in laying its hands on Southwest Africa, Togo, the Cameroons, Kenya and Tanganyika territories in Africa. Belgium acquired the Belgian Congo.

This was the famous "Scramble for Africa." It affected major parts of the Arabic-speaking world, establishing Christian domination over huge Moslem-inhabited areas.

Napoleon's attempt to make Egypt a French possession failed when Nelson annihilated the French fleet at Abukir and Trafalgar. Deprived of its ships, France was unable to hold Egypt. However, one generation after Napoleon's short-lived conquest of Egypt, France staged another major invasion in North Africa. Liberated from its reactionary Bourbon regime in 1830, France found an outlet for its regained vigor by conquering Algeria. No longer a part of the Ottoman Empire, that country could not count on outside help. Left to its own resources, it was facing a European army fully equipped with the most modern arms of the period. The armament of the natives of Algeria was primitive. But there arose among them a great leader: Abd el Kader, whose fame still lives in Islam. For more than ten years did this great general keep the numerically and technically far superior European army busy before he was forced to yield.

The next invasion of Moslem Africa again came from France. This time, Tunisia was the objective. Under its "deys" and "beys," Tunisia also had been a Barbary State. Here, too, the European armies had only local forces to contend with, as Tunisia also had long ceased to form a part of the Ottoman Empire. We have seen in an earlier chapter that the number of Italians and Frenchmen is about equal in Tunisia, each ethnic element numbering around ninety thousand souls. Tunisia had long been a center of Italian immigration, and when Italy became a single, united state in 1870, it began to cast longing glances toward Tunisia. Soon it became evident that Italy intended to seize that country. The French decided to "beat her to it." In 1881, they invaded Tunisia, making it a protectorate.

The next Moslem territory on the timetable of European conquest was Libya. It was a Turkish province. In 1911, the Italians invaded it. The Turks put up a stiff resistance. Enver Pasha, the "glamour boy" of the Young Turkish Revolution, handsome, inordinately ambitious, led the defense. From the beginning, it was a hopeless task, because Britain was on Italy's side and prevented the Turks from sending effective reinforcements, supplies and ammunition to Libya over the land route. Italy's fleet dominated the Mediterranean. Once again, valor alone was ineffective against vast numerical superiority, heavy guns, and huge quantities of modern equipment. The country was lost to the Ottoman Empire. A subsequent attempt by the Senussi warriors of Libya to shake off foreign domination was stifled in blood by Marshal Rodolfo Graziani. It was the hangman who silenced the Senussi.

Later, Graziani was succeeded as governor of Libya by Marshal Italo Balbo. Balbo had been one of Fascism's leading *squadristas*, the strong-arm men who did the killing, beatings-up and castor-oil-dispensing for Mussolini in the early days of his rule. Later, Italo Balbo became a moderate. He was appointed governor of Libya because Mussolini envied his popularity as an airman and politician in Italy. In Libya, Balbo tried to placate the natives by milder forms of administration.

Some time before Balbo went to Libya, I had a conversation with him in the Ministry of Aviation in Rome, of which he then was in charge. We discussed some problems pertaining to Islam, and I referred to the traditionally ruthless methods employed by European powers in Arab countries and elsewhere in Africa and the East. Balbo had the courage to agree, adding that if he ever got a chance to "work" in a Moslem country, as he put it, he would try sincerely to co-operate with the natives. He lived up to this contention when he assumed the governorship of Libya. Mussolini himself affected a pro-Moslem attitude, and affirmed it emphatically when I asked him about it in a conversation in Rome, in June 1927. Yet when Italo Balbo actually tried to put such a policy into effect in Libya, he was hampered by Mussolini himself. The Duce's jealousy of the popular Balbo proved stronger than political wisdom and statesmanship.

As for Egypt, Britain had long been taking a hand in its affairs. It had conquered the Sudan. There had been bloody fighting, rebellion, friction in every form. In the solidly Moslem Sudan, a rising of the population against the British took the form of open warfare in 1883, when native bitterness found a crystallization point in the person of Mohammed Ahmed, the famed "Mahdi." The Mahdi was a military genius. His ragged "army" of dervishes was actually a fighting religious confraternity, not unlike the Senussi of Libya today and the Almoravides in Morocco and Spain in the eleventh century. The Dervish army fought heroically. What the Mahdi lacked in weapons, commissariat, ammunition, and military training, he more than made up in natural strategic and tactical ability. He inflicted some dire defeats on the British, besieged Gordon Pasha in Khartum, took the city. When Kitchener, who later became "Lord

Kitchener of Khartum," finally arrived, Gordon was dead. Once again, it was the old story: European numerical and technical superiority versus native valor. The Sudan was definitely conquered.

Egypt itself remained nominally a Turkish dependency right up to 1914, its rulers, the Khedivehs, or Viceroys, being subject to Turkish suzerainty, although their throne was hereditary in their family. Actually, the Sultans of Turkey had not a word to say in Egyptian affairs. The country was ruled by the British, with the Khediveh as its figurehead. In 1914, the Turcophile Khediveh, Abbas Hilmy, happened to be in Turkey when the war broke out. He was deposed, being succeeded by his cousin, Fuad, who was proclaimed *King* of Egypt. But Abbas Hilmy did not hate the British. When I met him in great secrecy, in a back room of the restaurant in Berlin's famed Hotel Adlon, in the spring of 1922, he spoke of Britain with great moderation. This attitude apparently later convinced the British authorities that he was politically reliable, because, in the ninteen-thirtics, he was permitted to return to Egypt and live in retirement on his huge estates.

In 1936, England gave Egypt real sovereignty, and the two countries concluded a treaty of alliance. Subsequently, Downing Street came to the further conclusion that tolerance toward the Wafd party, mouthpiece of the huge majority of the population, was a wise policy. Since then, England, with that sound levelheadedness which is one of its greatest assets, and a moral greatness demonstrated by admitting mistakes, has been charting the right, the constructive course in Egypt.

Spain also entered the ranks of European aggressors in North Africa, slicing off the northern tip of Morocco. In 1911, the remaining part of that country was the last Moslem state in Africa still in native hands. Then came the French conquest, and the proclamation of the French protectorate over Morocco in 1912. Subsequent events in that country have been described in an earlier chapter. In 1926, however, Morocco found an "Abd el Kader," a "Mahdi" of its own, in the person of Abd el Krim. This native leader inflicted crushing defeats upon the Spaniards, who held the northern part of the country. In fact, an advancing Spanish army was almost completely wiped out by warriors of the Rif who fought under Abd el Krim, and were inferior to the Spaniards in arms, ammunition and supplies of every kind, not to speak of aircraft.

So catastrophic was the Spanish defeat that the Cortes, the legislature in Madrid, ordered an investigation of the responsibilities for the catastrophe. The really responsible person was none other than King Alfonso XIII himself. The Spanish drive in Morocco had been his idea. To avoid the political consequences of the debacle, the King conspired with General Don Miguel Primo de Rivera, then Captain General of Catalonia, in the creation of a dictatorship and the forcible dissolution of the legislature. This is how Spain got its first dictatorship inside the present century. It was later emulated by

Francisco Franco. Four-hundred-odd years after the fall
of Moslem Granada, a Moslem victory in Africa had
changed the political face of Spain.

The Spaniards now appealed to France for aid against
Abd el Krim. Trying to forestall a French offensive
through a preventive thrust, Abd el Krim attacked the
French himself. But now the brave band of Rif warriors found itself between two modern European armies.
It was forced to surrender. Abd el Krim was exiled to
the island of Réunion, in the Indian Ocean.

The whole of Moslem North Africa now was in
European hands. The Cross dominated the Crescent
from Casablanca to Cairo. But the European powers still
held designs on Moslem territories. France and England
both coveted regions in Asia that belonged to Turkey.
Germany's plan was to dominate the Ottoman Empire
"from within." Then, in Sarajevo, Gavrilo Princip's
pistol furnished the spark for the explosion of 1914. Contrary to the isolationist dream that in our age a major
war can rage without embroiling every major nation,
the world soon stood in flames. The Ottoman Empire
also was dragged into the conflict. That gave the diplomats of Europe their chance.

XII

WORLD WAR I IN THE LEVANT

𝒞HE GAME of the Wilhelmstrasse was to drag Turkey at all costs into the war on Germany's side, then establish domination over it, exploit its natural riches, finally give it the status of a glorified German colony. The Turkish cabinet was divided in its sympathies. Talaat Bey, Minister of the Interior, and later, as Talaat Pasha, Grand Vizier, was anti-German. So was Jemal Pasha. On the other hand, Enver Pasha, who had become a son-in-law of the Sultan and held a dominant position in Turkish politics, was rabidly pro-German. The Turkish government was still wavering, when the Germans forced its hand. Admiral Souchon Pasha, a German with a French name who headed the Kaiser's naval mission to Turkey, ordered his flagship and a Turkish flotilla to sail for the Russian naval base of Sebastopol, and shell it. The horrified Turkish cabinet had to bow before the irreparable *fait accompli*, a "Turkish" hostile action without a war declaration. The Ottoman Empire was at war.

Tsarist Russia was actually glad about the turn the events had taken. Here was a chance to get the Dardanelles without interference from Britain, which now was Russia's ally. Britain wanted the Arabic-speaking parts of the Ottoman Empire. But France wanted Syria.

So Downing Street and the Quai d'Orsay decided to try to co-ordinate their conflicting war aims in western Asia later.

Berlin, on the other hand, began to flood Turkey with German "experts" of every description, who were to prepare the exploitation of the country's forests, mines, and other rich natural resources by Germany. The construction of the Berlin–Baghdad Railway was pushed, to hasten the day of Germany's hegemony in Asiatic Turkey and its march to Iran and India.

Berlin sent Captain Niedermaier, of the Bavarian Army, to Afghanistan, to line up its ruler, the Ameer Habibullah Khan, with Germany, and induce him to invade India through the Khyber Pass. The Ameer received the German mission with courtesy, gave it a house in Kabul to stay in. But the Germans soon discovered that they were nominally guests but actually prisoners. Their movements were watched. When they called on the Ameer, they were listened to with the courtesy of a polite host, but got nowhere in their projects. After a few weeks spent in futile efforts to sow discord between Afghanistan and Britain, the envoys returned to Europe empty-handed. On his return journey, in Aleppo, Niedermaier himself, now a sadder and wiser man, told me the story of this German diplomatic fiasco on the western side of the Khyber Pass.

France had long enjoyed a privileged moral position in Turkey. It was the recognized protector of the Christians in the Levant. Throughout the Ottoman Empire it maintained grammar and high schools, even colleges, such as the University of St. Joseph in Beyrut. Practically every Christian in Syria and Palestine spoke French. So did almost every Jew, because the Alliance Israélite Universelle, with headquarters in Paris, operated a great number of schools in the Levant, and their language of tuition also was French. Inside the Arab population, the members of the educated middle class in the cities all spoke French. So did every cultured Turk. France was the spiritual home of every educated Christian, Jew and Moslem in the Levant. The rich bought their dresses in Paris' Rue de la Paix, many of them sent their sons to the Sorbonne.

French diplomacy used this privileged position as a battering-ram against the crumbling walls of the Ottoman Empire. When, following the outbreak of the war in 1914, Monsieur Bompard, French Consul General in Beyrut, returned to Europe, he committed the inexcusable blunder of leaving his secret archives behind. At this time, Jemal Pasha was Turkey's omnipotent proconsul and commander-in-chief in the Levant, including Palestine.

In Beyrut, then Turkey's biggest port in Syria, and now the capital of the Republic of Lebanon, Jemal Pasha seized the files of the French Consulate. To his amazement, he found that Bompard had left behind him complete records of his numerous secret palavers with leaders of the Arabic-speaking Moslem and Christian population, in which the parties had discussed a revolt against Turkish rule with French assistance. The rebellion was to be staged in Syria, Palestine and Iraq, and these parts of the Ottoman Empire were to form an independent Arab state, with close French affiliations. Today, we hear and read a good deal about the amazing exploits of Lawrence of Arabia, one of the truly heroic figures of modern history. But almost nobody, except a very few people, seems to be aware that, two years before Lawrence began his mission in Arabia, a "revolt in the desert" was being mapped out in the parlor of the French Consulate in Beyrut by Monsieur Bompard, who was certainly not one of the Seven Pillars of Wisdom.

Jemal Pasha had many among the compromised Arab notables imprisoned, others exiled, some of them hanged for treason. Through its agents, Britain had kept informed of the secret French moves. Downing Street also favored the dismemberment of the Ottoman Empire, but then still desired to inherit all the Arab regions itself and not to allow any of them to pass under French domination.

Germany, although officially Turkey's ally, was equally active in its efforts to establish domination over the Ottoman Empire. For example, in one region alone, namely, the important Syrian political and economic center of Aleppo, the German government spent sixty million gold marks — fifteen million dollars — inside two years on propaganda among the Arabs. This propaganda had a subtle slant against the Turkish element. The Germans wished to intimate to the Arab population that they would become their protectors and helpers against the Turks.

The Austro-Hungarian Ministry of Foreign Affairs also tried to deceive its Turkish allies in the Levant. With the war in progress and French influence temporarily eliminated, the political advisers of the late Emperor Charles of Habsburg felt that here was an opportunity to wean the Christians of the Levant away from France. These men hoped that if the Central Powers were victorious the Catholic house of Habsburg could replace France in the role of "protecting power" of the Christians of the Levant. However, on the whole the Austrians were more loyal to their Turkish allies than the aggressive Germans, and were liked by both Turks and Arabs.

As for the Germans, they were equally hostile towards their Turkish and their Austrian allies, as I can attest from personal experience. For example, my own battery of heavy mortars was temporarily assigned to the defense of the Gulf of Smyrna, in Asia Minor. Our logical base was Smyrna itself, a flourishing, rich, healthy city. But my guns were of Austrian make, my men mostly Viennese, and the Germans wished at all costs to prevent the population of economically and politically important Smyrna from coming into contact with the popular Austrians. This political jealousy actually overrode military considerations. It was the only reason why Trommer Pasha, German commander of the Turkish army corps responsible for the defense of the region, ordered us to establish our base in a small city called Menemen, about two hours from Smyrna. Menemen, which we called the "hell hole of Asia," is an arid spot where the summer heat becomes deadly and tropical diseases are rampant. Soon, *80 per cent* of our men were on the sick list with scorpion bites, sunstroke, and amoebic dysentery. The German still refused to let us move to the near-by, healthy base of Smyrna. Not until I had addressed a formal complaint to General Pomiankovski, Austrian military attaché in Constantinople, was the German general directed from "above" to put the manpower interests of Turkey above German jealousies, and allow us to proceed to Smyrna.

In 1918, after the collapse of Tsarist Russia, Berlin sent General Kress von Kressenstein to the Caucasus. His orders were to seize and hold for Germany those same oil wells of Baku which Adolf Hitler vainly tried to lay his hands on twenty-three years later. Baku was inside neighboring Turkey's direct sphere of interest, but the last thing its German "ally" had in mind was to make Turkey a partner in the venture.

To make the orgy of conspiracies and intrigues complete, the Germans themselves were split into rival factions. The German military attaché in Constantinople, Colonel von Lossow, had his own projects for subjecting Turkey to German wartime and postwar domination. Marshal Liman von Sanders, head of the German military mission to Turkey, commander-in-chief in Gallipoli and later in Palestine, was engaged in an unending, bitter feud with von Lossow and his henchmen. In this connection also, I was fortunate, or unfortunate, enough to get a close-up view of German intrigues in the Moslem East. In May 1916, I was Marshal Liman von Sanders' guest at his G.H.Q. in Banderma, on the Asiatic shore of the Sea of Marmora, whence Liman then directed the strategy of the Fifth Turkish Army. Again and again during that visit would I willy-nilly overhear "asides" which Germans in key positions in Turkey were making about their German comrades, Colonel von Lossow and "his gang."

The rivalry between the British and the French in the Arab question was eventually eliminated through the secret Sykes-Picot agreement, made while the war was still in progress. It gave Syria to the French, Palestine and Iraq to the British. It was rumored later that this agreement so incensed Lawrence of Arabia that he refused to accept any decoration or title of nobility. Lawrence had been instructed to promise the entire Fertile Crescent to the Arabs, and now he saw that they were to get no part of it. Although the Ameer Faisal, Sherif Hussein's second son, eventually became nominal head of French-ruled Syria, and later of British-controlled Iraq, Lawrence is said to have felt that he had been betrayed, and, in turn, had unwittingly betrayed the Arabs.

The rivalry between two other allies, Britain and Tsarist Russia, was believed among Turks to have caused the British campaign on Gallipoli. Turkish political circles thought that Downing Street was afraid that if the

Ottoman Empire collapsed, Russia would seize the Straits, and Britain, this time Russia's ally, could not intervene, as it had in the war of 1877.

It is generally remembered that, at first, the British tried to take the Straits through a major naval action, namely, shelling the Turkish forts into submission. The attempt failed. After the heavy guns of the Turkish coastal batteries had sunk several British ships and gravely damaged others, including the superdreadnaught *Queen Elizabeth,* the British navy broke off the engagement and withdrew. It is one of history's grim jokes, and still almost generally unknown, that the British could have planted the Union Jack on the minarets of Constantinople, had they continued the bombardment just ten minutes longer. At the moment when the British fleet broke off the engagement, Fort Hamidiyeh, key stronghold of the Dardanelles defenses, had two rounds of ammunition left. This secret of the First World War was then known to a handful of people in Turkish military and political circles. I first published it in America and Europe in 1920.

The war of 1914–1918 was notable also through the failure of the Turks to enlist the political support of the Moslem world. At the outbreak of the war in 1914, the Sultan-Caliph proclaimed that the campaign was a *jihad,* a Moslem holy war. The Ottoman government hoped that this measure would undermine the loyalty of hundreds of millions of Moslem people who lived in Allied territory, would induce them to hamper the Allied war

(213)

effort. Nothing of the sort happened. Those Moslem who served in the Allied armies did their duty without faltering. Here was convincing proof that there is no factual basis for a *political* Pan-*Islamic* movement, based upon general Moslem political solidarity, and distinct from a Pan-*Arab* movement. The latter is a reality, and is founded upon the common *political*, *economic* and *cultural* interests of the *Arabs*.

In January 1917, the British took Baghdad. In the fall of the same year, Lord Allenby conquered Jerusalem. In the night of September 18, 1918, the British pierced the Turkish Palestine front. Cavalry raced through the gap. The Royal Air Force rained bombs upon the retreating Turks. Lawrence of Arabia harassed the Turkish armies with his Bedouin guerrillas. Marshal Liman von Sanders, then Turkish commander-in-chief in Palestine, escaped capture through a miracle. The Ottoman Empire collapsed. The Allied fleets entered the Golden Horn. The British advanced as far as Aleppo, then ceded it to France, with the rest of Syria and the Lebanon. Palestine and Iraq became British mandates. The artificial state of Transjordan was set up, with the Ameer Abdallah, third son of Sherif Hussein, its nominal ruler. Hussein proclaimed himself King of Hejaz and Caliph of Islam. This brought Abdul Aziz Ibn Saud upon the scene. He defeated Hussein, took Hejaz, including the holy cities of Mecca and Medina. Hussein went into exile, died.

With the exception of Saudi Arabia, as Ibn Saud's

realm now became known, the dream of the Arabs had not come true. They had merely changed masters.

ᴄⱷꙆ   ᴄⱷꙆ   ᴄⱷꙆ

Then came the hectic postwar years in western Asia. First, the Druses, under their hereditary chief, Sultan Pasha El Atrash, revolted against French rule. The rising was accompanied by anti-French riots in Damascus. Again we encounter the outworn cliché: heroic resistance by the natives, overwhelming European superiority in numbers and equipment. Soon, Druse resistance ceased.

In 1926–1927, Iraq revolted against the British mandatory power. This insurrection also was put down.

European domination of the one-time Arab parts of the Ottoman Empire has led to dismal failure. The British have had the greatness and wisdom to admit their mistakes in the administration of Iraq. They have given that country sovereignty and have replaced their mandate, actually their domination, by a treaty of alliance with an independent Iraq. This wise departure from the traditions of European power politics immediately paid dividends. Now, the British were able to secure the sympathetic co-operation of such Arab patriots as Nuri Pasha Es-Said. As Premier of Iraq, Nuri Pasha kept his country loyally in the Allied fold throughout the Second World War, after the *coup d'état* of the German puppet, Rashid Ali El Ghailani, had been crushed.

In Syria, Léon Blum, who became French Premier at the head of the "Popular Front" government in 1936, used moderation and wisdom — two words for the same thing. He substituted a policy of co-operation and understanding for the previous policy of force. His government negotiated a treaty with the Syrians, along the lines of Britain's treaty with Iraq. Renouncing its mandate over Syria and Lebanon, France recognized the independence of these countries and made a military alliance with them.

But in 1938, when the Blum administration fell in France, the ratification of these treaties was sabotaged by the reactionaries inside the French Chamber of Deputies, influenced by Pierre Laval. In 1943, Syria and Lebanon were eventually granted independence by the French. It is to be hoped that the truly democratic elements in France finally put a stop to the recurrent sabotage of France's real interests by a group of incorrigible reactionaries. France must become one of the major factors in the cultural and political regeneration of the world. And France's prestige as a progressive nation demands that it follow the British example by substituting *co-operation* for *domination* in the Levant.

In the postwar world, when the project of a Pan-Arab Federation, referred to in a subsequent chapter, will begin to take shape, the Western powers generally will have a spectacular opportunity to give the peoples of the East further proofs of wisdom.

A Lesson in Humility: Our Arab Heritage

XIII

THE SPIRIT OF ISLAM

*T*HE HUMAN personality is a symbiosis of thoughts and thought habits, held together by memory. So is the collective personality of a community. In this case, common tradition represents the collective memory which holds the thought habits of the community together. In fact, what actually constitutes a people, or any kind of community, is common tradition, including the tradition that it *is* a people or community. And no link inside a people is stronger than common tradition — that is, collective memory.

This rule transcends all national, geographic, ethnic, racial or other limitations, and applies equally to civilizations.

In a *psychologic* sense, then, a civilization is the totality of the common traditions of a group of people, regardless of their geographic or even ethnic affiliations. *Technically*, a civilization is the sum total of the achievements of a community in the fields of science, applied science, industry, social organization, literature, the fine arts, and in other fields of *intellectual* activity.

That is *civilization. But it is not culture.* Culture does not consist of intellectual achievements. It is *a state of mind*, a permanent condition of an individual soul, or of

(219)

the collective soul of a community. Culture is a purely ethical concept. It is a wholly spiritual, intangible, yet clearly perceptible residue formed in a soul, or in a community, through consistent thought and action along ethical lines. Civilization is a fertile subsoil for culture, but often exists without it. Conversely, a person or community can have the highest culture without "civilization" — that is, without what we commonly call education, and without proficiency in mechanics, science, or literature.

Airplanes, fountain pens, anti-typhus serum, are products of civilization. The use of an airplane for the transportation of anti-typhus serum in an epidemic, the use of a fountain pen for signing a check for the benefit of a charitable institution, are manifestations of culture.

In the sense of the foregoing, the Arabs have built up a flourishing civilization, actually one of the greatest of all time. They have also accumulated a highly evolved culture. We have seen that in its *ethnic* sense the term "Arab" applies solely to the Bedouin of the Arabian Desert. In addition, two centuries after its foundation, the huge Arab empire had already disintegrated. But the collective personality of the Arabic-speaking world survived the political changes, because the criterion of a collective personality, of a civilization — common tradition — was never extinguished.

That common tradition is deeply rooted in, and conditioned by, Islam. Since culture is wholly a spiritual condition, it is natural that Arab culture also should have sprung from the religion of the Arabs. So, both their civilization and their culture have been decisively conditioned and shaped by their faith.

And here we come to the fundamental difference between the Occidental and the Oriental, including the Moslem.

In the West the average person's daily occupations, social, hygienic, and other activities, are totally independent of religious views or the tenets of religion. In the East, they are conditioned and constantly influenced by religion, by metaphysical concepts. This applies to the primitive and to the advanced Oriental alike, to each in his own way.

A metaphysical outlook — in other words, religion — is a *compartment* of the Occidental's life. With the Oriental, it is the very *basis* of life. To the Westerner, metaphysical beliefs are a *creed*. To the Oriental, they are one uninterrupted *living experience*.

The Oriental is a mystic. The Westerner is a rationalist. He thinks that this renders him superior to the Oriental. Actually, the opposite is true. The average Occidental feels that to be an efficient "realist," a sociable "regular guy," he must repress, or at least limit, his spiritual interests and man's deep-set metaphysical and spiritual yearnings. He is unaware that in the sense in which it is used in "regular guy," "regular" is a synonym for "average," and "average" for "mediocre." As we have said, one compartment of the Westerner's life is religion. The other is Business, with a capital B.

(221)

The first is to be explored Sunday morning, the second during the rest of the week.

One of the direct results of this is that the intellectual and spiritual interests of the Occidental, "if any," seem to conflict with his professional interests. It often seems to him that the time spent on them is stolen from that which should rightfully belong to his professional work. Somehow he feels guilty about them, like a schoolboy playing truant. At best, he fails to detect any connection between his intellectual or spiritual interests and his profession. He cannot see how they could "help him in his job," and looks upon them as a higher kind of hobby. It is this dismal traditional attitude which is primarily responsible for the Occidental's lack of psychic poise and spiritual equilibrium.

Suicide is rare in the East, nervous breakdowns literally unknown. They simply do not occur. The reason is that a "nervous" breakdown, like the state of mind leading to suicide, has nothing to do with the nervous system. The nervous system is made up of neurons, nerve fibers, not of thoughts, thought habits, states of mind, aspects of morale. The nervous breakdown, a form of *psychosis* restricted to, and endemic in, the West, especially in America, is a state of psychic collapse, the victory of a fear complex over the normal "morale complex."

The Westerner becomes a victim of this form of psychosis because, having unconsciously, but methodically, repressed or segregated his spiritual and metaphysical leanings, he has no metaphysical beliefs strong enough to support him when his accumulated, self-fabricated fears threaten to overcome him. Nor has he then the support, or even the consolation, of spiritual interests other than metaphysical. He cannot even use them as vehicles for psychic escape. He had drawn the color line against them. Now, he has no power to summon them when they are needed.

The Oriental's position is fundamentally different. To him, his metaphysical beliefs are the key to every aspect of life — the professional, recreational, intellectual, spiritual. The average Moslem achieves this simply by following the tenets of Islam. Islam is much more than a religion. It is a complete system of life, ethics, social organization and social contact, including etiquette. Many of its rules are laid down, not in the Koran, but in *hadith*, a voluminous collection of actual and reputed sayings of the Prophet. Islam underlies jurisprudence, science, art, philosophy, and every other major activity of a Moslem community and individual. Orthodox Islam represents theology in the form of a complete code for both secular and spiritual life. So, the *average* Moslem lives inside his *theology*.

The *advanced* Moslem lives inside his *religion*.

We constantly confound theology and religion. Actually, theology is an intellectual system of rules and iron-bound dogmas, projected onto religion, which is a system of metaphysical concepts that transcend the intellect. Theology is a rationalistic stockade of man-made regulations and taboos, inside which we try to corral the Deity. Theology tries to put a harness of scholastic thought, of logic, upon that all-embracing, indivisible, cosmic thought-process, Universal Mind, which is above logic, and which we have no reason not to call the Deity.

Both the average and the advanced Oriental have much more integrated personalities than have Westerners of a corresponding social or intellectual level. The *simple* Moslem sees Allah's will in everything. Therefore, he is free from the fear of things that usually do not come, anyway. He believes in Kismet, in Destiny. He is a stoic. He is just as active as the Occidental, and just as shrewd in business. Try to buy a carpet in an Eastern bazaar, and you will see whether a stoic cannot be a supersalesman. But when that supersalesman is faced with real or fancied disaster, he suffers no nervous breakdown, is not a suicide. Allah willed it so. He begins life anew.

The truly *advanced* type of Oriental strives after the highest goal of every major Eastern religion, which was also the goal of the stoic school of philosophy in ancient Greece and Rome. He systematically trains his mind to achieve what the ancient stoics called *ataraxeia*, what the Buddhist calls *nirvana*, the Hindu Vedantist *jivân mûkti* or *kaïvalya*, the Sufi Moslem *fahnah* — *self-induced liberation*. Liberation of the mind from self-made misery. It is achieved by the recognition that *happiness* is not a matter of "good luck," wealth, or money, but simply *a spiritual state*, characterized by the absence of suffering.

Suffering is a product of autosuggestion. What goes on round you is beyond your control. *Your reaction to it is inside your control.* Hence the enlightened soul, having become familiar with the mechanics of the mind, rises above its own mind, ceases to fabricate those autosuggestions which are the cause of suffering and misery.

This is not as difficult as it sounds. It is achieved through the gradual reintegration of the personality. This, in turn, is obtained through the co-ordination of the daily round of activities with one's metaphysical beliefs and spiritual interests, by ceasing to look upon any of these fields as a separate compartment of life.

Psychologically and spiritually, the liberation of the soul from self-made misery results in that permanent state of serenity which the Christian mystic calls the "peace that passeth understanding." It is characteristic of the spiritually advanced type of Moslem and of spiritually advanced Orientals generally. The average Occidental visitor in the East confounds this state of mind with apathy, with inability to act with energy. Nothing could be more remote from the truth. Haste, the Westerner's permanent companion, is the manifestation not of energy but of nervous tension. Nervous tension, the Occidental's deadly enemy, is the result of anxiety.

Conversely, absence of anxiety leads to the absence of nervous tension. The resultant serenity, absence of fear and worry, not only prolongs life but gives the mind a chance to reflect, to draw on intuition, to unfold. Says an Arabic proverb: "Haste comes from Satan."

The serenity of the average Moslem comes from his *aslamah*, his "surrender" to his personal concept of the Deity, which is actually his surrender to *Theology, as a comprehensive code for secular and spiritual life.* By contrast, the serenity of the advanced Moslem thinker is due to the thoroughly conscious identification of his self with that higher Self, the World Soul, the pantheistic concept of a Universal Mind, in Arabic, *el ahkyl el kully*.

സ   സ   സ

In the light of the foregoing we begin to understand why "Oriental" and "Occidental" are psychologic, not ethnic or geographic concepts. Geographically, the European would be an Oriental to the American. Psychologically, he is in one category with him.

We begin also to understand why it is that Islam has such a deep hold upon its followers, be they humble souls or advanced thinkers. Nothing could be more significant in this connection than the amazing fact that today, when the overwhelming majority of Moslem are politically under the domination of Christian powers, Islam should continue to be by far the most effective proselyting religion. The number of Chinese, South Sea Islanders and other people whom Christian missionaries convert each year is small compared to the hundreds of thousands, chiefly in Africa, who, year by year, voluntarily become Moslem. There are several Moslem missionary societies in the East, especially in Egypt. No temporal power is behind them. On the other hand, the Christian missionary has the unrestricted support of his government. Yet Islam continues its march, which it began thirteen centuries ago. What are the reasons for this?

We have seen what comprehensive guidance in every phase and aspect of life the Moslem derives from his faith. Another reason is Islam's freedom from social stratification. In India, the Moslem convert is automatically liberated from the caste system, he is treated as an equal by his fellow Moslem, because Islam knows no castes. In Africa, when the Negro tribesman becomes a Christian, he still is a Negro to the whites, a social pariah, relegated to manual labor, excluded from higher education. On the other hand, Islam knows no color line. The Negro convert to Islam is a Moslem, the equal of all other Moslem. He is accepted in every Moslem school, all professions are open to him if he shows ability. On his pilgrimage to Mecca he meets in the holy city fellow Moslem from the most remote parts of the globe. Malays, and Moros from the Philippines, meet mountaineers from Bosnia and Albania; full-blooded Negro tribesmen from the heart of Africa pray, eat, live, side by side with the highly cultured Moslem of Syria and Egypt. The Moroccan Berber warrior meets the Moslem Ph.D. from Delhi or Peshawar, the Afghan merchant from Kabul, and the Chinese Moslem scholar from Sin-kiang. There are no social barriers inside Islam. Many Negro slaves have become generals, viziers, Grand Viziers. During my residence in Aleppo, Syria's largest city, I knew several Negroes who held commissions in the Turkish army, commanding *white* troops. At the same period, a Negro was the head of Aleppo's excellent school of handicrafts — whose teachers and students were exclusively white.

It is worthy of note that several Occidentals of the highest intellectual and spiritual level have become Moslem, by no means merely in order to be able to visit Mecca, or study Islam at close range. Among these are the famed British explorer, Harry St. John Philby, who traveled extensively in Arabia, especially in Saudi Arabia; Professor Snouck Hurgronje, celebrated Dutch Orientalist; and Professor Julius Germanus, one of Europe's leading specialists on Islam, who assumed the Moslem name "Abdulkarim" and made the pilgrimage to Mecca, thereby acquiring the coveted title of *hajj*.

The *voluntary* conversion of a Moslem to Christianity, Judaism, or any other religion is extremely rare. Having seen how and why Islam has such a firm hold upon its followers, we should have no cause for surprise.

At the time when slavery still was general in Islam, the status of the slave in Moslem society differed from that of his brother in the West, including America. We have seen that a liberated slave often attained to the highest office in the state. In Egypt, for about three centuries, ex-slaves actually ruled the country as Sultans. This was the famous "Mameluk" dynasty. Actually, the word is *mamlook*, which means "he who is owned."

The Prophet taught that one of the most effective ways of atoning for sin, and one of the actions Allah likes most, is the liberation of slaves. In Islam, from its very beginnings, a slave woman who had a child from her master could no longer be sold or otherwise alienated. The child of such a slave mother was free. No such humane custom existed in our own slavery days in America.

In order to show to what extent the established customs of Islam dominate every aspect of the life of the faithful, I do not consider it an improper anticlimax to refer to certain hygienic usages that are seldom mentioned. The married Moslem woman depilates her *mons veneris*. This habit came to Islam from the Byzantines, who had it from the ancient Greeks and Romans, as every Greek or Roman statue of a nude woman, in contrast to statues of nude men, proves. Nobody can deny the hygienic advantages of the habit.

Islam knows another habit of even greater hygienic significance. The Moslem of the old school washes his rectum after defecating. He uses only his left hand for the purpose. Consequently, it is exceedingly bad form among Moslem people to use the left hand for the *temenna*, the traditional Moslem form of greeting. Hemorrhoids are almost unknown in the Arab world. This is a direct consequence of the habit I have just referred to. In fact, Dr. Ladislas Lenhossek, well-known professor of anatomy at one of Europe's leading universities a generation ago, used to recommend to his students to follow up the usual cleaning process employed after defecating by washing their rectum. He rightly asserted that this was an almost infallible method to prevent hemorrhoids.

Here then, for a change, we encounter a very prosaic but very useful habit that the West can learn from Islam. Said the Prophet: "Cleanliness is a part of religion." Said the ancient Romans: "What is natural cannot be vile."

∽   ∽   ∽

From the very beginning, the Arab empire had direct relations with four major civilizations: the Chinese, the Indian, the Byzantine, and the Sassanid Persian. Its contact with India and China was close and intense. Travel and trade with these countries were operated on regular schedules. Hindu teachers stood in high favor at Baghdad's famed university.

Byzantine civilization was a direct continuation of the Greek, under a thin veneer of Christian doctrine. Egypt and Syria were Byzantine provinces when the Arabs conquered them in the first half of the seventh century. Only a hundred years earlier had Emperor Justinian of Byzantium abolished the great and glorious Academy of

Athens, a bulwark of Greek education ever since the days of Plato, nine centuries before.

The Sassanid Persian Empire had been a revival of the ancient Achaemenid. Aside from its lofty metaphysical system, based upon the Zoroastrian teachings, the neo-Persian Empire had been heir to high artistic traditions, originally evolved from the Babylonian civilization.

On the other hand, the Bedouin Semites who had conquered the gigantic region between Gibraltar, India and China brought with them three principal intellectual and spiritual assets. One was a keen, virginal intelligence, waiting for outlets of a constructive nature. The other was the tremendous spiritual momentum of religious enthusiasm, intensified by an all-embracing religious system. The third asset was an innate gift for poetry, for the beauty and power of thought and speech, with the resultant general appreciation of intellectual and spiritual interests. With the exception of an amazingly advanced poetic literature, the desert Arab had no literary, technical, scientific or artistic accomplishments of his own to look back upon. But he had a tremendous respect for them, and so, as an empire builder, something to look forward to.

All parts of the Moslem world stood in closest cultural and commercial contact with one another, so that every major cultural achievement soon became the common property of the faithful everywhere. As a result, inside a century the world of Islam became the crucible and the vehicle of one of the most important civilizations and cultures the world has ever seen. With the major phases of Moslem conquest completed, the Arabs' tremendous collective urge for self-realization, now given creative outlets, blossomed forth in a rich harvest of technical, scientific, industrial, economic, social, hygienic, literary, artistic and philosophical achievements. They laid the direct foundations for our present culture and civilization in the West.

The Arab's principal points of contact with the West were Spain, Sicily, Asia Minor, and at the time of the Crusaders also Syria and Palestine. As indicated in earlier chapters, there were long periods of peaceful political and economic contact between the Moslem world and the Crusader states which flourished for about two centuries in the Levant.

The culture and civilization that Spain and Portugal possess today are almost entirely of Moslem origin. Through the conquistadors, many features of Moslem civilization were brought to the Americas. Life in South and Central America, including Mexico, and to a great extent also in the United States, is influenced by Arab culture and civilization. Only thirty years before the conquest of Mexico, Granada still was a flourishing Moslem state. Like the Spaniards of today the conquistadors were racially a mixture of Berber and Arab blood, with a small dash — hardly more than 10 per cent — of the Visigothic and Ibero-Roman. While speaking Spanish and professing the Christian faith, these men, like their present-day successors in Spain and Portugal, were unconsciously, but very definitely, Moslem in many an aspect of their lives, in their proverbs, social habits, even gestures and manner of speech. Even today, to an observant traveler familiar with the world of Islam, the inhabitants of the Iberian Peninsula reveal themselves as people of Arab-Berber blood and largely Moslem mentality and habits.

As a matter of fact, from our own contact with Mexicans, and the one-time Mexicans of Texas, California, and our Southwest, we derive numerous Arab-Moslem habits, hitherto perhaps never recorded. They clearly stand out from the general Europeo-Anglo-Saxon background of our North American civilization. We shall see some of them later.

As early as the eighth century of our era, Moslem culture and civilization had become fully manifest. They reached their climax in the ninth and tenth centuries. Where was the West then? Our "dark Middle Ages" had not even begun! The Occident was as yet a cultural desert, inhabited mostly by nameless savages, ruled over by a few sanguinary kings. The howling savagery of heretic- and witch-burning, of the unchecked domination of nobles and kings over the social structure, was only to come! No contrast could be greater than the methodical suppression of free thought and research in medieval Europe and their enthusiastic encouragement in the Arab world both in the Middle Ages and later. To be sure, there are fanatics in every human community, whether Christian or Moslem. But it is a simple fact that, in diametrical contrast to conditions in the Christian world, opposition to advanced thought in Islam was mostly casual and unorganized. The rule was tolerance.

This tolerance was partly due to the characteristic fact that many Caliphs, especially those of Baghdad and Córdoba, were liberals even in matters of religion. Many among these men held the fanatics inside the community and priesthood in check and encouraged free thought not only in matters of science, literature and the arts, but in the field of religion itself. No Inquisition, no methodical heretic-hunting, beclouded Islam's civilization. The matter of witches never even arose.

The great Caliph Mamun, who ruled in Baghdad in the ninth century, a son of the more celebrated though much less great Harun-er-Rashid, was a religious freethinker. When he appointed a Christian as the *shaykh* — today we should say "president" — of a famous college in Damascus, he said to his critics: "I have appointed this learned man to guide me in matters of science, not of religion." Picture a Moslem President of a Christian college either in the medieval or in the contemporary West!

XIV

OUR DEBT
TO ARAB CIVILIZATION

𝒯HE ARABIC language
still spans an enormous territory. The Koran was its
principal vehicle. Every Moslem reads the Koran in
Arabic. The Turkish translation of the Koran is a very
recent venture, initiated by the late Kemal Ataturk,
founder of the new Turkey. In some form or other,
Arabic is actually spoken in Iraq, Palestine, Syria, Egypt,
Malta, North Africa, Nigeria, the Sudan, the western
Sahara, the island of Zanzibar off the east coast of Africa,
and even in parts of East Africa.

Arabic was the language of the Balearic Islands and
Sicily until the end of Arab domination in those regions.
Up to the eighteenth century, it was spoken on the island
of Pantelleria, situated between Tunis and Sicily, and
the scene of an Allied naval operation in the Second
World War.

The Arabic script was gradually developed from the
Phoenician of the eighth and ninth pre-Christian centuries. It is used in a number of non-Arabic languages,
just as many non-Romance languages use the Latin
script. Various Berber idioms, Persian, Urdu, are written
in Arabic characters. Until Kemal Ataturk's reforms,

(235)

enacted in the nineteen-twenties, the Turks also used the Arabic script.

Calligraphy is actually one of the fine arts among the Arabs. In its zeal in fighting idolatry, orthodox Islam forbids the reproduction of human or animal forms. Shiite Persia, almost always in opposition to the rest of the Moslem world, disregards this rule, and Persian miniatures, whose style is influenced by Chinese and Indian art, are famous. But on occasion, Sunnite Moslem also have disregarded the prohibition of sculpturing or painting man or beast. In Granada's fabulous Alhambra I have seen frescoes picturing kings of Granada. These paintings hail from the fourteenth century, and in artistic advancement surpass most Western paintings of the same period, which still struggle against the stiffness of Gothic concepts of art.

In Moslem architecture, calligraphy has become a major decorative element. It was and still is generally used on walls, where it is combined with the other, geometric and floral ornamental elements so characteristic of the Moslem style. One of the ancient forms of Arabic script, often used in this way, is the *kûfi*. With its angular lines, it is particularly fitted for decorative purposes.

The influence of the Arabic language upon other tongues is proportionate to the influence of Arab civilization and culture upon other nations and communities, including Christianity. In Turkish, practically every single abstract word is borrowed from the Arabic, if not from the Persian, just as the West borrows practically every abstract and scientific term from the Latin and Greek. But our Western languages also contain many words of whose Arabic origin we are totally unaware. To quote a couple at random, no one would think that our word "hazard" comes from the Spanish *el azar*, which, in turn, comes from the Arabic *es-zar*, meaning "a die." And indeed, to their grief, the West and the East alike know the close relationship between dice and hazards. The original meaning of our word "magazine," of course, is that of a warehouse, or a receptacle for military stores. In French, *magasin* means "a store." The word comes from the Arabic *al-masen*, also meaning "a store or storehouse."

Spanish, of course, teems with words directly borrowed from the Arabic. Moreover, hundreds of geographic names inside the Iberian Peninsula have simply retained their Arabic form, sometimes slightly altered. Various Spanish cities, such as Seville, Segovia, Toledo, and others, have their "alcázar." "Alcázar" is a corruption of *al qasr* — Arabic for "fortress." *Alcalde*, the Spanish word for "mayor," is the Arabic *al kaïd*, meaning "the chief of a tribe or of an administrative district."

In order properly to evaluate Arab-Moslem civilization and culture at its peak, in the ninth and tenth centuries, we must realize that at that time no city in Europe, except Constantinople, had more than thirty thousand inhabitants. In the West, everybody except a handful of monks and laymen was illiterate. There were no higher schools, no hospitals. Cities were unpaved and had no sewer systems. Soap was unknown. Even kings and high nobles seldom took a bath, and owned only one or two washable undergarments of linen. Politically and socially, anarchy reigned in Europe. The Vikings and Danes ravaged England. The Normans had turned France into a shambles.

At this time, Baghdad, Damascus, Córdoba, and later Cairo, were big cities. Baghdad and Córdoba vied with each other, and at various periods Córdoba outshone even Baghdad. In the tenth century, Córdoba, seat of Abd-er-Rahman III, who had proclaimed himself Caliph, had half a million inhabitants, and Moslem Spain thirty million. Córdoba had three hundred public baths, more than a dozen colleges, at which theology, philosophy, medicine, jurisprudence, and other branches of science were taught. Not only was the overwhelming majority of the population of Moslem Spain literate, but collecting books had become a hobby among the rich and poor alike. From China, the Arabs introduced paper to Europe. In Syria, they built several paper mills. The Arabs of Spain also had several, the largest being at Xátiva. The Cordovese Caliph, Al Hakim, sent scholars to all parts of the Moslem world, including Iraq, Syria, Persia and northern India, to have all major scientific and literary works copied. Over eighty thousand shops flanked Córdoba's paved streets. The city had more than a score of public libraries. The rich vied with the Caliph in building up large private libraries. Some of the latter actually contained more than a hundred thousand volumes, one had more than four hundred thousand. Even three hundred years later, the Canterbury Library, then the largest in England, was made up of 698 volumes.

Not only were the streets of Córdoba paved but they were regularly flushed from oxcarts, and lighted by lamps attached to the outer walls of the houses. The Caliph's palace in the Cordovese suburb of Madinat-es-Zahra has been described in detail by contemporary travelers, and must have been one of the wonders of the world.

The typical Arab house was and still is a modification of the ancient Roman. An open court, which the Romans called *atrium*, is surrounded by the living rooms, the Roman *cubiculae*, which open onto the court. The center of the court is not roofed. A basin in the middle catches the rain water, and is usually adorned with a fountain. This court is the famed patio of "Spanish," actually Arab, architecture. The luxurious homes of the well-to-do on our West Coast, built in the "neo-Mexican" style, are simply replicas of Arab houses.

Soap was invented by the Arabs, and one traveler reports that in Moslem Spain poor people spent their pennies on soap rather than on food. That every wealthy person's house had its own bathroom has already been mentioned. Similar conditions existed in Baghdad and Cairo. Like Córdoba, Cairo, Damascus and Baghdad each had several colleges. The first actual university in Islam, a methodical co-ordination of a number of colleges, with a systematized curriculum, was founded in Baghdad in 1065. It was richly endowed by the Abassid Caliphs. Maintenance was provided for both teachers and students.

There is a detailed record of a hospital for the poor being inaugurated in Baghdad in 918 A.D. The chronicler mentions the amount of its monthly endowment from the Caliph's treasury. It corresponded to about fifteen hundred dollars in our money. Another hospital had a staff of twenty-four physicians. A hundred years later, Baghdad had six thousand medical students and nine hundred physicians. Another hundred years later Damascus had a big medical school directly attached to its central hospital. At this time, the principal hospital in Cairo had buildings that surrounded four large courts, provided musicians for the amusement of the patients, and paid five gold pieces to each poor patient who left the institution, in order to help him tide over the period of convalescence.

Some of the most important mosques of the early Arab period still stand. In beauty, the famed mosques of Damascus, Jerusalem and Córdoba lead the rest. The first, built by the Omayyad Caliphs of Damascus, shows a splendor and perfection that make it a famous landmark. Equally famous is the Mosque of Omar in Jerusalem. The great Mosque of Córdoba, however, can be called one of the wonders of the world. It was begun by the great Abd-er-Rahman I, enlarged and completed by his successors. The visitor finds himself in a forest of columns, with the light throwing intricate patterns upon them and upon the three gloriously beautiful *mihrab*, or prayer niches. In accordance with Moslem custom, these niches face the direction of Mecca. They are covered with designs of subtlest charm and artistry, executed in gold mosaic.

Inside the mosque, which the Spanish conquerors of Córdoba turned into a cathedral, there stands the wonderful chapel of Ferdinand of Castile, Christian conqueror of Moslem Córdoba. It was built and decorated by Moslem architects and artists, entirely in the Arab style. The rulers of the various Christian states that later existed side by side with the minor Arab kingdoms in the Spanish peninsula regularly employed Moslem artists and architects. This Moslem art applied to Christian religious and secular uses is known in Spain as *mudéjar* art. The famous Alcázar of Seville, which still stands, is a masterpiece of such *mudéjar* architecture, having been built by Moslem architects and craftsmen for the Christian king, Peter the Cruel of Castile, in the fourteenth century.

Some elements of the style which has become typical of Moslem-Arab architecture were derived from Achaemenid Persian art by way of the Sassanid Persian, which was a revival of the former. To this category belongs the famed stalactite pattern, sculptured around arches and the upper parts of alcoves and recesses. The *ajímez*, or twin window, so characteristic of Arab art, also comes from the Sassanid. The religious taboo on paintings and statuary directed the attention of the Moslem architect to the decorative side of art. Three decorative elements cover the walls of mosques and secular buildings. One is decorative script. Usually, it reproduces passages from the Koran. The second element is the arabesque, a name clearly indicating its Arab origin. It is usually a composition of flower designs. The third is the *entrelac*, made up of interlacing geometric designs. It is difficult to imagine the wonderful effects achieved by the combined use of these three motifs in such fairylike specimens of Arab architecture as the Alhambra of Granada, the Alcázar of Seville, and the tombs of the Sa'adite Sultans in Marrakesh.

To this must be added the copious use of the glazed tile. We have seen that it was popular in the neo-Babylonian Empire, and also generally used by the ancient Persians, the Parthians, and the Sassanid Persians. The Arabs perfected this industry, gave it favored application in their religious and secular architecture, brought it to Europe through Sicily, and especially through Spain. The general use of glazed tiles in contemporary Spain, Portugal, and Latin America, including our own "neo-Spanish" or "neo-Mexican" houses, is a direct heritage from the Arabs.

Arab architecture has had a profound influence upon the Christian. The Gothic arch was inspired by it. The Tudor style, our conventional style for college buildings in America, and once in wide use at Oxford, Cambridge, and everywhere in England, is derived from the

Arab. It represents a methodical application of the so-called Cluny style. But the monks of the famed French monastery of Cluny had originally come to France from Spain. Many of these monks were architects. They borrowed and slightly modified some basic elements of Arab architecture. One was the flame-shaped arch, later known as the "Cluny" arch. Another was the *ajímez*, or twin window, consisting of two narrow windows set side by side and separated by a narrow strip of masonry. A third Arab element borrowed by the Cluny architects was the elaborate interlaced design of the upper parts of the windows. So the Tudor style, and its direct source, the Cluny style, are basically Arab. So is the so-called "flaming Gothic," which is actually another name for the Cluny-Tudor style. So is the more elaborate, decorative plateresque style, which became fashionable in Spain around 1500, less than ten years after the fall of Moslem Granada. It is mainly a combination of the Arab-inspired, pointed, flame-shaped arch with rich sculptured arabesque designs. The so-called churrigueresque style, "invented" a hundred years later, around 1600, by the Spanish architect Churriguera, carries the combination of the plateresque style with the arabesque and *entrelac* to excess. The "Spanish baroque," in its turn, is a combination of these Arab decorative elements with the European baroque. In each instance, most of the dominant elements of the style are Arab.

The plateresque and churrigueresque styles subsequently became very popular in Spanish colonial America. Many churches in Mexico offer gorgeous examples for these styles. Unique in this connection is the façade of the church of Acatepec, just off the road from Mexico City to Puebla. Its churrigueresque style, combined with yellow, green and blue glazed tiles, which cover the whole façade, is a riot of decoration and color in its exotic, exaggerated application of basically Arab elements.

Both the round and the pointed forms of the "horse-shoe" arch, and the arch forming more than a semicircle, with its various modifications, also are typical elements of Arab architecture. Many among Venice's beautiful private palaces are decisively influenced by this style, which originally came to Italy from Moslem Sicily. The façade of the celebrated Cà d'Oro, the "Golden House," one of the jewels of Venice's Grand Canal, is a particularly effective combination of Arab decorative elements. We have seen that almost all synagogues in the West are built in the Arab style.

οↄ   οↄ   οↄ

It was said earlier in this book that the commerce, crafts, arts, industries, and agriculture of Spain had been created by the Arabs, the Jews, the *conversos* or forcibly converted Jews, and the Moriscos or forcibly converted Moslem. We contended that the Spaniards were mainly warriors. Surely, then, at least such characteristics of the medieval Western warrior as the higher type of horsemanship, and the institution and the tradition of knighthood, must be chalked to the credit of the West?

No, it must be chalked to the credit of the Arabs. Knighthood is a Moslem Arab invention. So is the *haute école*, the art of superior horsemanship. So, as we shall see later, is even the famed medieval Christian institution of the troubadour.

The Arab horse has retained its world fame. Along with the art of horse breeding, the Arabs developed the art of horsemanship. It was Charles V of Habsburg, inside whose empire the sun never set, who rescued the traditions of Arab horsemanship from oblivion in the Christian world. He transferred some of the masters of this art from Spain to Austria. Later, the Habsburgs organized the famous stud of Lippizan, south of Vienna, where the noblest strain of Arab horses is bred to this day. These famous white stallions are used in the equally famous "Spanish Riding School" of Vienna, until recently one of the Austrian capital's greatest attractions. But as we have seen, its name should be actually "Arab Riding School."

To this day, the Arabs are masters of equestrianism. The Arab rides stallions only. He has no geldings, and mares are reserved for breeding. The Arab horse has an amazing degree of intelligence, is lively and nervous but exceedingly good-natured. In battle, it will not desert its fallen or wounded rider. It often follows its master like a dog.

The three widely celebrated specialties of Vienna's "Spanish" Riding School, which never failed to impress the tourist, are known as the levade, the piaffe, and the capriole. In the first, the horse rests on its hind legs, sitting up in a way that recalls the rabbit and the squirrel. In the second, it jumps up vertically to a height of some three feet, without taking a run. In the capriole, this trick is combined with a violent kick while the horse is in mid-air.

Each of these tricks is of Arab origin. In fact, the capriole was more than a mere trick. It is unknown to our contemporary experts on equestrianism, including the members of Vienna's Spanish Riding School itself, that it originally served a military purpose with the Arabs. The Arab cavalry used it when fighting infantry at close quarters. It is easy to imagine the effect of the capriole if we realize that in combat the Arab horseman would occasionally turn his mount round, performing the capriole that way. Those terrible kicks at the height of the adversary's chest or stomach must have simply mowed down the enemy's infantry.

When I first rode a horse in the Moslem East, I was surprised to see that it constantly tried to fall into a gait that I had not known before. It would touch the ground with three hooves at a time, which seemed to tire the animal much less than the gallop. Later, I found that this gait, known to the Arab as *rakhwan*, is generally used for long-distance travel in Arab countries. It is totally unknown in Europe. Characteristically, it is widely used in our American West and Southwest, and is known as the "lope." How is it that the lope is unknown in Europe but popular in America? Because the lope — more precisely, the Arab *rakhwan* — was brought to the Americas by the conquistadors. They had it direct from the Arabs of Spain, still masters of Granada when many of Cortéz' men were boys. The *charro*, the Mexican equivalent for our cowboy, brought the *rakhwan* to Texas, California, Arizona, New Mexico. With our acquisition of these regions, it automatically became an "American" gait. This is why the lope, completely forgotten in Europe, flourishes only in the Arab world and in America.

The idea and ideals of knighthood came to Europe from Arab Spain, and from Moslem Syria, through the Crusaders. The nobles in the petty duchies and kingdoms that had survived the Arab conquest in the north of Spain took the institution over from the Arabs. From Spain, it spread to the South of France, thence to the rest of Christendom.

The knightly tournament, including the joust, is an Arab invention. In Spain, Moslem women were not veiled and enjoyed greater freedom than their sisters elsewhere in Islam. Long before knighthood became known in Christian Europe, the Arabs of Spain had their tournaments, with the spectators sitting round a ring. The women of the upper classes sat in the front rows. On his blunted lance, the Arab cavalier carried a scarf in his lady's favorite color, and the tilting was done in honor of the combatants' chosen ladies. The Arab knights wore coats of chain armor, and over them tunics, or surcoats, of crimson or blue velvet, embroidered in gold. This later became the regulation uniform of Europe's Christian knights.

These Arab cavaliers indulged also in a relatively humane kind of bullfighting, which has survived in a specific form in Spain and Portugal. In Spain, it is known as the *corrida real*, or "royal corrida." The Arabs had no professional bullfighters, no *picadores*, *banderilleros*, or *espadas*. The bull was not tortured as it is today. It was met in the ring by a superbly mounted cavalier with a short, heavy spear in his right hand. The sport consisted of allowing the bull to charge the rider, then, through sheer horsemanship, making it miss him by inches. In this, closest co-operation between the highly trained horse and its rider was indispensable. But the Arab stallion, more intelligent than the best-trained polo pony, was fully aware of the nature and spirit of the game, and thoroughly enjoyed it.

I have seen this type of bullfight in Portugal. There was no doubt about the horse's conscious participation in it. The stallion taunted the bull on its own account, by prancing in front of it, then side-stepped its charge with the skill of a trained boxer. The horses used for the *corrida real* and its Portuguese replica are not blindfolded. They are of the choicest breeds, often worth a fortune. In this type of bullfight the horse is almost never killed or hurt, so accomplished is its master's horsemanship and its own co-operation with him. The bull is painlessly killed through a thrust with the *rejón,* the short spear, into its medulla oblongata, the posterior part of the brain forming the direct continuation of the spinal cord. In the Portuguese version of the *corrida real,* the bull is not killed, and no blood shed. The greatest master of this more sportsmanlike Portuguese form of bullfighting in our generation is Simão da Veiga, a worthy disciple of the Arab art of superior horsemanship.

The origin of our religious orders of knighthood also goes back to the Moslem world. They were slightly modified Christian replicas of such religious fighting confraternities as the Almoravides of Morocco and Spain in the tenth and eleventh centuries. A late Moslem revival of this institution was the dervish army of the Sudan, which fought the British under the leadership of its Mahdi. We shall see later that the institution and the poetry of the troubadours also are an Arab heritage of the Christian world.

Military science is another among our Arab heritages. Moslem Granada of the thirteenth century had a full-fledged war college, where the military sciences were taught in a regular curriculum. In 1325, at the siege of Baza, the Moslem army of Granada used a device which "threw big balls of iron and stone over long distances amidst flames and smoke" — possibly some precursor of the cannon. It has long been established that gunpowder was first invented in China, and that its invention was gradual, the discovery going through various stages. We have seen the permanent and close commercial and intellectual relations between Islam and China, millions among whose inhabitants still are Moslem.

We may also recall from former chapters the perfection which Arab military architecture reached in such structures as the citadels of Aleppo, in Syria, and Almeria, in Spain. There can be little doubt that Vauban, famed military architect of Louis XIV, had studied Arab military architecture. The basic architectural elements of his fortifications — the escarp, the *contreescarpe*, and the *glacis* — are modifications of Arab originals. Even some of our present-day military terms show our Arab education in military matters. Thus, "arsenal" is the Arabic *dar-es-sanah*, meaning "house of industry."

Pigeons as a medium for conveying military information and urgent mail were methodically used by Egypt's *mamlook*, or "Mameluk" Sultans. The most elaborate records were kept of the pedigrees of these birds.

We shall see presently that the basis of our knowledge of navigation also comes from the Arabs. So does even the title "Admiral." Its original form, as used in Christendom, was the French, which is *amiral*. But *amiral* is merely the arbitrarily amputated Arabic term, *ameer-al-bakhr*, with the *bakhr*, which means "sea," lopped off. The meaning of *ameer-al-bakhr* is "commander of the sea."

Our Debt to Arab Civilization

The most coveted possession of a Christian knight was an Arab sword of Toledo or Damascus make. The Arabs brought the fabrication of steel to a high degree of perfection. The damascene and Toledo blades are famed to this day. But Arab industry embraced other fields also. Brass and copper ware, richly inlaid with gold and silver, still is a familiar feature of Moslem craftsmanship, and has survived as an industry in Toledo and other one-time centers of Moslem civilization. We have seen how the industry of glazed tiles had been perfected by the Arabs. Incidentally, our word "majolica" for a fine, soft, enameled kind of pottery comes from the name of the Balearic island of Majorca, for centuries a dependency of Arab Spain, where Moslem artists and craftsmen had introduced the art of making glazed pottery. Specimens of early Moslem glazed pottery, with its beautiful iridescent tints, are among the most treasured objects of our museums.

Italy introduced the glazed tile from Moslem Sicily. One Italian industrial center which later specialized in it was the city of Faenza, which gave its name to faïence. Dutch merchants brought this Moslem art to Holland, where Delft became a famed center of the industry. The conquistadors brought it to the Americas.

The Oriental carpet, a typical product of Moslem lands, still is the most distinguished feature of the cultured Western and Eastern home. Throughout Iran, Iraq, Syria, Turkey, and North Africa, carpet weaving still is a flourishing industry. Unfortunately, the old, mellow vegetable dyes now are almost generally replaced by aniline dyes from the West. Originally, carpet weaving was an accomplished art in Sassanid Persia, where the Arabs learned it following their conquest of the country. Subsequently, they introduced the carpet to the Western world.

The textiles of the Arabs still arouse the admiration of the West. The word "damask" comes from Damascus, and the fabric so named originally was a product of Syria. The term "muslin" is derived from the name of Mosul, in Iraq, which was one of the original centers of this industry. Taffeta also was originally an Arab product, and its name comes from the Arabic *taftah*. To this day, cordovan is our designation for a particularly fine kind of leather, whose secret came to Christendom through Moslem Córdoba. Morocco also was, and still is, a center of a highly evolved leather industry. Morocco is our name for a particularly fine quality of leather.

In the field of agriculture, the contribution of the Arabs to civilization is unique. They made irrigation a general feature of farming and brought its methods to highest perfection throughout their vast empire. The hills of Andalusia, later left barren by the Spaniard, were terraced and cultivated under the Arabs. At the time of Arab rule, southern Andalusia had three to four crops a year! Today, in poverty-stricken Spain, we find traces of Arab-built dams, six to seven hundred feet long, with reservoirs three miles in circumference. After Spanish religious fanaticism had wiped civilization off the map of the country, they were allowed to crumble.

In Arab Spain, as elsewhere in Islam, irrigation systems included huge water wheels, many of them a hundred feet in diameter. Some such wheels still are in operation at Hama, on the Orontes, in Syria, where they are a famous landmark.

The Arabs introduced to Spain, through Spain to Europe, and through the conquistadors to America, spinach, asparagus, coffee, pomegranates, peaches, almonds, dates, oranges, apricots, bananas, melons. They planted them everywhere, gave regular courses to the farmers on their cultivation. Sugar came to Christendom from Moslem Syria, where the Crusaders first saw sugar cane and its industrial utilization. Before the crusading knights brought sugar back to Europe with them, Occidentals used honey for sweetening their food. The word "sugar" itself is directly derived from the Arabic.

 convo convo convo

In the field of science, our debt to the Arabs is equally great. This is due in great measure to the methodical encouragement of free thought and scientific research by the various Caliphs. One of the most advanced thinkers who ever sat on a throne was the Caliph Mamun, son of Harun-er-Rashid. His name has repeatedly appeared on the pages of this book. He held that all holy scriptures must conform to reason if they are to be followed. In this, he anticipated Rousseau, Voltaire, Thomas Paine, and the Encyclopedists of the West by nine hundred years.

The principal role of Islam in the field of science and secular philosophy was to conserve, consolidate, co-ordinate, and develop further the stock of thought and knowledge that the ancient Greeks and Hindus had accumulated. To this stock, the Arabs added many original achievements of the first magnitude.

We Occidentals owe our numerals to the Arabs. That is why we call them Arabic numerals. Actually, they were brought to Baghdad from India in the late eighth century, and forthwith struck roots throughout Islam. With them, the Arabs brought the decimal system and the concept of "zero" to the West. Without the Arabic numerals and the "zero," we should still be using the abacus, and higher mathematics and algebra would be impossible. Trigonometry is mainly the original creation of the Arabs. So is analytical geometry, and algebra, whose very name is Arabic. The Arabs solved cubic equations by geometric construction. Following their revolutionary achievements in trigonometry, they invented celestial navigation, still the basis of a modern naval officer's training. Even "our" terms, as used in modern navigation — "azimuth, zenith, nadir" — are Arabic. The magnetic needle was discovered in China, but it was the Arabs who adapted it for navigation, inventing the mariner's compass. They invented also the astrolabe.

With the support of the great Caliph Mamun, Arab

mathematicians measured the length of a terrestrial degree. This amazing operation — in the ninth century! — was carried out in western Iraq and the Syrian Desert. They erred by not more than three thousand feet, and *proceeded from the assumption that the earth was a sphere.*

Geography is another field in which the Arabs were prominent. The works of a very great number of Arab travelers and geographers are preserved. Many were translated into Latin for the benefit of the West in the late Middle Ages and during the Renaissance. Ibn Beithar was a famous Arab geographer, a professor at Moslem Granada's celebrated university, which flourished in the thirteenth and fourteenth centuries. Besides, during his many travels he collected also new plants, both for scientific purposes and in order to promote agriculture. Probably the greatest Arab geographer was El Idrissi, who flourished in Palermo, at the court of King Roger II of Sicily, in the twelfth century. Seven centuries before Stanley, he actually located the sources of the Nile as being "on the highlands of Africa." For King Roger, he wrote his famous work on geography. For Roger he made also a terrestrial and celestial planisphere six feet in diameter. *El Idrissi also contended that the earth was round.*

The Egyptian Fatimid Caliph Mo'izz and his son, Al Aziz, paid the equivalent of fifty thousand dollars for a unique map of the world, made in gold embroidery upon a huge sheet of silk. In the tenth century, the royal library in Cairo included almost six thousand works on astronomy and mathematics alone.

In the same century, both Moslem Spain and Moslem Persia had botanical and zoological gardens. Botany and zoology were greatly cultivated among the Arabs. Among the many scientific works on botany, still preserved, one, richly illustrated, runs to fifty volumes. The science of geology also was popular. The famed, great Avicenna, one of the world's greatest physicians and philosophers, whose correct name was Ibn Sina and who flourished in Persia in the eleventh century, wrote also on the formation and classification of minerals. It is practically unknown in the West that Omar Khayyam is even better known to the Moslem world as an astronomer and mathematician than as a poet. But he was also a geologist, and proved that large areas of land had once been covered by the sea!

It has long been known that the works of Roger Bacon were almost entirely based upon Arab works, principally those of the great Arab physicist, Al Kindi. To Bacon's honor be it said that he often openly refers to his Arab sources. In the field of physics, Arab and Persian Moslem scholars published extensive studies on gravitation, capillary attraction, the velocity and weight of bodies. By studying the properties of oscillating bodies, the Arabs discovered the principle of the pendulum clock. Subsequently, they constructed the most intricate clocks of this kind for the various Sultans and Caliphs, and one, which became famous for its beauty and intricacy, for Roger II of Sicily.

Al Hazen laid down the foundations of the science of optics, published amazing results of his observations of the functions of the human eye, and made a relatively good estimate of the height of the earth's atmosphere. He explained twilight by the refraction of light.

There are hundreds of early and later Arabic works on chemistry. The most famous among the many Moslem chemists was "Geber," a Western corruption of the name Jabeer ibn Hayyan, who lived in the eighth century. He was both an alchemist and a scientific chemist, two fields of research which were by no means in conflict. It is said that it was he who discovered nitric and sulphuric acid. Arab chemists and alchemists used such chemical processes as filtration, sublimation, calcination, distillation. They discovered, or invented, alum, borax, silver nitrate, aqua regia, which they used to dissolve gold, and corrosive sublimate. Their achievements form the basis of our present-day chemistry, and the great Western scientific chemists of the eighteenth century merely continued from where the Arabs had left off many hundred years earlier.

Medicine and pharmacology are probably those branches of science in which the Arabs have most decisively influenced our present-day researches. Here it should be mentioned that, as in other fields of Arab science and thought, so also in medicine, hundreds of Jews vied with their Moslem brothers. We have seen that they and the Christians were well treated in Islam. But nowhere did the Jews ever enjoy such a measure of equality and opportunity as inside the Arab civilization. Jews were famed professors at the University of Córdoba, savants in other Moslem centers. They held the posts of viziers to sultans. Several were made ameers, or princes. Jews were highly popular physicians, astronomers, geographers, merchants of repute and great wealth.

The Jewish merchant of Moslem Sicily and Spain was instrumental in spreading Arab culture and civilization to the Christian West. Traveling from Córdoba, Granada or Palermo to the cities of France, England, Germany and Italy, the Jewish merchant brought with him physical and astronomical instruments, Oriental herbs, medical preparations, spices, textiles, weapons and numerous Latin translations of the major Arab works in all fields of science and philosophy.

The methodical translation of thousands of Arabic works was a flourishing industry, and the Jews were both its promoters and the leading translators. In the South of France, many hundred learned Jews, masters of Arabic, Persian, Latin, Greek, Spanish and French, were constantly engaged in translating the latest scientific, philosophical and literary works of the Arabs, and also the work of Jewish philosophers and scientists inside the Arab world, who wrote in both Arabic and Hebrew. Thus, the Jew carried out an important cultural mission as a direct intermediary between the flourishing Arab civilization and the spiritually still barren world of Christendom.

The greatest of all Arab translators was a Nestorian

Our Debt to Arab Civilization

Christian, Hoonayn ibn Ishaq, later known to the West as Joannitius, who lived in Baghdad in the ninth century. He was in official charge of a corps of translators on the Caliph's payroll. Upon the latter's orders, Hoonayn and his assistants translated into Arabic Galen's and Hippocrates' medical works, Plato's *Republic*, and the major works of Aristotle. Hoonayn himself translated the Old Testament into Arabic, using the Greek text of the Septuagint. He was also a prominent physician, and was widely revered for his noble, unselfish character.

We have seen that the Arab world had regularly endowed hospitals almost a thousand years before they became a feature of public life in the West. By preserving the medical knowledge of the Hindus and that of the Greeks, and transplanting both to the West, the Arabs saved the former from isolation, the latter from oblivion. In addition, they themselves brought medicine to an astounding level of development. Scores of names of celebrated Arab physicians still are familiar to the Moslem scholar. Probably the greatest among them was Ar Razi, known to the West as Rhazes, chief physician of Baghdad's great central hospital, who lived in the late ninth century and the early tenth. Instructed by the Caliph to select the site for a new hospital in the city, Ar Razi hung up pieces of meat in various parts of Baghdad, then chose the site where the meat was last to putrefy. He wrote a classic on chemistry, later translated into Latin and considered a standard handbook in

Christian Europe. Roger Bacon quoted copiously from it four centuries later. Ar Razi's treatise on measles and smallpox is a classic in the history of medicine.

Another star on the firmament of Arab medicine was Avicenna, more correctly, Ibn Sina, a scientific and philosophic genius who, as we have seen, lived in Persia in the eleventh century. His medical encyclopedia was the basis of our medical knowledge until the seventeenth century. Maïmonides — Moses ibn Maïmoon — the great Jewish philosopher, was also one of the leading physicians of his century, the twelfth. Born in Arab Spain, he later went to Egypt and became the personal physician of the great Sultan Saladin, Moslem hero of the Crusades. "Averroës," correctly, Ibn Rushd, a Spanish Arab of the twelfth century, who vitally influenced Christian scholastic thought, also was a great physician, besides being one of the greatest philosophers of all time. His teacher in medicine, the famed Ibn Zoohr of Seville, was a celebrated specialist for the treatment of sciatica. *Arab surgeons operated for nine forms of cataract of the eye.*

In many regions of the Arab world, a regular diploma was required for medical practice, and also for the profession of apothecary. The first drugstores and apothecaries' shops were operated in the Arab world. There were many of them in Córdoba, Baghdad, Cairo, and other Moslem cities. The Arabs brought to Europe such drugs as rhubarb, camphor, myrrh, ginger, nux vomica. *They composed the first pharmacopoeia in history.* In his classic on medicine, Avicenna alone enumerates more than seven hundred drugs.

What was, then, the relationship between the Christian precursors of scientific research in the Western world, and the Arabs? We have seen that Roger Bacon, considered the founder of natural science in Europe, owed his knowledge to the Arabs. Gerbert, who later became Pope Sylvester II, preceded Bacon in scientific research. It has been conclusively proved by de la Salle de Rochemaure, Gerbert's biographer, that this highly educated Pope had lived as a boy at the court of the Count of Barcelona, who took him to Moslem Córdoba, where he studied under Arab professors. In his works, Albertus Magnus, the learned German monk of the thirteenth century, constantly refers to more than a half-score Arab writers and scientists, whose books he knew well from Latin translations. And Raymond Lully, the great Catalan chemist and alchemist, philosopher and mystic, was a native of the Balearic Islands, which had been completely Arabicized, and spoke Arabic like an Arab.

ση   ση   ση

There still exist old Arabic scientific works on the theory of music. As regards popular music, including the folk song, with the exception of the Wahhabi sect of Saudi Arabia and some other small groups of Moslem puritans, it played and still plays a major role in the world of Islam. Our lute, on which the troubadours of medieval Europe accompanied their compositions, came from the Arabs, as did the troubadour song itself. Even the word "lute" is Arabic, the original name of the instrument being *al ut*, pronounced "al oot." Al Ghazali, one of Islam's greatest philosophers and intellectual mystics, wrote: —

"To God Most High belongs a secret, consisting in the relationship of measured airs to the souls of men, so that the airs have a wonderful effect upon them. He whom the spring with its blossoms does not move, nor the lute with its strings, is corrupt of nature. There is no cure for him."

And Ali ben Othman: "He who has no pleasure in sounds and melodies and music, is either a liar or a hypocrite, or he is not in his right senses, and is outside the category of men and beasts."

Arab music, and Oriental music generally, is characterized by the principle not of harmony but of rhythm. We have a perfect, unadulterated survival of Arab folksong technique in the Christian world in the form of the so-called *flamenco* singing. The Spaniard calls this form of song *cante jondo*. It still is one of his favorite popular entertainments, as it is in many places in Latin America. The *cante jondo* is sung not "from the diaphragm" but "from the head," in a kind of falsetto. Its lyrics are the so-called *coplas*, short verses, each independent of the rest. They deal mostly with love, and similar aspects of life dear to the optimist, with a little practical philosophy thrown in.

Actually, what the Spaniard calls the *copla* is a typical Arabian poetic form. The particular technique of the "Spanish" *cante jondo* is the classic technique of the Arab song, as still sung from Morocco to India. Another survival of Arab music, this time in a slightly modified form, is the Portuguese technique of popular song, the *fado*. Modern Spanish music, as composed for the orchestra, for chamber music, and also for the zarzuela, Spain's famed popular form of operetta, is largely a direct survival of Arab motifs.

Poetry is nearest to the Arab's heart. We have seen that the illiterate Bedouin of the desert is a born poet. In conversation with these simple and warlike folk, whose daily interests are camel and horse breeding and search for food and loot, the traveler is amazed at the elegance of expression, diction and elocution, the beauty and poetic force of metaphors, quite casually introduced into a trivial phrase. It is as if a stevedore or lumberjack spoke to you in the language of Edgar Allan Poe or Oscar Wilde. There is nothing affected about this. It is age-old Semitic tradition, clearly apparent in David's psalms. King David had the Bedouin Semite's characteristic love for the poetic and musical aspect of speech, coupled with that rhythm which the Semite, and the Oriental in general, *applies to thought and speech* as well as music. This, incidentally, is one of the Oriental's fun-

(263)

damental characteristics. The style and composition of the Old Testament, and of Buddhism's sacred *Dhammapadda*, are cases in point.

The Bedouin still is a creator of impromptu poetry of real merit. Arabic literature can actually boast of hundreds of excellent poets, scores of whom have highest literary value by strictest international standards. There exist great collections of Arabic poetry of the pre-Islamic period. They are known as *diwans*.

During some two hundred years, pre-Islamic poetry was preserved for posterity by wandering bards, the *rahwees*, before being collected in anthologies. The most celebrated form of Bedouin poetry is the *qaseedah*, a highly elaborate ode, usually up to a hundred lines in length. Many *qaseedah* composed by illiterate Bedouin warriors in the sixth and seventh centuries are gems of world literature, incandescent in the combination of beauty and power. Some poets, like the great Antarah ibn Shaddad, who flourished in the sixth century, were simple Bedouin tribesmen. Antarah was the son of a soldier and a Negro slave. Others, like the equally great Ta'abbatah Sharrah, and Shanfarah, were *harameeyah* by profession — highwaymen and outlaws, who composed immortal poetry between attacks on peaceful caravans. Others again were kings and princes. The number of kings, ameers, sultans, and caliphs who were poets in their own right also is indicative of the cultural advancement of the Arab East. Almost the only "literary" products of crowned heads in the West other than Frederick the Great are the *Tales of the Queen of Navarre,* which even Boccaccio might have hesitated to write.

Among the various Arab rulers who were poets of real merit, though not geniuses, we can mention the Omayyad Caliphs Yazid I, who ruled in Damascus in the seventh century, and Walid II, who flourished in the eighth. There were two other royal poets in the Arab world whose works are justly famous. One was King Mutamid of Seville, who lived in the eleventh century. He was important. The other, Amroo'ul Qais, of the sixth century, was a member of the Kinda tribe, of royal blood. He was a genius.

Among Arab poets who rank with our Tennysons, Brownings, Shelleys, and Whitmans is the great Abu'l Ala, a Syrian, still widely famed in Islam, and possibly the most deeply human among the lyric poets of the Arabs. Among the mystic poets, Ibn Farid and Ibn 'Arabi rank foremost. Ibn 'Arabi was born in Moslem Spain and died in the Levant. It is difficult to find in Occidental literature analogies to those flights of the spirit, couched in words of striking beauty and power, that characterize the poems of this genius.

I have already indicated that the troubadour song of the Christian West originally came from the Arabs. Love, the favorite theme of the troubadours, was the favorite subject of many Arabic poems of the early Islamic period. Two great Meccan poets, Omar and Jamil, specialized in love lyrics. Platonic love inspired the works of Majnoon, and of a famous poetess, Lailah. Among the famous poetesses of Moslem Spain were Aïsha and Princess Walladah, both of Córdoba, Algasaniah and Safiyah, both of whom lived in Seville. It was in Arab Spain that the actual lyric of the troubadour type was developed to a high art, and from there it spread to the South of France, thence to the rest of Christian Europe. Its greatest master in Arabic was Ibn Quzman, who flourished in the first half of the twelfth century.

Rhyming prose, known as *maqamah*, is one of the most characteristic of Arab literary inventions. The popular romances and story cycles, such as the famous *Arabian Nights*, do not represent major achievements of Arab literature, although, characteristically, the *Arabian Nights*, largely of Sassanid Persian inspiration, are the best-known product of Arabic literature in the West.

It is noteworthy that as early as the eighth and ninth centuries we find Arabic books on polite education and etiquette. Etiquette is elaborate in the East. The Oriental is instinctively aware that etiquette is actually a ritual, governing man's relations with his fellow men, while ritual is a system of etiquette, governing man's relations with his metaphysical concepts.

The beautiful fables of Bidpai were translated into Western languages, and undoubtedly inspired the great La Fontaine. Experts agree that the first historiographer who deserves that name was an Arab, the great Ibn Khaldoon of Granada, who lived in the fourteenth century. Before him, the world knew no real work on history since the days of the Greeks and Romans. What passed in the West and the East under the name of history writing was the chronicle, the drab, soulless enumeration of events. It was Ibn Khaldoon who approached history from a pragmatic angle, taking into consideration the influence of social environment, the climate, the soil, and other factors that are the basis of historiography as we know it today.

In concluding this cursory survey of Arabic literature, let me call attention to one feature of it that is more eloquent than any enumeration of names, dates and works could be. We Occidentals rightly pride ourselves on the encyclopedia, spiritual child of that spiritually great century, the eighteenth. The Founding Fathers were nurtured on the spirit enshrined in that monument. In fact, the spirit of the encyclopedia is to modern democracy what the spirit of the Bible is to Christianity.

The encyclopedists of the Arabs, the Diderots and d'Alemberts of Islam, however, lived four, five, six and eight centuries before their Western brothers! The first regular encyclopedia in Arabic was composed by a society that flourished chiefly in Basrah, Iraq's great port on the Persian Gulf, in the latter part of the *tenth century!* These men, divided into four orders, called themselves *Ikhwan es-Safa'i*, "Brothers of Purity." Their composite work, consisting of fifty-one treatises, covers practically the entire knowledge of their time in mathematics, logic, natural science, and theology.

The next two Arabic encyclopedias were much more voluminous and comprehensive. Yet each is the work of a single person! The author of the first, Noowayri, lived in the late thirteenth and early fourteenth centuries. The creator of the other, Ibn Fadlallah, was his contemporary. Another encyclopedia was written by Qalqashandi, who died in 1418. About five hundred years later, Qalqashandi's work was printed in Cairo. It filled *fourteen large volumes.*

Indicative of the scientific zeal of the Arabs, and of the great number of their poets, writers of prose, scientists, and thinkers, is another branch of Arabic scientific literature: the dictionary. An outstanding example is a vast dictionary of the Arabic language, the Arabic counterpart of our Oxford Dictionary, or Webster's. But there is a difference between them: this Arabic dictionary had a single author, Safahdi, and he lived in the *fourteenth century.* A hundred years before him, Ibn Qifti wrote an encyclopedic work, entitled *History of the Philologists!* Yahqoot wrote a *Dictionary of Men of Letters,* Ibn Abi Usaibi'a the *Lives of the Physicians.*

It is usually a thankless job to enumerate names, titles and data. But some data carry a lesson. In this instance, they reveal that, to a very great extent, we Occidentals are the spiritual children of the Arabs.

XV

WHAT MOSLEM THOUGHT
CAN TEACH US

$\mathcal{T}$HE SPIRITUAL life
of the Arabs was not restricted to science, art, and the
humanities. Arab thinkers soared to the greatest heights
of philosophy and metaphysics. They derived some of
their ideas from the Platonic, Aristotelian, and neo-
Platonic schools of thought, and from that combined
system of philosophy, cosmogony and mysticism known
as Gnosticism, which flourished round the Mediterranean basin in the first six centuries of our era. India
was another source of spiritual influence upon Islam. As
we have seen, commercial and intellectual intercourse
between India, China, and the empire of the Caliphs
was intense, and a number of Hindu thinkers and savants
actually lived and taught in Moslem Baghdad. Through
these influences, India's so-called Vedantic pantheism,
and the various systems of yoga, became known to the
Moslem world long before the Moslem empire of the
Moguls was founded in India.

Among the many philosophers of Islam, Avicenna and
Averroës had the most immediate influence upon Western thought. We have already met both these men as
physicians and medical writers. Avicenna was also a
great philosopher, in which capacity he was surpassed

only by the even greater Averroës. The latter's works, like Avicenna's, were translated many times. They were well known to the Christian scholastic thinkers of the Middle Ages, including Thomas Aquinas.

Averroës was a philosophical pantheist, a spiritual precursor of his Christian and Jewish brothers, Giordano Bruno and Baruch Spinoza. But pantheism became also the basis for the higher forms of Moslem mysticism. It is my considered opinion that Moslem mysticism has directly influenced the thoughts of such celebrated Christian mystics as Raymond Lully and St. John of the Cross, and of Jewish mystics like Moses de León. The latter is the author of that famous book of the Cabbalah, the pantheist *Zohar*, which he wrote in Spain, about 1280 A.D. He undoubtedly spoke Arabic. So did Raymond Lully, famed Spanish-Catalan alchemist and Christian mystic of the fourteenth century. St. John of the Cross, a highly educated man who lived in sixteenth-century Spain, probably knew the principal Arab-Moslem mystics through some of their many translations, which circulated in Spain at the time.

Ibn 'Arabi, a poetic and religious genius of the first magnitude, ranks not only among the greatest Arab-Moslem mystics, but also among the most advanced souls of all time. It is undoubtedly in Sufism that Moslem mysticism has reached its spiritual climax. Sufism and Baha'ism, a beautiful offshoot of Sufism, have made many converts in twentieth-century America and Europe.

The motto of the Sufi is: *God is the All, and all is God.* Sufi poets are among the greatest in Islam. Many of them wrote in the Persian language. One of the greatest, but by no means the greatest, is none other than our old friend, Omar Khayyam. We have seen that this great man was also a mathematician, astronomer and geologist. But there ·were greater Sufi poets than Omar. Among these, Jelaleddin Rûmi, Ferideddin Attar, Jiluwi, rank first. Ferideddin Attar's didactic poem, "The Parliament of Birds," is a gem of mystic philosophy and poetry. The "birds" are the human souls, and the poem, couched in symbolic language, deals with the stages in self-development that the Sufi experiences.

It is time that, in the interest of an easier evaluation of the spirit of Islam, the veil of secrecy be lifted from the hidden meaning of the poetry of Omar Khayyam and of his Sufi fellow poets.

To the orthodox Moslem, pantheism, and therefore Sufism, is just as much of a heresy as is pantheism to the orthodox Christian or Jew. Therefore the Sufi poets, including Omar Khayyam, had a regular "code," a secret vocabulary, in which they couched their thoughts, the real, deeply hidden meaning of their poetry. Sufi poems, including Omar Khayyam's famed *Rubá'iyát*, have two distinct meanings. One is exoteric, intended for the uninitiated. The other is esoteric. It is the real meaning, and is intended for the fellow Sufi. If you read the *Rubá'iyát*, the quatrains seem to deal solely with wine, woman and song. If you know the Sufi code, you will find that they deal with the loftiest kind of mysticism. We have a Western analogy in *Faust*. Read *exoterically*, it is a glorious, lofty tragedy, with a deep symbolic meaning. Studied *esoterically*, it reveals that Goethe, who knew many things but perhaps did not know the Sanskrit term *Iñana Yoga*, actually was an *Iñana yogin*, an advanced intellectual pantheist mystic of the *highest* order.

In the code of the Sufi poets, "wine," or "the grape," stands for the spirit of God, as experienced by the mystic through ecstatic union with the Deity, achieved through the practice of meditation. "The beloved" means God. The "tavern" is the innermost aspect of the mystic's soul, into which he retires when meditating. The "keeper of the tavern" is the Sufi's spiritual guide, who gradually prepares the disciple for mystical experience. "Sleep" is meditation on God's perfection. "Perfume" stands for the hope of divine inspiration and of the supreme experience of the soul's identity with God. "Zephyrs" represent the grace of God, which eventually descends upon the mystic. A "kiss" or "caress" is the ecstatic experience of the soul's identity with God, including the state of ecstatic trance, the *samâdhi* of the *yogin*. "Beauty" is the perfection, the spiritual beauty, of God. "Love-locks" stands for the radiance of God's glory. This erotic imagery applies solely to religious concepts and has no erotic meaning whatever.

Now, let us consider some of Omar Khayyam's immortal quatrains in the light of the above. First, in their customary, camouflaged form, intended for the uninitiated.

> And lately by the tavern door agape
> Came shining through the dusk an angel shape
> Bearing a vessel on his shoulder; and
> He bid me taste of it; and 'twas — the Grape!
>
> The Grape that can with logic absolute
> The two-and-seventy jarring sects confute:
> The sovereign alchemist that in a trice
> Life's leaden metal into Gold transmute.
>
> And this I know: whether the one True Light
> Kindle to love, or wrath-consume me quite,
> One flash of it within the tavern caught
> Better than in the temple lost outright.

And here, in a free rendition, is the secret teaching which this alleged bard of wine, woman and song desires to impart to his fellow mystics: —

"The other day, when I had opened the door of the tavern, that is, of my inner soul, through meditation, I had the ecstatic vision of an angel. The vision was accompanied by the Grape — that is, by ecstatic union with the spirit of God.

"This ecstatic union with God is a much more real experience of the Deity than any of the doctrines of the 'seventy-two,' that is, of the many conflicting religious sects of humanity, is able to give. It is the sovereign alchemist who, in an instant, transforms lead into gold, that is, changes the human soul, which actually is only the human aspect of the Deity itself, into the non-human, the cosmic aspect of God.

"And this is certain: whether the True Light, that is, the mystic, ecstatic experience of man's essentially divine nature, arouses in me universal love for humanity (the latter is a familiar concept among Sufis, being known to the *Hindu* mystic as *Sattva*); or whether this overwhelming mystic experience of terrific intensity actually consumes my spiritual energy, depriving me of my sanity: a single flash of this supreme experience of my identity with God, caught in the soul, is worth more than being lost in prayer in the temple."

That is the rendition, in modern Western philosophic terminology, of Omar Khayyam's secret message to his fellow mystics. To the general Moslem and Christian reader, Omar Khayyam and the other Sufi poets are inspired bards of the art of earthly life. To the advanced Sufi, their songs are inspired didactic poems, descriptive of Life in its highest, divine aspect.

ᲬᲰ   ᲬᲰ   ᲬᲰ

It is characteristic of the religious tolerance inside Islam that it should have several monastic orders generally known to profess pantheism, that is, to be heretical, without being molested. In fact, these orders are greatly respected. Many among their members are intellectual leaders of their communities. Some Moslem religious confraternities known as "dervishes" are not pantheistic. Some consist of uneducated, primitive people. But such dervish orders as the pantheist *Mewlewi* are made up of intellectuals. Many of these monks are teachers, writers, scientists. Several orders have lay brothers also. The Turkish Sultan, Mehmed Reshad, who succeeded his tyrannical brother Abdul Hamid II in 1909 and died during the First World War, was a lay brother of the *Mewlewi* order. One of the intellectual, pantheist dervish orders, the *Bektashi*, occasionally accepts non-Moslem members, as I can affirm from personal experience.

The new Turkey has abolished the dervish orders, but they flourish everywhere in Islam outside Turkey.

The *Mewlewi* are known also as the dancing dervishes, or whirling dervishes. This name is derived from the specific technique which they employ as a part of their spiritual discipline. When performing their "dance," they turn round on their bare feet for ten to fifteen minutes at a time, moving their feet in a way much resembling the waltz step. A flutist accompanies the ceremony, which strangers are permitted to attend. The "dance" of the *Mewlewi* is a perfectly conscious, often tested and proved, strictly technical psychologic "prop." Its purpose is to create a state of spiritual elation and ecstasy, through the physical medium of rhythmic motion. Earlier in this book, when I referred to the ecstatic states of Mohammed, Jeanne d'Arc, Luther,

Swedenborg, and Beethoven, I emphasized that there is nothing eccentric about ecstasy, that ecstasy of a higher order simply is a psychologic state in which the channels of higher perceptive and creative intuition are wide open.

There are, of course, other, base forms of ecstasy. The war dances of primitive peoples create an ecstatic condition, but stir up blood lust. Another inferior kind of ecstasy, actually a veiled form of erotic semi-ecstasy, is created by some of our Western dances, such as the original form of the rumba, the *son cubano*, the *béguine*, and the like. When we whirl round a ballroom, engrossed in rhythmic motion unconsciously intended to produce erotic semi-ecstasy, we call it dancing, and look upon it as a perfectly natural, pleasant occupation. But when we see the *Mewlewi* dervishes, many of whom are intellectuals of the highest order, engrossed in rhythmic motion consciously intended to produce ecstasy of a very definite spiritual nature, we are inclined to consider their action ludicrous. Nothing could be more characteristic of the average Western tourist's unthinking, self-centered approach to things seen in the East, than this example.

The ritual of the *Nakshbendee* dervishes resembles certain forms of yoga. On the other hand, the *Jelwetee* pray on their knees, Christian fashion.

Hamzawee dervishes offer a striking analogy to the Quakers. They meditate in silence, inviting the manifestation of the *noor*, the "Inner Light," or "Divine

Light." Ever since I first met Quakers and observed their admirable relief work in the war-torn Old World, I have looked upon this sect as a ray of sunshine in the wilderness of a decadent world. Incidentally, I am inclined to believe that some Quaker teachings, such as their doctrine of the "Inner Light" and their practice of collective meditation, can be traced back to Western contact with the East.

Much has been written about the howling dervishes, or *Rufa'iyah*, who shout the name of the Deity, and sway their bodies, in a steadily accelerated rhythm, to achieve a state of transportation. I have repeatedly watched them during their ceremonies, to which outsiders, even non-Moslem, are admitted. The *Rufa'iyah* are not a monastic order. They form a very loose confraternity, and come from the lowest social and intellectual stratum of the community — dock laborers, weight carriers, and the like. We all seek escape from the self-made misery of our lives. Some people are privileged to use more advanced kinds of "escape," such as philosophy, higher forms of religion, literature, music, the theater. Undeveloped souls have only primitive forms of escape at their disposal. In the East, some of these become howling dervishes. In the West, some of them seek escape through certain kinds of revivalist meetings, with their ecstatic shouts, convulsions, hystero-epileptic fits. These pseudo-religious practices bear a Christian label. If some cultured Moslem tourist in America saw them, or watched our "holy rollers" and "holy jerkers," his reaction would be the same as ours is when we watch the howling dervishes of his homeland.

It is a fact that the howling dervishes, certain primitive religious confraternities in the Sudan, and the so-called *Aïssaouas* of Tunisia, display paranormal faculties while in a state of hysteric semi-trance. I have seen howling dervishes, fakirs, and also people of a very high degree of education, versed in certain methods of psychic training, performing such "miracles." Among these were fire walking, kissing a red-hot iron bar without getting hurt, and the healing of wounds. I put the word "miracles" inside quotation marks because a paranormal phenomenon is a miracle, or "para"-normal, if you choose to be amazed by it, but becomes normal if you realize that Mind rules supreme over every manifestation of life. Mind is the All, and all is Mind. There is only one kind of Mind — Universal Mind. It has two simultaneous aspects: as so-called human Mind and as extra-human, cosmic Mind. The World Soul, or the Deity, or Universal Mind, is all-pervading, indivisible. Universal Mind not only runs the universe. It *is* the universe.

From this supreme cognition spring two other key truths. One is that the words "thought, idea, impression, belief, autosuggestion, conviction, obsession," are all synonyms, merely expressing the same thing in various degrees of intensity. The other key truth is that *the one and only criterion of so-called "reality" is sufficient in-*

tensity of belief. This is one of the master cognitions of life. It is also the key to the self-induced liberation of the soul from both physical and emotional pain, the latter being known as unhappiness.

Everybody knows that in a sufficiently intense hypnotic state the "subject" feels no pain. If he is made to think that the thrust of a knife causes him no pain, it does not. If he is caused to believe that a kiss hurts him, he will yell with pain when kissed. But even in hysteric fits, in which consciousness is partly retained, the patients are often insensible to pain.

During their pseudo-religious practices, many howling dervishes feel no pain when burned or wounded, although they retain full consciousness. They believe that this is due to the direct intervention of the Deity. But you don't have to go to the East to see such "miracles," caused by sufficiently intense belief, or autosuggestion. In 1936, Kuda Bux, an educated Moslem from Kashmir, performed fire-walking in England before a committee of the medical faculty of London University. The photographer of London's famous *Times* took many pictures of the event. In 1938, Kuda Bux repeated his thoroughly genuine performance in New York's Radio City. He is one of the relatively numerous people who possess the faculty of great concentration in the waking state. Through concentration, he is able to impart unusual intensity to the arbitrarily chosen *momentary belief, or autosuggestion,* that he cannot burn himself by walking on red-hot coals. As a result, his mind

(279)

has complete control over the epidermis of his soles, and he does not get burned. Many doctors know that the so-called "bewitching away" of warts is a fact. The actual fact is, however, that the wart disappears not through the intervention of the old woman who says she can perform the trick, but because of the sufficient intensity of your autosuggestion, that is, belief, that she can do it. This autosuggestion, if strong enough, activates your subconscious will, and dominates your epidermis so completely that the wart actually disappears.

And if only you believe *with sufficient intensity*, in the full waking state, that your physical ailment will be cured by the famed spring at Lourdes, it *will* be cured. Not by the spring, but by your autosuggestion, or belief, that you will be cured. The more intense your belief, the more freely are you able to draw upon the *unlimited* resources of energy of your unconscious mind, that is, of Cosmic, Universal Mind in its human aspect. Through the medium of autosuggestion, Mind momentarily establishes unrestricted control over your blood vessels, bones, muscles, nerve fibers, cells. You leave Lourdes cured.

I repeat: Mind is the only Reality. The one and only criterion of *so-called* reality is sufficient intensity of belief. This rule governs *every aspect* of life. It is also the secret of the primitive howling dervish, who feels no physical pain, and does not get hurt, when kissing a red-hot iron bar. And it is also the secret of the advanced Moslem thinker and mystic, who feels no emotional pain, does not suffer spiritually, and *therefore cannot get hurt* in the whirlpool of life.

He knows the power of the Mind. He knows that autosuggestion, or belief, which is the primary product of the Mind, can operate both ways. It can conjure up the illusion of suffering and misery, just as it can create the feeling of *absence* of suffering and misery. Therefore, let us learn from the advanced Moslem thinker. Let us realize that what happens round us is largely outside our control, *but that the way we choose to react to it is inside our control.*

⁓   ⁓   ⁓

We have briefly covered every major aspect of the civilization and the culture of the Arabs. We have seen that the Arabs were the intermediaries between the East and the West in almost every field of endeavor and knowledge, were our teachers in almost every branch of civilization and culture, and can still teach us many things.

And, as we have also seen, even that all-embracing efflorescence of Occidental culture and civilization which we call the Renaissance was an Arab gift to the West, which came to us by way of Sicily and Moslem Spain.

That is our Arab heritage.

(281)

The Arabs in the Postwar World

XVI

THE PAN-ARAB FEDERATION

ONLY DURING the last thirty or forty years has science begun to discover that Nature is not governed by iron-bound rules. The revised form of the Quantum Theory assumes a "Principle of Indeterminacy," and we now speak, rightly, of a "statistical conception" of the universe.

It would be simpler to say that the universe is not a factory, turning out products in standardized patterns, is not governed by "laws," subject to a few "exceptions." Actually, the cosmos is not a factory but a laboratory, constantly experimenting with new forms, discarding some, developing others. The saurians were an experiment. Their gigantic, unwieldy bodies proved impracticable patterns of Nature. They died out. So do obsolete, impracticable concepts about the universe, and about everything else.

The cosmos is governed, not by laws, but by *trends*. These trends, which the mystic might call the thought habits of the World Soul, or Universal Mind, that is, of the Deity, allow a wide margin for experimentation.

These cosmic trends extend, of course, to the collective life of the various species, including the human species. The study of the collective life of the human species, as observed in Space, is labeled "sociology" and

(285)

"international relations." Its study, projected into Time, is called "history."

In our generation, a new historic trend is becoming manifest: the age of imperialism and colonization is over. Despite the recent political experiment of Japan's militarist group, empires, in the form of an agglomeration of exploited colonies, now face the alternative of *transformation* or *disintegration*.

Without any desire to be flippant, one might say that all is over except the shooting. More explicitly, the task of substituting Western partnership for Western tyranny in the East is a question no longer of principle, but solely of time. The problem is merely whether that partnership will come about through more wisdom or through more bloodshed, through postwar *agreements* or postwar *wars*.

When inevitable historic trends first become manifest, the Lord Norths look the other way. They reap the Boston Tea Parties. Real statesmen face facts. They listen to complaints. They know that fear is a poor substitute for esteem.

There is no reason at all why the nations whose governments now hold down peoples in Africa and Asia should be afraid to change that policy. The change is inevitable. For empires as for individuals, *the secret of survival is timely self-adjustment to inevitable change.*

Says Marcus Aurelius, the sage who administered the world from Scotland to Arabia in the second century: "Are you afraid of change? Yet, what can materialize without change? What is more pleasing or more suitable to Nature? Can anything be accomplished without change? Don't you see that change *inside yourself* falls under the same law, and is equally indispensable to Nature?"

It would be unfair to accuse any individual Western power in connection with the domination and exploitation to which Africa and Asia have been subjected. These methods are not even characteristic of the West alone. They are typical of human nature generally, and have been used by Oriental conquerors also. But that is no excuse for continuing them. How is progress possible if we perpetuate mistakes merely because they are time-honored mistakes?

Today, the Arab world lags behind the West, not in culture and spirituality, but in science and industry — that is, in civilization. Why?

Because it has lost its independence, is dominated and exploited by the West.

Civilization can just barely survive under foreign domination, but cannot progress under it, because it lacks the spiritual incentive of liberty. The Spirit is a plant that needs the fresh air of freedom. Conversely, in the course of history we see how, again and again, the genius of a people soars to hitherto unscaled heights when the fetters of foreign domination fall from it. Hardly had Greece shaken off the invading armies of Achaemenid Persia, when it rose to the apogee of its civilization in the great fifth century B.C. Immediately after the liberation of the Netherlands from the Spanish yoke, Dutch vitality blossomed forth in the creation of a great empire.

The East, including Islam, is by no means in a state of decadence. Tremendous creative energies are latent there, under the lid of Western political domination and economic exploitation. These creative energies will become manifest as soon as the Atlantic Charter has really ceased to be merely Atlantic, and is fully applied to Africa and Asia.

The governments of the Western powers have consciously and methodically prevented the industrialization of the Arab and non-Arab East. They have administered these huge regions, not from the viewpoint of the prosperity of the natives, or even of the joint prosperity of the governing and the governed, but primarily in the interest of the Western imperialist powers. The East was and still is, not a partner of the West, but an object of methodical exploitation *by* the West. Major industries must not be in native hands, so that the Western industrial colonial powers can exploit the Oriental markets for their own benefit. To the West, the East is above all a source of raw materials, obtained largely without compensation to the natives except labor wages and conditions which would land the same employers in jail at home. The living standard of the natives, their nutrition and housing, often is actually such that millions are chronically underfed and their physical growth stunted.

The Pan-Arab Federation

The Oriental's somnolence, his lack of the "knack" of handling machinery, are a time-honored fable. What the Occidental takes for somnolence in the East is absence of haste, not absence of energy. The statement that the Arabs — or, for that matter, any other people with an old civilization of its own — are unable to acquire skill in modern science and industry is foolish. Let it be said again: by repeating an untruth we make it not a truth but a prejudice.

Inside our own generation, the Turk and the Russian have given the lie to the same dogmatic claim that they are unable to handle machinery, to become machine-conscious. Once they had the machinery, and the chance to build up industries, the Russians and the Turks both showed that they are the equals of the West in modern civilization also.

So firmly rooted was the dogma of Russian incompetence in matters of industry and engineering that the Russians themselves accepted it. They used to consider the Germans paragons of perfection in these fields, and referred to them as *khitri nyemets* — "the smart German." There was a saying in Russia that even the Moon had been made, and was being constantly renewed, in Hamburg. Following the Second World War, the Moon will probably be made in Magnitogorsk or Dniepropetrovsk, and its light made available to the Germans by special license from the Kremlin.

When I first met the late Kemal Ataturk, founder of modern Turkey, in Aleppo, in 1917, he was one

(289)

among many major generals in the army of the "somnolent" Ottoman Empire. Ten years later, Ataturk was the chief executive of a thoroughly modernized country. In another memorable conversation with him, this time in Ankara in the summer of 1923, I asked him point-blank whether he did not think that the pace at which he was introducing reform after reform would arouse bitterness and opposition among his people.

Ataturk replied: "Don't underrate our sense of progress. All we want is liberty. We are neither better nor worse than anybody else. Up to now, we were denied political and economic freedom. We have established it through our own strength and vitality. Unless we are attacked again, we intend to be a peaceful neighbor to other nations. We will vie with them, not on the battlefield but in the field of human progress."

The voice was Ataturk's. It was the entire East that spoke.

ᴏᴡᴏ   ᴏᴡᴏ   ᴏᴡᴏ

The first task of the Western powers in the postwar East lies in the field of ethics. The East generally, and the Arab East with it, must be made a partner, cease to be an object of exploitation for the sole benefit of Western political overlords.

I repeat that no individual Western nation is to blame

for present and past methods of domination in the East. These methods are inherited, traditional. But so was slavery in our South. It was not invented by the people who lost their slaves through the Civil War. Yet we had to put an end to slavery. The same truth applies to the outworn methods of imperialism and colonial policy.

Elsewhere, I have presented a general plan for post-war reforms in the Eastern Hemisphere, including Asia, Africa, and Europe.[1] Here, I shall deal specifically with those features of the plan, and those major postwar problems, which concern the Arabs.

France has done much good in modernizing Morocco, Algeria, and Tunisia. It has not done well in Syria and Lebanon, where unimaginative men who were sent there, and reactionary elements in metropolitan France, committed grave blunders. A prosperous France is an absolute necessity for the further progress of humanity. The overwhelming majority of Frenchmen are demo-cratically-minded, liberal, progressive people, with a lot of warmth and a lot of common sense. Following the ravages of the *furor teutonicus*, France has a doubly important mission to fulfill in the postwar world.

But like every major country, without exception, France also has its minority of incorrigible, narrow-minded imperialists and reactionaries. Let Frenchmen put their house in order in the postwar era. Let them use their healthy intuition, and keep the reactionary

[1] *A Five-Year Peace Plan*, by Edward J. Byng. New York, 1943.

minority in their midst from holding back French progress. This applies also to France's postwar policies in its overseas possessions.

The bulk of Algeria's Moslem population has no electoral vote. The small French element in Algeria has. So Frenchmen, who form less than 20 per cent of the population, represent Algeria in the Chamber of Deputies and the Senate in Paris. The decree promulgated by the French Committee of National Liberation in Algiers in 1943, giving a number of Algerian Moslem the vote, was tangible proof of French statesmanship. But it is necessary to extend the vote to all Moslem of Algeria. However, if the entire Moslem population of Algeria got the vote, that country would undoubtedly send Moslem deputies and senators to the French national legislature in Paris. In the postwar period, that legislature is very likely to be made up once again of many numerically weak parties and groups, neutralizing each other. Thus, the votes of Moslem Algeria might occasionally be instrumental in deciding major French issues of a purely domestic character in the French parliament.

There is a way to avoid this without withholding from Algeria's Moslem population its right to vote and thereby to manage its own affairs. Algeria should be given a new status. It should no longer form a part of metropolitan France, as it does now. Instead, Algeria should become a full-fledged self-governing dominion, on the British model, inside the French Empire. Then, native animosity will be replaced by fruitful native co-operation in the common destinies of the French Empire, which should be transformed into a *French Commonwealth of Nations.*

Inside that symbiosis of peoples, Tunisia also should become a dominion, living under French *guidance, not* French *domination.* There is no reason why the Beys of Tunis should not continue to be the hereditary heads of their country. If Tunisia becomes a dominion, and gets a constitution, it makes no difference whether the nominal head of its constitutional government is appointed, or whether he inherits his office. It is just as immaterial whether his title is Bey, or Governor General.

Morocco is not yet ripe for far-reaching self-government. Its social structure still is thoroughly feudal. As we have seen, powerful feudal lords still play a part in its affairs, tribal allegiance often transcends loyalty to the community as a whole. Here, the French will have to assist for a while in the actual administration of the country before it can become a full-fledged *member* of the French Empire.

But when Morocco eventually reaches that state, it might then prove more expedient politically and economically to merge Algeria, Tunisia and Morocco into a single unit, forming one single self-governing dominion inside a French Commonwealth of Nations.

Whatever may be the permanent political affiliation of *Libya* in the postwar world, it should advance from the status of a colony, which it held under Italian Fascism, to that of a protectorate, with very far-reaching facilities for native self-government. Libya is too poor in natural resources, and too poor in intellectual leaders versed in *modern* methods of administration, economics, and social organization, to be set adrift without a transitional period of constructive help from the outside. The *official* form, or title, of protectorate, however, must be avoided at all costs. It smacks of unadulterated Western imperialism, and is an insult to the natives. Besides, Hitler, with his "protectorate" over Bohemia-Moravia, has dragged this word down into the quagmire of his own diseased, sadistic mentality.

There is no reason why, after a transition period of perhaps ten years, Libya should not be allowed to go one step further. It should then exchange its status of a *de facto* protectorate for that of a dominion on the British model, working in full and equal partnership with whatever power may be assigned to co-operate with it. Libya is too barren, industrially too undeveloped, to exist without a partner.

As to the identity of its partner, we are faced with three distinct possibilities. One is a renewed co-operation between Libya and Italy, but with a democratic Italy. The other possibility is that Libya co-operates directly with that permanent central organization for the preservation of peace which may be eventually set up in the postwar world, and for which, in my book, *A Five-Year Peace Plan*, I have coined the name "Union of Nations." By co-operation between this organization

dling oil reserves has made it a business partner of Saudi Arabia. American interests operate Arabia's oil fields. Soon, an American pipeline will connect Saudi Arabia with the Mediterranean. Our political, economic and personal relations with the Arabs have suddenly become important, close, permanent. We are entering upon these relations with a clean political conscience. The United States is the one and only power that enjoys real popularity in the Arab East, because we have never indulged in imperialism.

So, we must not bungle. We have a reputation to lose. In dealing with the Arabs and their governments, in discussing treaties and economic concessions with them, we must painstakingly avoid driving sharp bargains, such as the European powers used to "put across" in the East. The Arabs trust us. We need the Arabs. If we use traditional Western methods in dealing with them, they will distrust and dislike us, too, and ultimately *we* shall be the losers.

Honesty still is the highest form of wisdom. And wisdom is the direct opposite of foxiness.

XVII

THE ARABS IN THE
RUSSO–AMERICAN CENTURY

$\mathcal{O}$N ST. HELENA, Napoleon predicted that a hundred years after him Europe would be "either Roman or Cossack." He meant that in our days Europe would be under the dominant influence of either the Vatican or Russia.

In the latter respect, the prophecy is proving amazingly correct. We are entering upon the Russo-American century. The postwar world will live in the sign of American influence in the Western Hemisphere and the Pacific and Russian influence in Europe and major parts of Asia.

This does not mean that Russia will try actually to control any country outside the Baltic and Balkan spheres. Its power will be so great that there will be no need for such conquests. For generations, irrespective of its regime, Russia will influence the outcome of every vital international issue. This will not exclude Britain from the councils where history is made. On the contrary, Britain, with its stouthearted and levelheaded people, will continue to be an important factor in the world's affairs and progress. But just because they are levelheaded, the British will be the first to recognize Russia's permanent dominant position. Instead of opposing it, England's future leaders will, and will have to, co-operate methodically with Russia.

In the world of today, the life of nations is so closely interdependent that if two major powers turn their backs upon one another, it is merely a statistical question as to how many months or years precede a sanguinary war between them.

Russia has its regime, we have ours. We believe that the democratic form of life is the best, and we shall, and must, see to it that no one interferes with our democratic ideals. But that is a question of domestic policing, not of international relations. International relations must be conditioned not by emotion but by wisdom. Wisdom is a synonym for self-restraint. The basic cause of wars is fear — warranted and unwarranted fear. Self-restraint alone can eliminate fear between men, as between nations. If either Russia or the Western powers allow their handful of fanatics and opportunists to exploit the delicate problems, and even conflicts, that will inevitably arise between these countries from time to time, a third world war is a certainty. If they hold the political mediocrities and cynics in their midst in check, mutual fear and distrust, and therefore war, can be prevented, constructive co-operation assured, conflicts eliminated, problems solved.

The *principal* basis for world peace during the rest of the century is active co-operation, and the absence of fear and distrust *between Russia and the United States.* As we have indicated, Britain is practically certain to promote this objective, alike in the interest of world peace and of the British Commonwealth of Nations. In fact, it is likely that Downing Street will repeatedly have the important mission of mediating between America and Russia, of helping to avoid and eliminate occasional friction, until a permanent condition of mutual trust is established.

At the same time, it would be a mistake to leave France altogether out of the picture in connection with the major problems of the postwar era. France will be by no means a negligible quantity. It will remain a great power. It will retain its huge empire, with millions of Arabic-speaking and other Moslem inhabitants. And in fairness to France it should be stated that inside its empire it has not created that artificial social gulf between a so-called "white élite" and the so-called "natives" which has caused so much bitterness elsewhere in the East. French participation in world affairs, including the solution of economic problems, is essential if the postwar world is to achieve real stability.

As for Russia, permanent access to the world's trade through warm-water ports has long been a vital issue in Moscow's policies. It was the dream of Peter the Great. By seizing the Dardanelles for this purpose, Russia might sow the seeds of an eventual war with Britain. America would not let Britain perish. Russia knows this. So the straits question will be solved in another way. I think postwar Bulgaria will be just as openly pro-Russian as past Bulgarian governments always have been, with the exception of Hitler's puppets in Sofia during the Second World War. On the other hand, Russia might actually procure for postwar Bulgaria that access to the Aegean which Bulgaria had until 1919, when it lost it through the peace treaty of Neuilly. In such a reinstated "Bulgar corridor" to the Aegean, the U.S.S.R. would probably enjoy a privileged status. Actually, this strip of land might constitute Russia's permanent postwar outlet to the Mediterranean.

In addition, it is more than likely that postwar treaties between Egypt, other Arab states, and the U.S.S.R. will enable the latter to operate permanent airlines between North Africa, the Arab East and Russia. The principal stopovers on these air routes will probably be Cairo, Damascus, Baghdad, Teheran, Baku and Moscow. Russia's new Holy Synod, re-established in 1943, will almost surely regain the direct moral and political influence over the Greek Orthodox elements in the Levant which the Russian Church had under the Tsars. Russia's present influence upon neighboring Iran also is likely to grow in the postwar years.

As a result of all these factors, Russia's political, economic and strategic influence in North Africa, western and midwestern Asia, will have to be taken into account in connection with the Indian, Persian and Pan-Arab problems. There can be no doubt that, true to the attitude it has adopted ever since the days of Lenin, the U.S.S.R. will side with India and the other peoples of Asia and Africa in the matter of granting them real self-government. Therefore it will be wiser for the European powers to turn a new leaf in their ledger of colonial affairs, by giving the peoples of the East their liberty, before those peoples look to Russia for assistance. It would be well if the diplomats of Europe kept this in mind.

Not that Russia would foment rebellions, or go to war to help the East. It will need peace as much as we shall need it ourselves. But its moral support of the Oriental nations could hardly be ignored. It was generally observed in the pioneer days of our American West that if a man was six feet tall, weighed two hundred pounds, and carried two guns, even his humblest and meekest suggestions were given serious consideration.

The Occident still can win the respect and friendship of the East by making a clean slate of an inglorious past. It would be both unfair and unwise to procrastinate. If the various peoples of Africa and Asia are given self-government only after Russia has intervened, that concession will have lost its value as a moral asset for the West in subsequent dealings with the peoples of the East.

ოუ   ოუ   ოუ

But another role also awaits Russia. Once again, I wish to make it crystal clear that we must distinguish between peoples and their regimes, and must remember the obvious fact that regimes are solely *political* structures.

It is in the light of this observation that attention should be called to the important *cultural* mission which the Russian *people* will be called upon to fulfill during the next three or four generations. I have expressed the conviction that a politically free Arab world will once again be a bridge between Eastern and Western thought. By giving the Arabs free access to our industrial and scientific achievements, we shall get new cultural and spiritual values in exchange. The Russian people will share this spiritual and cultural role with the Arabs. And Russian spiritual influence upon the West will gather momentum from Russia's dominant political position.

To the Asiatic, the Russian is an Occidental. To the European, he appears as an Oriental. Actually, spiritually and culturally the Russian *is* an Oriental. That is one of his greatest assets. Today, he shows a scientific skill, and an inventive originality in industry and engineering, which are in no way inferior to ours. Russia has performed miracles in this connection. But in addition to this the Russian has a traditional appreciation of spiritual values, a bent for mysticism, and the Oriental's automatic co-ordination, instinctive integration of professional activities, intellectual life, and purely spiritual interests. The present atheistic phase in Russia's intellectual life is an episode, will soon be a matter of the past.

The doctrinary spirit of mid-Victorian atheism, which was at the root of it, is dying out everywhere. The time is not distant when the thinking Russian will rediscover the truth that religion is not necessarily dogmatic, that it is merely another word for metaphysics, and that theology and religion not only are not identical concepts but are opposites in many ways. Then, he will no longer neglect his deeply ingrained, typically Oriental metaphysical inclinations, and will eventually integrate his traditional Oriental approach to life with his newly found "machine-consciousness."

It is my firm belief that the otherwise inescapable complete collapse of our Western civilization of the machine will be averted by a spiritual wave of Russian, Arab, Hindu, and other Oriental influence in art, literature, philosophy, and mysticism, which will sweep over western Europe and America in the coming years and decades. It will be supplemented and intensified by an Arab renaissance, the first symptoms of which are already discernible in such events as the relatively recent foundation of an "Arab Academy" in Damascus, on the model of the French Academy.

The curse of our contemporary Western civilization is the worship of the single-track expert, the idolatry of soulless information. We confound a good memory with a good intellect, the memorizing and retention of information with thinking. Surrounded by a petrified forest of facts and data, we are unable to find the

(306)

clearing that opens on to the blue sky of creative intuition.

Advanced souls are rare in both hemispheres. But while advanced people in the West have *intelligence*, advanced souls in the East have *wisdom*. Even now, thousands in America and Europe study Sufism, Baha'ism, Vedanta, yoga, and other Oriental systems of thought. These people feel the haunting emptiness that comes from the entanglement of the consciousness in that jungle of self-made worries and fears which it calls "reality."

Say the advanced *yogin* and the Sufi: "I am not identical with my body. I am not my nerves. I am not my emotions. I am not 'my' mind. I am the one, all-embracing, indivisible, cosmic Universal Mind, in its human aspect." This attitude of detachment from our own self, through identification with the supreme Self, does not disable us for practical work. On the contrary. *By refusing to identify ourselves with our ephemeral problems*, by rising above them, we give our higher insight, our *noor*, our Inner Light, our higher intuition, a chance to guide us out of them.

Let us learn this from the advanced thinkers of the East. Then, we shall have souls free from inherited prejudice, souls that can be "serviced" anywhere, far away from their home bases. We must begin to integrate our professional, private, and clearly spiritual interests. We must understand that life has no compartments. We must learn to transcend our factual knowledge, retaining the faculty of the intuition to pass freely in and out of it, instead of being stifled by it.

And, in a spirit of constructive self-criticism, we Occidentals must give up our puerile superiority complex, which blinds us to the higher aspect of culture. For, in the last analysis, culture is to have a soul to be proud of and not to be proud of it.

Index

INDEX

ABBAS HILMY, 203
Abbasids, 140, 141, 148, 152, 160
Abdallah, 112
Abd el Kader, 14, 204
Abd el Krim, 204, 205
Abd-el-Mumen el Moahid, 148, 167
Abd-er-Rahman, 140–142, 149; the Third, 238
Abd-er-Rahman Ibn Abdullah, 139
Abdul Aziz Ibn Saud, 45, 51, 214, 298
Abdulhalik Renda, xvii
Abdul Hamid, 192, 194
Abdulkarim, 228
Abdul Medjid II, Caliph of Islam, xvii, 160
Aboo-r-Reehah, 79
Abraham, 40, 67
Abu Bakr, 115, 119, 130, 134
Abukir, 199
Abu'l Ala, 265
Abu Talib, 113
Acatepec, 244
Achaemenids, 83, 231, 287
Achilles, 158
Acre, 183, 184
Aden, 62
Adrianople, 58, 191
Adrooh, 129
Aegean, 303
Affrit, 20, 46
Afghanistan, 135, 196, 207
Africa, 28; North, 46
Aghlabites, 29, 185
Agra, 13
Ahkyl, 45, 52, 107
Ahmed, 113

Ahmed Izzet Pasha, Marshal, 58
Ahoggar Mountains, 14, 18
Aïn Sefra, 15
Aïn Sofar, 80
Aïsha, poetess, 266
Aïssaouas, 278
Ajímez, 241, 243
Akhenaton, 103
Alaska, 295
Al Aziz, 255
Albania, 110, 191
Albertus Magnus, 261
Albizensians, 168
Alcázar, 241
Alembert, d', 267
Aleppo, 10, 25, 181, 207, 209, 228, 250, 289
Alexander, 133, 134, 144
Alexander III, 196
Alexandria, 36, 135; Library of, 142, 143
Alexios Comnenos, 179, 181
Alfonso XIII, 204
Algasaniah, 266
Algeria, 3, 14, 19, 135, 140, 291
Al Ghazali, 262
Algiers, 15, 18
Al Hakim, 238
Alhambra, 12, 169, 236
Al Hazen, 257
Alhucemas, 5
Ali, 66, 115, 119, 131, 132
Ali ben Othman, 262
Allah, 84, 95, 112, 113, 115, 119
Alleih, 80
Allenby, Lord, 77, 81, 131
Alliance Israélite Universelle, 208
Allies, 58
Almeria, 168

Index

Almohade dynasty, 148, 151, 152, 167
Almoravides, 151, 166, 202, 249
Altai Mountains, 92, 153
Amasis, 106
Ameenah, 112, 113
Ameer Abdallah, 214
Ameer Chékib Arslan, xvi
Ameer Faisal, 212
Ameer Ibn Rashid, 53
America, 125, 302, 307
American University of Beyrut, 81, 82
Amr ibn-el-As, 134, 135, 146
Amroo'ul Qais, 265
Andalusia, 252
Anese, 47
Ankara, 39, 59, 156, 181, 290
Antarah ibn Shaddad, 264
Anti-Atlas, 6
Anti-Lebanon, 79
Antioch, 184
Aphrodite, 71
Arab Academy, 306
Arab Empire, 126
Arab movement, 38
Arabia, 37, 45, 54, 95, 112, 113, 123, 132
Arabian Desert, 37, 43, 52, 93, 94, 109
Arabian Nights, 11, 73, 266
Arabian peninsula, 37, 57
Arabs, 37, 108, 109, 115, 120, 305
Archangel Gabriel, 114, 115, 118
Archimedean Theorem, 117
Aristotle, 167
Arius, 36
Armenia, 39
Armenians, 40, 147
Ar Razi, 259, 260
Arslan, Ameer Chékib, xvi
Asarhaddon, 81
Asia, 109, 110, 115, 125, 141
Asia Minor, 11, 21–23, 39, 58
Asir, 34, 57, 66

Aslamah, 226
Assur, 67
Assyria, 69
Astaroth, 71
Astarte, 71
Ataraxeia, 224
Ataturk, Kemal, 59, 60, 290
Atlantic, 6, 133, 136
Atlantic Charter, 130, 288
Atlas, 6, 8
Atrium, 239
Austria-Hungary, 191, 198
Avaris, 102
Avars, 92, 153
Avatara, 87
Averroës, 167, 260, 269, 270
Avicenna, 256, 260, 261, 269, 270
Avignon, 139, 149
Aztecs, 22

Baal, 29
Baal-Marduk, 69
Babylon, 29, 67–69, 71, 119, 147; architecture of, 65
Babylonia, 99, 231
Bacon, Roger, 256, 260, 261
Badis, 5
Baghdad, 67, 73, 74, 141, 152, 214, 230
Baghdad Railway, 49, 76
Baha'ism, 270, 307
Bahrein Islands, 62
Baku, 211, 303
Balbo, Marshal Italo, 201, 202
Bald Mountain, 13
Baldwin, King, 184
Balearic Islands, 173, 235
Balfour Declaration, 67
Balkan War, First, 195, 198; Second, 197
Balkans, 150, 156
Banderma, 212
Baron de Prorok, 28
Basrah, 73
Bayazid, Sultan, 156

(312)

Index

Baybars, 184
Baza, 249
Bcherre, 80
Beaconsfield, Lord, 197
Bedouins, xiii, 19, 38, 39, 41–49, 73, 93, 94
Beethoven, 276
Béguine, 276
Beka'a Valley, 79, 80
Bektashi dervishes, 275
Belgrade, 159
Benghazi, 33
Beni Harb, 47
Berbers, 4, 21, 39, 42, 151
Berlin, 203
Berlin-Baghdad, 197, 199, 207
Bernadette Soubirous, 118
Berne, 121
Berytos, 80
Beth-Sheba, 40
Beylerbey Palace, 194
Beyrut, 80, 81, 184, 208
Beys, of Tunis, 27, 293
Bible, 40
Bill of Rights, 172
Biskra, 16
Bizerte, 27, 30
Bliss, Dr., 82
Blum, Léon, 216
Boabdil, 169
Boghazkeny, 39
Bokhara, 135
Bombay, 135
Bompard, 208
"Book of Wisdom," 87
Bordeaux, 139
Borglum, Gutzon, 13
Bosnia, 110, 191
Bosporus, 156, 194
Boston Tea Party, 286
Bouillon, 181
Bourbon, 199
Boxer Rebellion, 143
Boyars, 125
Boy Scouts, 154

Britain, 73, 74, 300
British, 48; Museum, 100; Mediterranean Squadron, 135
"Brothers of Purity," 267
Browning, 265
Bruno, Giordano, 270
Brusa, 155
Brutus, 124
Buda, 189
Budapest, 189
Buddhism, 117, 264
Buddhists, 117
Bulgaria, 190, 195, 302, 303
Bulgars, 92
Bundschuh revolt, 125
Bursa, 155
Byng, Dr. Maxim, xvii
Byzantine, 112, 123, 126, 136; Empire, 134, 135, 156, 188; Fleet, 135
Byzantium, 156–158

CABBALAH, 270
Cà d'Oro, 244
Caesar, 133–135
Cairo, 23, 36, 205
California, 51
Caliph, 136, 137, 214; Abdul Medjid II, xvii; Omar, 32; Abu Bakr, 134
Caliphate, 66, 132, 157; in Spain, 42, 152; Abbasid, 152; of Córdoba, 165
Caliphs, 127–131, 140, 149, 152
Cambridge, 242
Canaan, 40, 103
Cannae, 109
Cante jondo, 262, 263
Canterbury Library, 239
Carchemish, 40, 41, 76
Carpathian Chain, 92
Carthage, 28, 65, 81, 109, 135, 136
Casablanca, 205
Castile, 167, 168
Catalonia, 204

(313)

Index

Catholic Kings, the, 174
Caucasus, 110, 211
Central Powers, 210
Ceuta, 5
Chaldean, 94, 96, 97
Charlemagne, 92, 113
Charles Martel, 139
Charles of Habsburg, 210
Charles V of Habsburg, 245
Charro, 247
Chékib Arslan, Ameer, xvi
China, 22, 35, 39, 87, 109, 125, 133, 139, 143
Chinese-Turkestan, 110
Chott, 27
Christ, 36
Christianity, 117
Christians, 36, 66, 75
Cicero, 107
Cincinnatus, 122
Civil War (American), 291
Cluny, 243
Coburg, 191
Code Napoleon, 99
Cologne, 180
Colomannus, King of Hungary, 180
Columbus, 173
Committee for Union and Progress, 193, 194
Constantine, département of, 15
Constantine, Roman Emperor, 22
Constantine XII, Byzantine Emperor, 157, 158
Constantinople, 49, 58, 141, 156, 158, 159, 181, 191, 211
Converso, 173, 176, 244
Copernican System, 117
Coplas, 262
Copts, 36
Córdoba, 41, 42, 141, 142, 149, 151, 165, 168, 238
Corrida real, 248
Cortes, 204
Cortéz, 137, 247

Count Waldersee, 143
Crane, Charles R., 35
Crete, 39
Crimea, 93, 191, 195
Crusaders, 34, 77, 82, 83, 180–184
Crusades, 168, 179, 180, 184
Ctesiphon, 134, 141
Cubiculae, 239
Cusco, 178
Cyprus, 39
Cyrus the Mede, 66
Czermak, Dr. William, xvi

DAMASCUS, 75, 79, 112, 131, 134, 135, 137, 140, 234, 306
Dandolo, Enrico, 184
Danes, 238
Da'ood, 145
Dardanelles, 144, 213, 302
David, King, 40, 45, 53, 263
Dead Sea, 75
de la Salle de Rochemaure, 261
Delft, 251
Delhi, 225
Demir Kapu, 49
Départements, 15
Derna, 33
Dervish army, 202
Dervish, Howling, xiii
"Devil Worshipers," 83
Dhammapadda, 264
Dhimmi, 146
Diderot, 267
Diwans, 264
Djemah el Fnah, 11, 12
Djerablus, 76
Dniepropetrovsk, 289
Dog's River, 81
Dome of the Rock, 31, 32
Don Quijote, 61
Downing Street, 203, 212, 302
Druses, 83, 84, 86, 87, 151, 215
Duce, the, 202

ECSTASY, 115, 117
Ed-Deresi, 84

(314)

Index

Eden, Garden of, 62, 67
Egypt, 4, 36, 74, 95, 135, 142, 295
El Ahkyl El Kully, 85, 226
El Azhar, 36
Elbe, 92
El Bedi Palace, 12
Eleusinian Mysteries, 85
El Gharb, 6
El Glaoui, Si Hammu, 9
El Glaoui, Sidi Thami, 8
El Gundafi, 8
El Hooz, 6
El Idrissi, 57
El Idrissi, geographer, 255
El Jerz, 14
El Moahid, 151
El Moahideen, 84, 151
El Mutawakkil, 160
El Qoreish, 111
El Walid, 138
Encyclopedists, 254
England, 190, 301
Entrelac, 242
Enver, 193, 194, 201, 206
Ephesus, 154
Ephron the Hittite, 40
Eridu, 67
Eroica, 117
Er-Romdan, 27
Ertoghrul Shah, 154
Esdraelon, plain of, 76
Es-Samh ibn Mahlik el Khow-
    lahnee, 139
Esther, 71; Book of, 71
Etemenanki, 68–71
Ethiopia, 36
Etruscans, 22, 23, 108
Euphrates, 40, 71, 72, 76, 141
Europe, 109, 307
Exodus, 102, 103, 106

Fado, 263
Faenza, 251
Fahnah, 224
Faisal, Ameer, 212

Fatih, 159
Fatimah, 131, 151
Fatimids, 84, 87, 151, 255
Faust, 272
Fellah, 93
Ferdinand, 6, 169, 171, 174; of
    Coburg, 191
Ferghana, 196
Ferideddin Attar, 271
Fertile Crescent, 93, 95, 107, 212
Fez, 6, 10
Fezzan, 19
Finns, 92
First Balkan War, 195, 198
First World War, 147, 199, 213
Five-Year Peace Plan, A, 291, 294
Flamenco, 262
Foreign Legion, 16, 18
France, 122, 124, 139, 190, 291
Franco, Francisco, 205
Franco-Prussian War, 14
Franks, 139
Frederick, "Barbarossa," 183
Frederick of Hohenstaufen, King
    of Sicily, 187
Frederick the Great, 265
French Academy, 306
French Morocco, 5
Freud, Siegmund, 103
Fronde, 125
Fuad, 203

Gabes, 27
Gabriel, Archangel, 114, 115, 118
Galata, 156
Galen, 259
Gallipoli, 211
"Geber," 257
Genesis, 40
Genoa, 173
Gerbert, 261
German, 92, 142, 289; General
    Staff, 122; Roman Empire, 124,
    159
Germanus, Julius, xvi, 228

(315   )

Index

Germany, 118, 125, 209
Ghardaïa, 15, 16
Gibraltar, 5, 30, 136, 142, 231
Giordano Bruno, 270
Giralda, La, 32
Glaooee, 8
Glaoui, 8
Godefroy de Bouillon, 181
Godounov, Boris, 125
Goebbels, Joseph, 170
Goethe, 272
Golden Horn, 156, 214
Goondahfy, 8
Gordon Pasha, 202, 203
Government of Jebel Druse, 78; of Latakiyeh, 78
Granada, 6, 12, 38, 148, 165, 168, 169
Grand Inquisitor, 174
Grand Rabbi, of Baghdad, 147
Grand Shaykh Ahmed, 34, 35
Graziani, Marshal Rodolfo, 34, 201
Great Atlas, 15
Greater Lebanon, 78
Greece, 190, 195, 224
Greeks, 58, 108
Gueroosh Castilla, 7
Gundafi, 8
Guy de Lusignan, 182

Habibullah Khan, 207
Habsburg, 159, 191
Hadhramaut, 63-65, 94, 113
Hadith, 223
Hadrian, Emperor, 77
Hafid, Moolay, 8-10
Hagia Sophia, 159
Haifa, 48, 73, 76
Hail, 53, 56
Haïreddin, Barbarossa, 161
Hakim, 84, 87
Hama, 253
Hamburg, 289
Hamid Bey, Abdul Hakk, xvii

Hamidiyeh, Fort, 213
Hamitic stock, 17; nomads, 21
Hammurabi, King, 99
Hamza, 85
Hamzawee dervishes, 276
Han dynasty, 125
Hannibal, 29, 109
Harun-er-Rashid, 59, 234, 253
Hashish, 83
Hashishin, 83
Hassan, 66, 131, 132
Hattin, Battle of, 182
Haute école, 245
Havarith, 102, 103
Hebrew University, 296
Hebrews, 102
Hebron, 40
Hejaz, 34, 37, 48, 56-58, 66, 113, 138, 214
Hejira, 120
Hermes, 105
Herodotus, 68
Herzegovina, 191
Heth, 39, 40
High Atlas, 6, 15
Himyaric, 96
Hippocrates, 259
Hitler, 92, 124, 173, 174, 211
Hittites, 38-42, 76
Hodeida, 65
Holy City, 131
Holy Land, 39, 67, 296
Holy Roman Empire, 187
Homs, 166
Hoonayn ibn Ishag, 259
Hotel Adlon, 203
Howling Dervish, xiii
Hulagu, 152, 160
Hungary, 92
Huns, 92, 153
Hürriyet, 194
Hussein, 66, 132
Hussein, Sherif, 214
Hussein ben Ali, 27
Hyksos, 95, 100-103

Index

IBERIAN PENINSULA, 95, 140, 233
Ibero-Roman, 136
Ibn Abbas, 140
Ibn Abi Usaibi'a, 268
Ibn 'Arabi, 265, 270
Ibn Beithar, 255
Ibn Fadlallah, 268
Ibn Farid, 265
Ibn Khaldoon, 266, 267
Ibn Qifti, 268
Ibn Quzman, 266
Ibn Rashid, 53, 56, 57
Ibn Rushd, 167, 260
Ibn Saud, 45, 51–57, 61, 214
Ibn Sina, 256, 260
Ibn Zoohr, 260
Ifrica, 28
Ifrikeeyeh, 28
Ikhwan, 56
Ikhwan es-Safa'i, 267
Imam, 65, 66, 87, 128
Imam Yakhya, 57, 59, 195
Imayegh, 20
Imaziren, 4
Imghad, 20
Iñana yoga, 272
Iñana yogin, 272
India, 64, 110, 117, 133–135
Ineunu, Ismet, General, xvii, 58
Inquisition, 6, 171, 174
Iran, 66, 95, 131
Iraq, 48, 49, 51, 66, 67, 72–74, 96, 97, 113, 131, 215
Isabella, 6, 169, 174
Ishtar, 71, 72
Ishthar, 71
Isidore, 107
Isidoros, 107
Isis, 107
Islam, 31, 64, 66, 91, 108, 117, 121, 123, 219
Ismaïl, Moolay, 6
Ismaïlites, 82, 87
Ismet Ineunu, General, 58, 59
Issa, 145

Istanbul, 157
Italy, 22
Ittihat wa Tarakki, 193

JABEER IBN HAYYAN, 257
Jaffa, 76, 77, 184
Jah, Azam, Prince of Berar, xvii
Jamblichus, 85
Jamil, 265
Japan, 286
Jarbah, 129
Java, 63, 110, 135
Jazygues, 153
Jeanne d'Arc, 118, 275
Jebel Druse, 78, 84
Jebel Shammar, 53
Jebel Tarig, 136
Jelaleddin Rûmi, 271
Jelwetee dervishes, 276
Jemal Bey, 193, 194
Jemal Pasha, 82, 206, 208
Jephtha, 45
Jerablus, 40
Jerusalem, 31, 76, 77, 111, 130, 145, 181, 296, 297
Jesus, 79, 85, 86, 145
Jews, 7, 29, 38, 39, 42, 66, 70, 71, 75, 103, 108, 111
Jihad, 213
Jiluwi, 271
Jinghiz Khan, 152, 153
Jinn, 46
Jivân mûkti, 224
Joannitius, 259
Jordan, 75
Joshuah, 107
Josiah, King, 76
Juda, 76
Judaism, 117
Judea, highland of, 75
Julian, the "Apostate," Emperor, 142
Julius Caesar, 124, 142
Justinian, Byzantine Emperor, 99, 112, 159, 230

(317)

Index

KA'ABA, 111, 112
Kabul, 207, 228
Kabyles, 17
Kadesh, battle of, 40
Kaïds, 7, 8
Kaiser, 92, 206
Kaïvalya, 224
Kala'at Shergat, 67
Kalmuks, 93
Kasbah, 7, 8, 18
Kasbah El Glaoui, 9
Kashmir, 279
Kel Tagilmus, 19
Kemal Ataturk, 59, 235, 289
Kerbela, 66
Kerkaporta, 159
Khabiri, 102
Khadiyah, 114, 119
Khaïrouan, 27, 31
Khalid ibn-el-Walid, 134, 135
Khan, 153
Khartum, 202
Khatti, 39
Khayan, 100
Khazars, 38
Khediveh, 203
Khiva, 135
Khyan, 100
Khyber Pass, 207
Kinda tribe, 265
King Hammurabi, 99
King John, 124
Kismet, 224
Kitab el Hikmet, 87
Kitchener, Lord, 202
Koldewey, Professor Robert, 70, 71
Konia, 11, 153, 154
Koran, 46, 55, 59, 113, 143, 159, 223, 235
Kossovo Polye, 155
Kremlin, 289
Kress von Kressenstein, General, 211
Krishna, 87

Kuda Bux, 279
Kufara, 33
Kûfi script, 236
Kufra, 33, 34
Kumans, 153
Kuweit, 62, 73

LA FONTAINE, 266
Lagash, 67
La Giralda, 32, 167
Lailah, 266
Lake Trasimenus, 109
Lao Tse, 61
Las Navas de Tolosa, battle of, 168
Latakiyeh, 78
Latin, 235
Laval, Pierre, 216
Lawrence of Arabia, 41, 44, 74, 209, 212
Lazarus, King, 155
Lebanon, 78, 80, 216, 291
Lenhossek, Dr. Ladislas, 230
León, 168
Levant, 79, 134, 172, 210
Libya, 4, 19, 32, 135, 151, 195, 200, 201, 293
Lima, 178
Liman von Sanders, Marshal, 211, 212, 214
Lippizan, 245
Litham, 19, 166
Little Atlas, 15
Logos, 86
Lója, 168
London, 279
London University, 279
Long Island, 81
Lord Allenby, 77, 81, 131, 214
Lord Beaconsfield, 197
Lord Kitchener, 202
Lord North, 286
Lossow, Colonel von, 211, 212
Louis, 124, 177, 184, 250
Lourdes, 118, 280

Index

Lucifer, 84
Lully, Raymond, 270
Luther, 118, 275
Lyon, 139

MACEDONIA, 144, 191
Machpelah, cave of, 40
Madinat-es-Zahra, 239
Magellan, 63
Magna Charta, 124
Magnes, Dr. Judah L., 296
Magnitogorsk, 289
Magyars, 92, 153
"Mahdi," the, 202, 249
Maïmonides, 182, 260
Majnoon, 266
Málaga, 168
Malaya, 63, 64, 110
Malta, 81
Mameluk dynasty, 184, 229
Mamre, 40
Mamum, Caliph, 234, 253, 254
Mandarins, 126
Maqamah, 266
Maqnah, 129
Marc Antony, 107
Marco Polo, 82
Marcus, 107
Marcus Antonius, 107
Marcus Aurelius, 286
Marcus Tullius, 107
Marduk, 71, 72
Maronite, 188
Marrakesh, 6, 8
Marshal Ahmed Izzet Pasha, 58
Matmata, 31
Mauretania, 176
Mayas, 22, 97
Mecca, 31, 34, 56, 111–114, 120–122, 145, 214
Medina, 31, 56, 120–123, 131, 145
Mediterranean, 15, 48, 75, 80, 95
Medjid, Abdul II, Caliph of Islam, xvii

Mehmed Reshad, 275
Mehmed Talaat, 193, 194
Meknes, 10
Mendelssohn, 80
Menemen, 211
Mercury, 105
Merv, 196
Mesopotamia, 67
Mewlewi dervishes, 275
Mexican, 137
Mexico, 22
Mexico City, 178
Michael Romanoff, 125
Mid-Atlas, 6
Midhat Shukry, 193
Mihrab, 241
Minaean, 96
Mindanao, 63, 64, 135
Misurata, 33
Moaviyyah, 131, 132, 140, 151, 157
Mocca, 66
Moguls, 92, 153, 162, 269
Mohammed, 63, 66, 95, 112–115, 117–123, 126, 128, 129, 131, 145, 275
Mohammed Abu Abdallah, 169
Mohammed Ahmed, the "Mahdi," 202
Mohammed Ibn Abdallah, 120
Mohammed Ibn Abdul Wahab, 56
Mohammed Ibn Rashid, 53
Mohammed II, Turkish Sultan, 147, 157–159
Mo'izz, Caliph, 255
Mongols, 38, 39, 92, 152, 153
Monreale, 186
Montenegro, 195
Moolay Mohammed, 6, 9
Moorish architecture, 175
Moors, 17, 64, 176
Mordecai, 71
Moriscos, 6, 176, 177
Morocco, 3, 5, 42, 135, 140, 141, 148, 291

Index

Moros, 64, 227
Moscow, 302, 303
Moses, 104, 107, 118
Moses de León, 270
Moslem, 66, 75, 113, 117, 119, 121, 123, 269
Mosque of Omar, 77
Mossul, 49, 67, 73
Motamid, King of Seville, 166, 167
Mount Carmel, 76
Mount Hermon, 79
Mózarabes, 148, 175
M'tooggy, 8
M'tuggi, 8
Mudéjares, 175, 241
Mumtaz Mahal, 162
Murad, 155
Murcia, 168
Musa, 135, 136, 138–140, 145
Mussolini, 201, 202
Mutamid, 265

NABATAEAN, 96
Nakhr-el-Kelb, 81
Nakshbendee dervishes, 276
Naples, 142
Napoleon, 34, 133, 134, 140, 199, 300
Napoleon III, 81
Narbonne, 139
Nasrid dynasty, 169
Navajos, 22
Nazareth, 184
Nazis, 42, 125
Nebuchadnezzar, 69, 70, 72, 76
Nejd, 52, 53
Nejef, 66
Nekho, Pharaoh, 76
Nestorian, 148, 258
Netherlands, 288
Netherlands East Indies, 63
Neuilly, 303
Nicholas II, 196
Niedermaier, 207

Nigeria, 19, 110
Nile, 102
Niniveh, 67
Nisibin, 49
Noor, 276
North Africa, 46, 81, 95, 132, 135, 138, 141, 142, 193
Nuri Pasha Es-Said, 74, 215

OBERON, 80
Okba ben Nafi, 32
"Old Man of the Mount," 82
Old Mexico, 22
Old Testament, 45
Oman, 62
Omar, Caliph, 130, 131
Omar, Meccan poet, 265
Omar II, 148
Omar ibn el Khattab, 119
Omar Khayyam, 256, 271, 274
Omayyad Caliphate, 157
Omayyads, 131, 135, 140, 141, 148
Oppas, 147
Oran, 15
Orient, 124
Orontes, 253
Osiris, 85
Osman, 154
Osman, house of, 130
Othman, 131, 132, 154
Ottoman, 154; Empire, 49, 58, 59, 74, 75, 126, 130, 146, 187, 188, 195, 199, 205, 213; Dynasty, 130, 154; Turks, 92, 153
Ouargla, 16
Ouled Naïl, 23, 25
Oxford, 242
Oxford Dictionary, 268

PAINE, THOMAS, 253
Palaeologos, house of, 157
Palermo, 185, 186, 255
Palestine, 7, 39, 40, 51, 58, 67, 73, 75, 77, 79, 95, 103, 111, 112, 132, 134, 211, 295, 297, 298

Index

Palmyra, 112, 113
Palmyranean, 96
Pan-Arab Federation, 38, 75, 216, 295–297; Movement, 214
Pan-Islamic movement, 214
Pantelleria, 235
Pantheism, 152
Papacy, 130
Papal State, 149
Paris, 15, 208
Parsees, 135
Pastoral Symphony, 117
Patriarch, 147; of Jerusalem, 182
Peking, 143; Library of, 143
Peloponnesus, 157
Persia, 131
Persian Gulf, 54, 134
Persian Sassanid Empire, 132
Persians, 72, 132
Peshawar, 225
Petchengi, 153
Peter the Cruel, 241
Peter the Great, 302
Petrie, Sir Flinders, 86
Pharaoh, 100, 101, 103; Akhenaton, 103
Philby, Harry St. John, 228
Philip II, King, 177
Philippines, 63, 110, 135, 227
Philistines, 39, 41
Phoenicia, 29, 80
Phoenicians, 65, 95, 103, 108, 109
Plato, 231, 259
Poe, Edgar Allan, 263
Poitiers, 139, 140
Poland, 38
Pombal, Marquis of, 173
Pomiankovski, 211
Pompey, 135
Popes, 168
"Popular Front" government, 216
Portugal, 149, 169, 173
President Woodrow Wilson, 35
Primo de Rivera, General Don Miguel, 204

Prince Electors, 124
Princip, Gavrilo, 205
Prophet, the, 109, 122, 123, 134, 140, 146, 151, 229
Prorok, Baron de, 28
Protestantism, 121
Pshemt, 101
Ptolemies, 7, 107
Puebla, 244
Punic, 29
Punjab, the, 85, 135
Pyramids of Gizeh, 117
Pyrenees, 109, 133, 139

QALGASHANDI, 268
Qaseedah, 264
Qoreish, 112, 114, 120–122
Quai d'Orsay, 207
Quakers, 276
Quantum Theory, 285
Queen Elizabeth, 213

RABBI SAMUEL, 148
Radio City, 279
Rahmy Bey, 193, 194
Rahwees, 264
Rahzoo, 44, 121, 123, 136, 137, 139
Rakhwan, 246, 247
Ramses, 104
Ramses II, 40, 81
Rashid Ali El Ghailani, 216
Razzia, 44
Red Sea, 58, 103
Rejón, 249
Renaissance, 185, 187, 255, 281
Renda, Abdulhalik, xvii
Republic, Plato's, 259
Resh Glutha, 147
Rhazes, 259
Rhine, 180
Rhineland, 180
Rhorfa, 31
Riadh, 53, 54
Richard the Lionhearted, 183
Rif, 5

Index

Roger II, King, 186, 255, 256
Roman Empire, 124, 142
Romanoff, 125
Romans, 108, 109
Rome, 107, 202, 224
Ronda, 168
Rong, 21, 23
Rousseau, 253
Roxelana, 161
Royal Air Force, 214
Rubá'iyát, 271
Rüdiger von Starhemberg, Prince, 162
Rufa'iyah, 277
Rudolph of Habsburg, 125
Rue de la Paix, 208
Russia, 38, 125, 130, 190, 289, 300–305
Russians, 109, 289
Russo-Japanese War of 1904–1905, 121
Russo-Turkish War, 196

SA'ADIS, TOMBS OF THE, 13
Saba, 112
Sabaeans, 96, 108
Safiyah, 266
Sahara, 14
"Saharan Oases," 15
Saïd, 183
Saida, 80
Saint-Simon, Duke of, 177
Saïs, 102
Saladin, 182, 183
Salmanassar II, 81
Salonika, 175, 193
Samâdhi, 272
Samarkand, 135
Samuel, Rabbi, 148
Sancho Panza, 61
San Sebastián, 38
San Stefano, 190
Sarajevo, 205
Sassanids, 83, 126, 134, 141, 231, 252, 266

Sattva, 274
Saudi Arabia, 45, 46, 51, 56, 73, 75, 214, 262, 295, 298, 299
Saul, 53
Scotland, 286
"Scramble for Africa," 199
Sea of Marmora, 156
Sebastopol, 206
Second Balkan War, 197
Second World War, 109, 215, 289, 303
Selim, 154
Seljuk, 153, 154; Turks, 153, 179, 181
Semiramis, Queen, 71
Semites, 37, 39, 40, 42, 91, 95–97, 108
Senussi, 33–35, 53, 151, 201, 202
Septuagint, 259
Serbia, 190, 195
Serbs, 155
Seven Pillars of Wisdom, 209
Seville, 32, 39, 165, 168
Sfax, 27
Shah Jahan, 162
Shakespeare, 80
Shammar, 47, 53
Shanfarah, 264
Shatt-el-Arab, 73
Shaykh, 45, 48, 49, 50, 67, 107, 130, 234; Saïd, 183
Sheba, 112
Shéhvar, Durru, Princess of Berar, xvii
Shekhinah, 86
Shelley, 265
"Shepherd Kings," 101
Sherif Hussein, 212, 214
Shia, 66, 131
Shibam, 64
Shiites, 66, 82, 87, 131, 133, 151
Shlooh, 6
Siberia, 92
Sicily, 29, 81, 142, 185, 235
Sidi-Bel-Abbès, 18

Index

Sidi Okba, 32
Sidon, 80, 184
Silesia, 92
Sinai Desert, 103
Sind, 135
Sinjar Mountains, 83
Sinkiang, 109, 135, 228
Slavs, 92, 153
Smyrna, 194, 210
Snouck Hurgronje, Professor, 228
Sobieski, Yan, King, 162
Sofia, 303
Soliman, 161, 189
Solomon, 40, 77
Son cubano, 276
Sooks, 30
Soorahs, 145
Sorbonne, 208
Souchon Pasha, 206
Sousse, 27
Soviet Russia, 73
Spahis, 16
Spain, 41, 136, 137, 139, 140, 142
Spanish Jews, 174
Spanish Morocco, 5
"Spanish Riding School," 245, 246
Spinoza, 270
Squadristas, 201
Stambul, 156
Stanley, 255
St. John, Gospel of, 86
St. John of the Cross, 270
St. John Philby, Harry, 228
St. Joseph, University of, 208
Straits Question, 196
Sudan, 110, 202
Sudeten, 92
Suevi, 136
Sufi, 307
Sufism, 152, 270, 271, 307
Suleiman, 145
Suleimanich mosque, 161
Suleiman Shah, 154
Sultan Pasha El Atrash, 215
Sultan Selim, 77, 160

Sultans, 49; of Nejd, 53, 54; of Egypt, 84
Sumatra, 63, 110, 135
Sumerians, 67, 95–97, 108
Sumero-Akkadians, 68
Sunna, 66, 131
Susa, 144
Swedenborg, 118, 276
Sykes-Picot agreement, 212
Sylvester II, Pope, 261
Syria, 10, 21, 39, 40, 49, 51, 58, 73, 74, 78, 79, 82–84, 113, 121, 131, 132, 134, 216, 291
"Syriac," 79
Syrian Desert, 46, 48, 49, 79, 112

Ta'abbatah Sharrah, 264
Taj Mahal, 13, 162
Talaat, 193, 206
Talib, 113
Tamerlane, 153, 156
Tancred of Hauteville, 186
Tangiers, 5
Tanis, 102
Tanit, 29
Tannenberg, Battle of, 109
Targi, 21, 23
Tarig, 136–138, 140, 147
Tartars, 93
Tchad, 19
Teheran, 303
Tel-Aviv, 297
Telouet, 10
Temenna, 229
Tennyson, 265
Terim, 64
Tetuán, 5
Teutonic Knights, 92
Thebes, 102
Theodosius, Emperor, 142
Thomas Aquinas, 270
Thot, 105
Thrace, 58, 191
Tibet, 66, 87

Index

Tifinagh, 21
Tigris, 67
Timbuctoo, 19
Times (London), 279
Timgad, 16
Titania, 80
Toledo, 138, 147, 170, 251
Toltecs, 22
Torquemada, Tomás de, 171, 174
Touggourt, 15, 16
Tours, 139
Tower of Babel, 68–71
Trafalgar, 199
Transjordan, 51, 73–75, 214, 295
Treves, 180
Tripoli, 33, 135
Trommer Pasha, 210
Tsar, 125, 303
Tsarataï Mosque, 154
Tsarist Russia, 124, 190, 198, 211, 212
Tuareg, 18–23, 33, 46, 166
Tudor style, 242
Tunis, 30, 31, 135, 136, 235
Tunisia, 4, 15, 27, 31, 200, 291
Tunisian Jewry, 30
Turcos, 16
Turkestan, 95, 110, 135
Turkey, 60, 73, 128, 130, 195
Turkish Republic, 59; Sultans, 48, 52, 155, 187, 191; Treasury, 49
Turks, 150
Tutmosis, 105
Tyre, 80, 184

Ukraine, 191
"Union of Nations," 294
Unitarian, 36, 84, 85, 152
United States, 301
Universal Mind, 85, 86, 224, 226, 278, 280, 285, 307
Ur of the Chaldees, 67
Urals, 92, 153
Urban II, Pope, 179

Urdu, 235
U.S.S.R., 303

Vabdalatus, 112
Vandals, 4, 136
Vatican, 300
Vauban, 250
Vedanta, 307
Venice, 244
Venus, 71
Versailles, 177
Vienna, 159, 162
Vikings, 238
Virgin Mary, 118
Visigoths, 136
Vistula, 92
Volga, 38
Voltaire, 253

Wadi Hadhramaut, 64
Wafd party, 36, 203
Wahhabi, 53, 55, 56, 151, 261
Waldersee, Count, 143
Walid, 265
Walladah, Princess, 266
Wartburg, 118
Washington's Farewell Address, 123
Webster's Dictionary, 268
Wilde, Oscar, 263
Wilhelmstrasse, 206
Wilson, President Woodrow, 35
Woolley, Sir Leonard, 41, 67, 76
World War, First, 147, 199, 213; Second, 109, 215, 289, 303
Worms, 180

Xátiva, 238
Ximenez de Cisneros, 170, 171

"Ya," 101, 106
Yahgoot, 268
Yahveh, 101, 106, 119
Ya-Khanaan, 101

Index

Yakub, 101
Yakub-Ba'al, 101
Yakub-Hal, 101
Yakub-Hor, 101
Ya-Mose, 106
Ya-Nathan, 101
Yazid I, 265
Yekeb, 101
Yekeb-Hor, 101
Yemen, 34, 39, 57, 59, 65, 66, 113, 195, 295
Yezdegerd, 134
Yezidi, 83, 84
Yoga, 307
Yogin, 272, 307
Young Turkish Revolution, 201

Young Turks, 192, 194, 195
Yussuf, Almoravide Sultan, 166
Yussuf (Sultan Saladin), 182

ZANZIBAR, 235
Zendavesta, 83
Zenobia, Queen, 112
Zerubbabel, 67
Ziggurat, 68
Zitoona mosque, 30
Zohar, 270
Zoroastrian, 83, 84, 135, 231
Zoroastrianism, 144
Zouaves, 16
Zurich, 121
Zwingli, Ulric, 121